SCHOOLS OF THEIR OWN

SCHOOLS OF THEIR OWN
The Education of Hispanos in New Mexico, 1850–1940

Lynne Marie Getz

University of New Mexico Press
Albuquerque

© 1997 by the University of New Mexico Press
All rights reserved.
First edition

First paperbound printing, 2010.
Paperbound ISBN: 978-0-8263-4955-2
13 12 11 10   1 2 3 4

Library of Congress Cataloging-in-Publication Data

Getz, Lynne Marie, 1956–
Schools of their own : the education of Hispanos in New Mexico :
1850–1940 / Lynne Marie Getz — 1st ed.
p. cm.
Includes bibliographical references and index.
ISBN 0-8263-1812-6 (cloth)
1. Hispanic Americans—Education—New Mexico—History—19th century.
2. Hispanic Americans—Education—New Mexico—History—20th century.
3. Mexicans—Education—New Mexico—History—19th century.
4. Mexicans—Education—New Mexico—History—20th Century. I. Title.
LC2674N6G48   1997
371.82968′0789—dc21   96-51266

For my father
Melvin E. Getz
And in loving memory of my mother
Alice Lorton Getz
1935–1996

Contents

	Acknowledgments	ix
	Introduction: Schools at the Crossroads of Cultures	1
1	Territorial Education: The Myth of Hispano Resistance	13
2	Preservation and Accommodation: New Mexico Education in Early Statehood	29
3	George I. Sánchez in New Mexico	48
4	Loyd S. Tireman: Contributions and Contradictions	66
5	Prospects for Enduring Reform: The Community School Ideal	87
6	The New Deal and Education in New Mexico	103
	Conclusion	118
	Notes	125
	Bibliography	149
	Index	165

Acknowledgments

I did not come to this study without my own personal baggage. My first awakening to the frustration and anger of young Chicanos occurred when I was a high school student in southern Colorado in the early 1970s. As my Chicano/a peers rebelled, I came to understand that they had experienced an entirely different relationship with the public schools. Where I had felt nurtured, enriched, and included, they had experienced ostracism, alienation, and neglect. Although we had gone through the same schools together for twelve years, our educational opportunities had not been equal. This book is an attempt, however limited in scope, to understand how such injustices could have transpired in a free society.

In spending nearly a decade working on this project I benefited from the assistance and support of numerous teachers, colleagues, friends, and family. Many of them must have wondered if this book would ever see the light of day: that it has is testimony to their faith and patience.

I have always been very fortunate in having excellent teachers who encouraged my love of history: my aunt Carol Ann Wetherill Getz; Dr. Shirley Fredricks and Dr. Norma Peterson at Adams State College; Dr. Paul F. Boller, Jr. and Dr. Donald E. Worcester at Texas Christian University. This study began as a dissertation at the University of Washington under the wise direction of Professor Lewis O. Saum. Professors Robert E. Burke and Carlos B. Gil read the manuscript and offered helpful counsel throughout the project. Don Worcester focused his editorial acumen on the manuscript and helped me improve some of my less than perfect prose.

Colleagues at Appalachian State University have supported me in innumerable ways. I am grateful to Dean Donald W. Sink of the College of Arts and Sciences and to Dean Joyce Lawrence of the Graduate School for finding the funds that enabled me to travel to collections. Chairs George Antone and Michael Wade of the History Department offered constant encouragement and allowed me schedules with time to write.

The Rockefeller Archives Center in Pocantico Hills, New York provided me with a Grant-in-Aid that enabled me to use its excellent collections and superb facilities. It was also a great pleasure to work at the New Mexico State

Records Center and Archives in Santa Fe. The staff, including Richard Salazar, Al Regensberg, Ron Montoya, Pat Garcia, and Arlene Padilla, consistently provided attentive professional service and warm hospitality during my numerous visits. At the University of New Mexico Terry Gugliotta and Nancy Brown guided me to many invaluable sources in the Special Collections of Zimmerman Library. Tim Blevins helped me find my way through the Rio Grande Historical Collections at New Mexico State University Library. Dianna Moody of Belk Library at Appalachian State University went beyond the call of duty in obtaining obscure items for me through interlibrary loan. Dr. Erlinda Gonzales-Berry of the Department of Spanish and Portuguese at the University of New Mexico graciously allowed me to read the transcripts from her oral history project, "And Gladly Did They Teach."

I thoroughly enjoyed working with Dr. David Holtby of the University of New Mexico Press. I am thankful for his editorial skill, patience, and tact in directing me through seemingly endless revisions.

My mother, Alice Lorton Getz, did not live to see this book published, although she had read the dissertation and eagerly followed each step of the publication process. She was the person I most wanted to read this book. The granddaughter, daughter, and mother of Western schoolteachers, she championed educational opportunity for all and was an excellent teacher herself. She and my father, Melvin Getz, always gave me their utmost encouragement, support, and love.

My family—George, Clio, F.B. and R.P.—enlivened my daily life and kept me from taking myself too seriously. And finally, I am deeply grateful to my partner Melissa Barth for sharing with me her joyful approach to life and her irrepressible repartee.

While the old cliche that I couldn't have done it without them holds true for the above-named, an equally timeworn disclaimer also applies. Any errors or mistakes within are my own. I also take full responsibility for the perspective presented here, knowing full well that I am dealing with controversial and sensitive matters. Someone will undoubtedly disagree with my conclusions, and indeed, I would be disappointed if this book did not engender a passionate and heartfelt response.

Introduction
Schools at the Crossroads of Cultures

In 1870 the *Santa Fe New Mexican* printed an article that had appeared in the *New York Times* on the prospects of statehood for New Mexico. The eastern paper scorned Santa Fe as "a decayed, decaying town, and so much unlike anything in America that one feels a stranger in a strange land." Albuquerque lying to the south was "younger, but with all the signs of ignorance and sloth." Progress beckoned, however, since "capital in the hands of intelligent labor has taken possession of some of the best mines and farming lands. Americans and English are swarming in. Even the towns are brushing up."[1]

The Hispanos of New Mexico have often suffered the indignity of being judged by another people's standards.[2] Nineteenth and early twentieth century observers denigrated Hispano culture even as they praised the rugged and beautiful New Mexico land. Historians have sometimes repeated the mistake of assuming that difference imputes inferiority, and this tendency may be all the more tempting when the topic is education. On few other subjects is there such pervasive agreement that American education is far superior to that of any other society. Tradition holds that the United States led the world in providing free common schools for the masses, in professionalizing the teaching corps, and in creating comprehensive school systems reaching from the grade school level to universities. Nineteenth-century Americans had nothing but contempt for other peoples who failed to exhibit the same enthusiasm for education.

We now understand that American educational patterns emerged out of a set of social and political circumstances unique to the United States. That these same circumstances were not replicated in other societies does not signify any inferiority in intelligence, character, or moral fiber of other peoples, although such conclusions were often reached in the nineteenth century and beyond. The success, or at least the perception of success, of American educational institutions had a tremendous impact on the destiny of New Mexico within the United States. New Mexico's lack of educational institutions was held up as the basis for perceiving Hispanos as dull, devoid of reason, incapable of self-government, and unwilling to improve themselves.

Today we readily recognize that New Mexicans were judged too harshly by nineteenth-and early twentieth-century critics. As first a Spanish colony and then as a Mexican province, New Mexico's political and cultural circumstances nurtured different institutional patterns. But the attacks upon its educational conditions were also unfair because the progress of American schools was much more uneven than tradition and nostalgia suggest. Americans long have been devoted to the idea of education, while they have resisted the practical burden of supporting schools. Consequently the rhetoric for and about education has often been greater than the actual accomplishment of the schools themselves. This was never more true than in the mid-nineteenth century, when attacks on New Mexican culture were the most vicious. Despite the fact that New Mexico's educational conditions passed through stages of development similar to those of other far western territories, Anglo critics heaped scorn upon Hispanos for their alleged resistance to schooling.[3]

If New Mexicans found it difficult to bear with such hypocritical affronts, they discovered in American educational patterns much that they could use for their own purposes. Local control of schools had been the backbone of educational policy in the United States since the early Republic; localism enabled Hispanos in New Mexico to shape the direction of their own schools to a great extent. The most significant reform efforts were those that capitalized on local needs and initiatives. This is not to suggest that New Mexicans determined their own educational destiny without interference, assistance, or guidance from anyone beyond the community level. New Mexicans, like other Americans, experienced the effects of three great periods of educational reform and change: the common school movement of the 1830s, 1840s, and 1850s; the progressive movement of the 1890s through the 1930s; and the New Deal of the 1930s. The following chapters examine in more detail the responses and contributions of New Mexicans to these movements.

A brief look at each major reform effort will put the New Mexican experience in perspective. Americans' long-standing faith in education began with the leaders of the early Republic. For their radical experiment in republicanism to succeed, the country needed a broad-based system of education to cultivate learning, nurture civic virtue, and disseminate knowledge. While many Americans agreed with these lofty ideals, few wished to construct the mechanism of centralized authority needed to achieve comprehensive school systems. Thus Thomas Jefferson's Bill for the More General Diffusion of Knowledge, calling for the creation of a system of free public schools, passed the Virginia Legislature in 1779, never to be implemented by the local citizenry. Political thinkers as opposed in outlook as Benjamin Rush and Nicholas Biddle favored a national system of publicly supported schools.[4] Yet no comprehensive system of free public schools emerged anywhere in the young Republic.

Although willing to extol the virtues of universal education, Americans clung stubbornly to the notion that local communities should decide what kind of schooling they ought to provide. Resistance to taxation often impeded the process of building schools and resulted in a bewildering hodgepodge of school systems in the early Republic. Few states supported public school systems with tax money before the 1830s, and many schools maintained by local communities offered a meager educational fare as a result of inadequate facilities, poorly trained teachers, and short school terms.[5]

In response to these dismal conditions, a number of reformers began in the 1830s to work for more centralized control of education, higher standards for teachers, and uniform classification of school grades. Horace Mann in Massachusetts, Henry Barnard in Connecticut, John Pierce in Michigan, and others articulated their crusade in the evangelical language of their reform-minded era. Schools did not exist merely to shape individuals but to reform society itself. In an increasingly heterogeneous society, the schools would serve as a great unifying force, giving every child a solid grounding in the common culture. These reformers favored a publicly supported education for all children, rich or poor, to ensure universal exposure to Protestant morality, republican principles, and capitalist values. Through the schools citizens would learn discipline, obedience, and order, regenerating the body politic in the process.[6]

It was in the heyday of the common school reform movement that Anglo Americans began to establish contacts with New Mexicans. The reforming zeal that drove Jacksonian Americans to demand so much from their fellow citizens carried over to their expectations of other peoples, even if they knew little about them. Zebulon Pike's journal of his 1806 expedition had introduced the American public to New Mexico, and tales of the mountain men fired imaginations about this little-known region. But it was not until after the Santa Fe Trail opened in 1821 that traders from Missouri hauled merchandise across treacherous terrain to Santa Fe and returned bearing witness to the many strange and wondrous attributes of New Mexico. Then the judgments began in earnest.

Anglo Americans traveling in New Mexico in the 1830s and 1840s came easily to accept and perpetuate a view of Hispanos as a depraved, superstitious, and lazy people. Their very nature created an obstacle to educational progress in the minds of these observers. Such an image confirmed what Anglos already believed about Mexicans as a race incapable of improvement and not likely to benefit from American institutions.[7] In his observations of New Mexico in the 1830s, Josiah Gregg offered a memorable depiction of Hispanos as a hopelessly ignorant people. He doubted "whether the habitual neglect and utter carelessness of the people, already too much inured to grope their way in darkness and in ignorance . . . could not eventually have neutralized all the good that [education] was calculated to effect."[8]

Skepticism about the educability of Hispanos lingered in the minds of the Anglo officials who came to New Mexico to serve in the territorial government after 1850. One of the most influential of these early publicists was William Watts Hart Davis, who served as territorial attorney general, acting governor, superintendent of Indian affairs, and superintendent of public buildings from 1853 to 1857. Despite his brief tenure in New Mexico, he prejudiced future perceptions of Hispanos through the 1857 publication of *El Gringo: New Mexico and Her People,* a document that congressional opponents to New Mexican statehood cited in 1889 as evidence that New Mexicans were not yet ready for statehood.[9] Davis pointed to the 1850 census, which showed that of New Mexico's total population of 61,547 inhabitants, 25,089 were unable to read or write.[10] "This great enmity to schools and intelligence," he complained, "can only be accounted for as follows:"

> that the people are so far sunk in ignorance that they are not really capable of judging of the advantages of education. From this result the cause of education has but little to hope for from the popular will, and the verdict shows that the people love darkness rather than light.[11]

Such a harsh rebuke ignored several realities: first, the record of educational support in the United States itself, where often a schoolman must have wondered if the common people did not "love darkness rather than light." And second, Davis and others dismissed as irrelevant the rich cultural patterns and educational efforts made under the most difficult of frontier conditions before the American conquest.

The land itself determined the direction of cultural development in New Mexico. The type of land available and the lack of rainfall precluded large-scale agriculture and instead encouraged small, self-sufficient farming and a ranching industry based upon range grazing. This resulted in a settlement pattern of small, communal villages, organized either as *plazas* or as *ranchos*.[12] The geography also created great isolation, first from the heart of Mexico and then from the center of Anglo America. That which emerged in New Mexico was very much a self-sufficient frontier culture. Forced by necessity to produce much of what they needed to live day-to-day, Hispanos developed a rich tradition of artisanship and craftsmanship, and they borrowed extensively from Native Americans, who knew the environment well. Psychologically they felt themselves to be on their own, and their loyalty to the mother culture and government of Mexico was always tenuous. Left mostly to themselves, their language, religious practices, cuisine, arts and crafts, economic activities, and even their racial composition evolved differently from that of Mexicans.

The educational legacy of the Spanish colonial period in New Mexico was a mixed one. Formal education fell under the purview of religious authorities, beginning with the first Franciscan padres who arrived with Juan de Oñate in 1598. The padres undertook to inculcate the native Pueblo and *genízaro* Indians in the values and knowledge of the dominant Hispanic culture. Ironically, as Ramón Gutiérrez has shown, education was used as a major tool in the "Hispanicization" of Native Americans, just as it would later be employed for the Americanization of Hispanos. The padres ladled out healthy doses of Christian doctrine while instructing their charges in European ways of making a living.[13]

Indians were not the padres' only students, however, or the only New Mexicans to learn to read and write. Primary schooling was provided, albeit inconsistently, for the children of soldiers and settlers, and parents or other adults apparently taught children to read and write in less formal settings. Bernardo P. Gallegos has estimated that one-third of the adult male population of New Mexico was literate in the mid-eighteenth century.[14] The means of education, in the form of books, paper, and school buildings, may have been chronically lacking, but the desire for education existed in colonial New Mexico. The few schools that did exist had remarkable consequences. Around 1805 Don Gerónimo Becero established a primary school in Abiquiu, where one of his pupils was Antonio José Martínez.[15] Martínez later went to seminary in Mexico and returned to northern New Mexico as an influential political, educational, and religious leader.

After achieving independence in 1821, the Mexican government intended to establish a public school system in New Mexico and required all town councils to set up primary schools. New Mexico's isolation and lack of funds frustrated this federal scheme, leaving only the church-sponsored schools to provide any education whatsoever. Little opportunity for education beyond primary schooling existed in New Mexico. Padre Antonio José Martínez established the first institution of higher learning of any kind in 1823, when he started his seminary school for boys in Taos. Prominent New Mexicans could send their sons to Mexico, the United States, or Europe for further schooling, but with few exceptions the sons of the poor and girls of all classes had little chance for higher education.[16]

Not only did nineteenth-century Anglo American observers dismiss the signs of educational interest that did exist in New Mexico, but they went on to disparage the character of Hispanos based on those misperceptions. Americans arrived in New Mexico with their Anglo Protestant heritage predisposing them to vilify the Spanish-speaking Catholics they found. Compounding this was their nineteenth-century American nationalist ideology, the same ideology that drove Horace Mann and other nervous educators to build schools for the attainment of a common morality. Unfortunately by the 1840s the American world view also had embraced an insidious racism that elevated the Anglo-Saxon race and denigrated all other groups.[17] Americans in the 1840s and 1850s met the world—and each other—in quite a striking mood: bold, arrogant, aggressively self-righteous, convinced of their moral and racial superiority, yet dangerously insecure and intolerant in the face of difference.

From the 1850s through the 1920s, most Anglo-Americans insisted that it would benefit Hispanos to adopt American customs and beliefs. Anglo American culture seemed to them to be the pinnacle of progress: English-speaking, Protestant, individualistic, acquisitive, hard-working, future-oriented, egalitarian, pragmatic. It was a formula for success, and no one could argue with success. If the institutions that carried the culture ensured that success, then the institutions had to be transplanted into the conquered territories. This was not necessarily a malicious assumption; naturally they believed that because their culture worked for them, it would work for others. So Anglo Americans brought with them the Protestant church, the bank, the land office, the legislature, the courts, and the school.

New Mexico Hispanos did not automatically either embrace or reject these unfamiliar institutions. Some welcomed the Anglo conquest and its promise of accelerated economic activity, enhanced transportation and communication, and better protection from enemies. But many Hispanos rightly understood the implications of Americanization and feared the loss of their own traditions and culture in the wake of the American conquest. As the territorial period progressed and statehood was achieved, Hispanos sought ways to maintain their ethnic distinctiveness.

The refusal of Hispanos to acculturate entirely reflects the centrality of ethnicity in people's lives. Hispanos tenaciously held on to their self-identity as defined by their religion, language, familial patterns, and other practices and attitudes of everyday life.[18] Their language, the symbol and vehicle of cultural unity, was Spanish. Roman Catholicism provided a rich spiritual life celebrated in annual festivals, processions, and art. This religion, with its sense of a close personal relationship with God, ideally suited the harsh realities of frontier life. Much of Hispano culture, in fact, depended upon the conditions of life in the isolated, rugged terrain of New Mexico. Hispanos placed great emphasis upon family ties and obligations, loyalty to one's community, and honor among friends. Because everyone had to work hard and no one could become inordinately rich, Hispano society was characterized by relatively egalitarian relationships between rich and poor, between men and women, and even between *patrón* and *peón*.[19]

Anglos failed to acknowledge the difficulty that Hispanos would face in rejecting the time-honored and cherished patterns of their lives. Judging Hispanos by their own standards—indeed they had no other standards on which to base judgments—nineteenth-century Anglos found New Mexico's economic and educational conditions abysmal. In 1870 Territorial Governor William Pile complained that "here exists the most schoolless, ignorant, and poverty-stricken people speaking a civilized, though foreign language, within the boundaries of the United States."[20] In his 1889 *History of Arizona and New Mexico*, Hubert Howe Bancroft took up this theme, when he asserted that

"Nowhere in the United States was popular education in so lamentable a condition as in New Mexico during this period."[21] Illiteracy rates remained high, few secondary schools existed, elementary school terms lasted only a few months, students made do with out-of-date textbooks, school buildings were inadequate, and teachers came ill-prepared to teach. Yet similar conditions could be found in rural areas all across the country. At similar stages in their territorial development, other western communities struggled with inadequate educational opportunities. In the decades following the Civil War, school reformers held up the common school ideal, while reproaching local farmers and businessmen for refusing to support better schools.[22] When it came to Hispanos, however, the attacks took on cultural and racial overtones.

Territorial schools as viewed by Hispanos might not have seemed so bad. In 1850 not a single public school existed in the territory, and only the children of the well-to-do became educated. On the eve of statehood, sixty-three thousand New Mexican schoolchildren, or 64 percent of the school-age population, attended schools.[23] In the most meaningful sense, this meant that tens of thousands more children attended schools in 1911 than in 1850. Only by looking at that change from an Anglo American point of view could one see no educational progress. From the Hispano perspective, this was a dramatic transformation, one that had occurred within a lifetime.

Understanding the differing ways in which Hispanos and Anglos viewed education points to the flawed logic that has undergirded the negative judgments made by educators and others in the past. In numerous ways the circumstances of Hispanic New Mexico differed from Anglo America, making it difficult, whether desired or not, for Hispanos simply to emulate the American example. Local political officials, in charge of building schools and hiring teachers, had other concerns, such as trying to maintain control over land and water rights, adjusting to new tax and legal systems, and participating in a changing economy. Territorial officials uniformly articulated support for education, but found their efforts stymied by lack of funds. Even William G. Ritch, secretary of the territory from 1873 to 1884 and a zealous critic of Hispanic educational efforts, admitted that the "chronic trouble . . . of public schools in New Mexico has always been how to raise a school fund. The necessity of schools were felt but where the people knew nothing about a property or direct-tax, . . . the raising of funds in any considerable amount was quite out of the question."[24]

Hispanos had no community memory of how schools had been run back in the States, as so many settlers did when they moved to frontier areas. Anglos brought with them ideas about how schools had been built, organized, and financed in older states. Hispanos had no such models and had to experiment with new methods of taxation, school administration, and curriculum suited to their own interests. Cultural attitudes about the role of the church and the duty of the family to inculcate moral education affected Hispanos' attitudes toward the public school ideal brought by Anglos. But neither a tolerance for church interference in the public schools nor the desire to control taxation meant that Hispanos resisted schooling. They rather show that people tried to find ways of educating their children that made sense within the established patterns of their lives.

Anglos' perceptions of educational progress in New Mexico during the territorial period of 1850 to 1912 were based upon the ideals articulated by the common school movement, not by the actual conditions engendered by those reforms. While considerable progress was made in increasing school enrollments and rationalizing school funding in some areas, great disparities in the quality and quantity of schooling existed across the United States.[25] As with most American educational reforms, the stated goals of the common school movement greatly outpaced the actual achievements. Yet the rhetoric of the movement was important in determining what people thought schools should be. Nostalgic educators carried an image of the idyllic "little red schoolhouse" in their mind's eye, while in fact that wholesome edifice had seldom actually existed.

In the period of great social and economic change following the Civil War, Americans once again found their schools inadequate. Not only had the sporadic success of the common school movement failed to create the harmonious cultural foundation that had been envisioned, but the demands on education intensified with changing American circumstances. Immigrants seeking a new life in the United States increased the cultural diversity of America, which to many Anglo Americans only amplified the chaotic dissonance of American society. The new arrivals joined migrants from rural America in rapidly expanding and increasingly disorderly industrial cities. In the unfamiliar terrain of the urban neighborhood, it seemed that the institutions traditionally responsible for American cultural values—the family, farm, workplace, and community— had broken down. In response to these disturbing trends, progressive reformers vested the school with a mission for social regeneration.[26]

The changes that most disturbed progressive reformers resulted from industrialization and urbanization. Factory work and city life, it was feared, could not nurture the same civic virtue or work ethic that an agrarian life had provided. Not wishing to halt the momentum of industrial capitalism itself, progressives sought to create alternatives for fostering virtues of hard work, civic responsibility, and community spirit.[27] John Dewey, usually identified as the father of the progressive educational reform movement, focused the progressive mind on the central challenge for the schools: to rejuvenate and ensure the success of a democratic society in an industrial and increasingly depersonalized economy.

By changing the nature of the school, Dewey hoped to provide a substitute for the agrarian way of life that was rapidly disappearing. He defined his new pedagogy in terms of the needs of the child, but his child-centered schools aimed at nothing less than the salvation of democratic society.[28] In *The School and Society* (1899), Dewey explained his educational goals in terms of the changed social conditions wrought by industrialization. Not so long ago, Dewey said, "the household was practically the center in which were carried on, or about which were clustered, all the typical forms of industrial occupation." In this world the "entire industrial process stood revealed" and everyone had a role to perform in the work. "The children . . . were gradually initiated into the mysteries of the several processes . . . even to the point of actual participation." This experience imparted to children a work ethic of discipline and responsibility, as well as acquainting them with the methods of economic production.[29]

In the urbanized modern society of the late nineteenth century, the schools had to compensate for the loss of contact with the simple industrial processes of rural life. Dewey believed that "manual training, shopwork, and the household arts" served this need to connect the child to the "primal necessities of community life." Industrial training, a vital aspect of the "New Education," made the school a "genuine form of active community life, instead of a place set apart in which to learn lessons."[30] The child learned basic skills and habits of industry and also came to understand something about the industrial process of the community at large. These lessons would have real meaning for the child, because they reflected what was going on in everyday life outside of the classroom. Hoping that his new pedagogy would engage pupils actively, Dewey wanted to infuse the curriculum with hands-on learning experiences that mirrored real-life occupations.[31]

John Dewey introduced a larger social vision of the school as a place where children would learn the values of society as well as the traditions of the past. He reiterated his ideas in *Democracy and Education* (1916), in which he spoke of the role of education in creating a common outlook among the youth of all classes. All persons in a democracy must share the same commitment and vision of community. "Since a democratic society repudiates the principle of external authority," he declared, "it must find a substitute in voluntary disposition and interest; these can be created only by education."[32]

Ironically, rural New Mexico offered the pastoral society and integrated communities that Dewey and other progressives idealized so nostalgically. Yet because Hispano culture differed so greatly from Anglo American standards, New Mexico's schools nevertheless became objects for progressive reform efforts. More than just a response to the new industrialization, progressivism embraced an intolerance for difference that threatened to disrupt people's lives if implemented wholesale in New Mexico.

Typically, progressives touted centralization as the means of achieving their desired reforms. They moved to apply business and industry models to the administration of schools, stressing greater cost efficiency, centralized control, and consolidation. Progressives attacked the haphazard standards and ungraded classes of rural schools as outmoded and ineffective. They attempted to consolidate rural schools and to place the administration of all schools in the hands of professional educators rather than at the whim of local politicians. As a means of eliminating amateur or politically oriented school direction, reformers at the state and city levels worked to build hierarchies of school administrators. Bureaucratization of the schools began in the nation's larger cities as early as the 1850s, gained momentum after 1900, and became pervasive during the 1920s and 1930s.[33]

The administrative reformers hoped to make the schools more businesslike and scientifically sound. They believed that schools could be more efficiently organized by dividing primary and secondary students into distinct grades by age, by requiring uniform textbooks, by giving standard examinations, and by differentiating curricula. Placing students in classes with others of like ability and age allowed teachers to focus upon the specific needs of a group of pupils, thus eliminating wasted time and energy. Testing enabled educators to sort students by ability and to provide different courses of study based upon the prospects of individual students.[34]

These national trends affected New Mexico in overlapping waves. Anglos moving to New Mexico from the 1880s through the 1910s brought a mixed influence of both common school and progressive ideals. There is no milestone marking the end of the common school movement and the beginning of progressivism; these educators do not easily sort into the categories used by late twentieth-century historians. The end of the progressive school movement is likewise hard to pinpoint. Unlike much of progressive reform generally, progressive educational reform continued well after the end of World War I. So pervasive was the impact of progressivism, that almost all the twentieth-century educators introduced in the following chapters might be said to have shared some progressive notions. Linking them was a commitment to reforming educational institutions by addressing the needs of children in the most efficient and scientific means possible. All progressives hoped to achieve a renewed democratic society grounded in a common culture of shared values. Yet they may not have spoken of themselves as progressives and perhaps should not be labeled progressive in retrospect. What is important is to follow the evolution of progressive ideas in the New Mexico setting, which clearly did not resemble the industrializing and urbanizing milieu in which progressivism developed.

For Hispano children progressive education left a mixed legacy. The commitment to meet the specific needs of any given child engendered a startling variety of interpretations depending upon who defined the child's needs. Progressives welcomed intelligence tests and other methods of quantification as the tools to determine what a child needed and how to meet those needs. Yet preconceived notions of racial hierarchies skewed the interpretations of IQ test results, compounding the tendency of Anglo educators to discount the abilities of non-Anglo children. In New Mexico a different interpretation of the progressive creed resulted in attempting to meet the Hispano child's needs by offering Spanish language instruction and lessons in native arts. New Mexican educators came to recognize that national educational trends had to be adapted to local circumstances rather than swallowed whole. Their innovative and unusual approaches to educating their children add another dimension to the multifaceted story of progressive education.

The last major educational development to be considered here did not purport to be a school reform movement at all. The architects of the New Deal had no intention of reforming the schools or of setting up centralized bureaucracies to exercise federal control over them. Yet in many ways the New Deal altered the educational landscape in a profound sense, by setting a precedent for federal intervention in schooling. While aiming to increase the earning and spending power of Americans through a myriad of government agencies, the administration of Franklin Roosevelt almost inadvertently directed huge sums of money to the construction of schools, the employment of teachers, and the provision of playgrounds, music programs, adult literacy classes, and other school-related activities. It is a measure of the centrality of education in the formula of American life that the New Deal ended up working through the schools in order to promote economic opportunity.[35]

New Mexico received much assistance for education through New Deal programs. For such a poor state, the infusion of federal funds offered a much-needed boost to the economy at a critical time. While the New Deal influenced few curricular developments, the largely nonacademic programs that were affected, such as vocational training, music, and arts programs, aimed to reinforce Hispanic culture and to improve the economic well-being of Hispanos. The self-consciously regional approach of state and local directors of New Deal programs in New Mexico helped to legitimize a commitment to cultural diversity and preservation. In a sense the New Deal shifted the national goal for education from that of achieving a common culture to that of providing an equal educational opportunity within a multicultural nation.

This study ends with the beginning of World War II, a major watershed in New Mexican history. The wartime influx of Anglos coming into New Mexico to work in the defense industries finally made Hispanos a minority in their own homeland. But even though they might be outnumbered, Hispanos and their culture would not be ignored. By World War II both Hispanic and Anglo New Mexicans had reached a consensus, for a variety of romantic, economic, and other reasons, that certain aspects of the unique history and culture of

Hispanos should be preserved. Many of the guarantees for the survival and cultivation of Hispano culture had been made through the efforts of educators working within the Hispano community in the decades preceding the war. In this regard education in New Mexico differed significantly from the policies of other southwestern states with large Spanish-speaking populations.[36] Yet even though Hispanos survived the Depression with renewed cultural integrity, their hopes for equal educational and economic opportunities had not been realized.

Hispanos attempted to preserve and sustain their culture even while learning to survive in a world dominated by Anglo-Americans. At the same time Anglo-Americans encouraged Hispanos to acculturate and assimilate into American society. The story of this tug-of-war between cultures was not as simple as that, however, for there were those Hispanos who readily adopted Anglo ways and those Anglos who respected the wish of Hispanos to retain their ethnic distinctiveness. Education played a key role in this dynamic relationship. Anglos and Hispanos alike recognized the power of the school to promote acculturation and assimilation. Whoever controlled the school and its curriculum had a hand in determining the fate of the culture and the welfare of the people.

I | Territorial Education
The Myth of Hispano Resistance

Eastern observers and territorial boosters alike shared an undisguised assumption that New Mexico's native-born Hispanos had squandered the rich potential of the land. Only the Anglos then entering the territory, they believed, could develop the mineral wealth and turn wastelands into fields of prosperity. To explain why Hispanos had not managed to exploit potential natural resources while Anglos would, observers often maligned the character of Hispanos as lazy, ignorant, and unambitious, while praising Yankee ingenuity and character. In making their charges, Anglos pointed to Hispanos' lack of interest in building schools as proof of their resistance to progress. Despite the newcomers' conviction that cultural factors impeded economic growth in Hispanic New Mexico, a closer look reveals a far more complicated set of variables at work than the stereotypes seized on by contemporary Anglo observers.

Hispanos did not so much resist education as face limited options for acquiring it. Funding schools presented the greatest challenge faced by New Mexicans. The Territory of New Mexico could not use the public lands designated for support of education until after the passage of the Fergusson Act in 1898.[1] This meant that all schools had to be supported by taxation, voluntary subscription, or fines. As large landholders, however, territorial leaders remained wary of imposing property taxes that would have a detrimental impact on their interests. Poor people, often short of cash in a subsistence economy, also found it difficult to adjust to new forms of taxation.

The first school law proposed in 1856 allowed for a system of common schools to be funded by a property tax set at a standard rate across the territory. Such a furor against the law arose in the Hispano-dominated counties of Taos, Rio Arriba, Santa Ana, and Socorro that the people there voted it down by a margin of 5,053 to 37. The law was repealed less than a year after it was passed.[2] The results of this referendum added weight to the belief that Hispanos did not care about education. Subsequent legislation, however, demonstrated that local people had not opposed schools or even taxing themselves to pay for schools, but simply wanted to have control over the local funding of education.

Territorial legislators passed laws in 1860, 1863, 1867, and 1872 setting up a county school system based on the principle of local control. In 1860 an "Act Providing for the Education of Children" gave county officials the power to appoint teachers, set school terms, raise fees to pay teachers' salaries, and require compulsory attendance. Although each county had to raise its own funds to support its schools, with no help from the territorial government, the skeleton of a public school system began to take shape.[3]

In 1863 and 1867 legislators further delineated the duties of the justices of the peace and probate judges of each county in administering the schools. Parents paid a sum of fifty cents per pupil per month as well as providing the books, paper, ink, and firewood for their children's schoolwork. Other funds derived from fines parents paid for failing to send their children to school, but the justice of the peace had the power to excuse children's absences for any number of acceptable reasons, including sheepherding duties. The 1872 laws authorized a poll tax and a property tax to be collected and distributed by county officials for locally determined needs. Elected school commissioners could raise voluntary subscriptions from wealthier persons to pay for the schooling of indigent children.[4]

Placing control in the hands of local officials diffused power over the schools and insured that not only upper-class Hispanos or Anglos would have a voice in education. Election returns show that Hispanos overwhelmingly elected their own candidates as county commissioners and school commissioners and were often appointed as justices of the peace by territorial governors. While most counties had few Anglos to elect to these offices, this pattern of Hispano domination prevailed even in counties with significant numbers of Anglos and prominent Anglo businessmen. In 1875 twenty-seven of thirty-four county school commissioners elected across the territory were Hispano. In 1878 thirty-three of thirty-nine elected school commissioners were Hispano, and in 1880 twenty-two of thirty-five school commissioners were Hispano.[5] These voting patterns indicate that Hispanos viewed the offices as critical enough that they should be kept in Hispano hands.

The mere election of school directors did not necessarily signify that schools were operated competently. As in other rural areas across the country, local school officials often held their positions as a result of party politics and patronage. Without doubt some local officials indulged in corruption. Governor Lionel A. Sheldon drew attention to abuses by school officials in his message to the territorial legislature in 1882: "Great complaint is made that in some localities schools are not established though taxes are paid, and in others that incompetent persons are employed—and that in some instances persons are employed and paid as school teachers and assigned to service as herders."[6]

Nationwide educational reformers denounced corrupt practices by local school directors and the disruptive effect of mixing politics and schools. These problems became the focus of reforming efforts within New Mexico just as they had throughout the nation. But not all reform came from outsiders or newcomers. In 1883 parents led by Don Eduardo Martínez complained about the teacher in the Anton Chico school, charging him with "incompetency and cruelty." The teacher, Julian Aragón, "dismisses school on all the feast days of the year, but is allowed pay for the same as if he had worked."[7] But the abuses were never the entire story in New Mexico or anywhere else. Corrupt local officials deserved blame for their misdeeds, but their cases should not obscure the honest efforts made by other local school directors and ordinary citizens, resulting in a steady improvement of schooling throughout the territorial period.

Perhaps the greatest difference in the perception of education between Hispanos and Anglos had to do with the acceptance of the church in school affairs. Hispanos overwhelmingly welcomed Catholic clerics as participants in public education. Catholic priests and nuns not only conducted private schools, but also served as county school commissioners, superintendents, and teachers for the public schools.[8] Local officials turned naturally to religious personnel for their expertise in education. Often a school that had started under church sponsorship was brought under public jurisdiction while retaining the nuns or priests as teachers. In 1888 the county began to pay the salary of the Sisters of Loretto who had operated the Annunciation Academy in Mora since 1868.[9] And many times a community would simply invite the church to send teachers or to donate a building for a school. When Bernalillo County commissioners began to organize Albuquerque's first public school system, for example, they asked the Jesuits to organize and staff the schools.[10] The Imprenta del Río Grande, a press established by Jesuits in 1872, published many of the textbooks used throughout the territory in the 1870s.[11]

The involvement of Catholic clerics in education outraged Anglos accustomed to the strict separation of church and state. William G. Ritch, secretary of the territory from 1873 to 1884, fervently believed in nonsectarian public education and laid the blame for New Mexico's education woes on the influence of the church since the arrival of Juan de Oñate.[12] He decried the "PRIESTLY INFLUENCE" that worked to "subvert the public schools and the school fund."[13] Ritch viewed the Jesuits as the most dangerous meddlers in the public schools. He believed that they interfered in the Albuquerque schools and had used their influence with the people of San Miguel County to control elections in order to take over school boards and appoint sectarian teachers.[14]

Anglo officials and parents, accustomed to the separation of church and state, understandably opposed sectarian influence in the schools. Hispanos, however, found this attitude perplexing and contradictory. The church had traditionally represented learning in New Mexican society, and Hispanos naturally assumed that church people should bring that experience to the aid of the public schools. As the Catholic Church under the leadership of Bishop Jean Lamy became more active in education through the 1870s, Hispanos showed greater willingness to support public schools through taxation. If the spread of education was the objective, then the resistance of Anglos to the work of clerics in the schools seemed hypocritical. By maintaining local authority over schools, Hispanos took control of this issue in practice, benefiting from the opportunities made available by the clerics.

Since the days of the early Republic, educational reformers had championed more centralized control over schools as the solution to educational problems. Local control suited neither the common school reformers nor the later progressive educators. Not surprisingly Anglo educators coming to New Mexico in the territorial period viewed centralization of authority within the territorial government as the antidote to the inadequacies they perceived in the schools of New Mexico. The struggle for control of the schools was yet another aspect of the larger interaction between Anglos and Hispanos, but it was one in which Hispanos had the upper hand, as long as the American tradition of local control prevailed.

As more Anglos moved into New Mexico Territory in the 1880s, pressure to secularize education and to bring the schools into line with American standards increased. Influential proponents of an Anglo American school system gathered in Santa Fe in 1886 to establish the New Mexico Educational Association. The NMEA's founding signalled an act of self-conscious professionalization on the part of educators anxious to secularize and improve schools through a central organization.[15] These educators did not stand alone. The editors of the territory's leading newspaper, the *Santa Fe Daily New Mexican*, called for centralization of authority under a territorial superintendent of schools who "should have complete control of the system and of the county superintendents, and should have an office at the capital."[16]

The reform-minded governor, Edmund G. Ross, urged the territorial legislature to pass new laws that would have raised taxes and centralized authority over schools in the Office of Territorial Superintendent of Public Instruction.[17] When the legislature refused to pass Ross's legislation, he appealed to the people of New Mexico: "Let us at once call public meetings in every town in the territory to memorialize congress, circulate petitions and write our friends at the national capital, praying congress to grant us now, a non-sectarian public school law."[18]

Congress did not come to the aid of New Mexico, and Ross's school reforms failed to materialize. The governor did however lay the groundwork for the 1891 school code, passed during the administration of and usually credited to Ross's successor, L. Bradford Prince. A member of the powerful Santa Fe Ring, Prince persuaded the large landowners of that faction to drop their antagonism to public schooling. With their support, "An Act establishing common schools in the territory of New Mexico and creating the office of superintendent of public instruction" passed the territorial legislature in 1891. The law strengthened the role of the territorial Board of Education and superintendent, who were now to enforce compulsory attendance and adopt uniform textbooks. But it also left local officials largely in control of their own schools. Each county would elect school directors and a superintendent, who organized and supervised school districts, apportioned funds, and sent reports to the territorial superintendent. Counties continued to collect their own funds, with an added provision that they could now issue bonds. Teachers were required to know English, but in those districts "where the only language spoken is Spanish, the teacher shall have a knowledge of both English and Spanish."[19]

While the intent of Anglo reformers had been to shift the locus of power from the county level to the territorial government, the new law left the funding of schools and supervision of teachers in the hands of local officials. Very little, in fact, changed as a result of the 1891 law. More schools were established, but an increase in the number of new schools had been in evidence for nearly two decades. County commissioners continued to raise what funds the people in their locale would bear and to do what they could with those funds. County school directors continued to use the services of Catholic clerics and to hire Spanish-speaking teachers. Even the adoption of textbooks, though now the responsibility of the territorial Board of Education, continued to reflect local interests and budgets. Local school directors provided textbooks in both English and Spanish, often using them for years after statehood.[20] Teachers continued to use Spanish as the language of instruction despite the efforts of territorial officials to enforce a policy of English use.

The 1891 school law does not stand out as a dramatic watershed when the whole of educational activity in the territorial period is taken into account. The numbers of schools, teachers, and enrolled students had increased slowly but steadily throughout the territorial period. When Governor Prince appointed Amado Chaves as the first territorial superintendent of public instruction in 1891, 24,297 students, or 54 percent of New Mexico's school-age children, were already enrolled in school.[21] The 1891 code did not, as was often asserted, signal a dramatic increase in school attendance.

Local control over schools remained the rule in New Mexican education at least through the 1930s, but the momentum of school reform favored centralized authority. It was through the centers of educational organization—government, normal schools, teachers' institutes, and the like—that new educational ideas filtered into the local communities, bringing both practical benefits and unavoidable losses. Hispanos welcomed lessons in English and other skills that seemed desirable as additions to Hispanic patterns. Too often, however, Anglos intended their innovations to replace Hispano ways, thus generating conflict and bitterness.

The career of Hiram Hadley illustrates the dynamic relationship between Anglo school reformers and Hispanos in territorial New Mexico. A native of Ohio and a member of the Friends' Society, Hadley had taught at the Friends' Academy and had started his own normal school in Richmond, Indiana. In 1887 he moved to Las Cruces, New Mexico, where he established Las Cruces College in a two-room adobe building. One room served as the primary department and the other held the eldest of the forty pupils who showed up for the first session in September 1888. When the territorial legislature granted Las Cruces the Agricultural College in 1889, the most advanced students of Hadley's school became the first class of the new college.[22]

Hadley exemplified the common school reformer, energetically extolling the virtues of public education. He became a well-known schoolman in the territory, serving as president of the New Mexico Educational Association in 1890–91. He was a member of the territorial Board of Education, high schools sought him out as a commencement speaker, and the governor put him in charge of organizing a school exhibit to represent New Mexico at the 1893 World's Fair.[23] In 1905 Hadley, then seventy-two years old, was appointed territorial superintendent of public instruction.

As territorial superintendent Hadley traveled throughout New Mexico to observe schools and direct teachers' institutes. The 1891 school law required school visitations and institutes to prepare teachers for certification. Hadley's predecessors in the office of territorial superintendent, Amado Chaves and José Francisco Chaves, started the practice of annual school visits and prepared courses of study for county institutes. Teachers with advanced training and administrators such as the president of the University of New Mexico conducted sessions at these institutes, lecturing teachers on the latest pedagogical theories and practices.[24]

Through his experiences Hiram Hadley developed a sympathetic though condescending view of the Hispano community. Their ignorance, he believed, derived from the Catholic Church having exercised "almost absolute and undisputed control of the minds and the hearts of the entire population." Hadley held the federal government of the United States responsible for the lack of education in the territory. "If the government had shown the same paternal interest in New Mexico that she has manifested towards the Philippines and Porto [sic] Rico," he charged, "the cry of 'illiteracy' would have ceased a quarter of a century ago." The only progress made in New Mexico and the only hope for the future derived from the arrival of Anglo-Saxon newcomers who "brought with them the idea of free, popular education firmly established in their own minds."[25] Hadley's notions of progress and distaste for the influence of the Catholic Church prevented him from recognizing the efforts made by Hispanos in education.

Hadley was not alone in his inability to acknowledge Hispanos' contributions to schooling. Belittling the work of Hadley's predecessors, the historian John H. Vaughan claimed that for fourteen years after the passage of the 1891 school law, "poor administration or no administration almost nullified the law."[26] Hadley represented the first "strenuous and progressive" administration of that office.[27] Vaughan considered a strong central authority at the very top of the educational hierarchy necessary in order to wrest control of rural schools from local authorities. In the minds of the administrative reformers, the local folks out in remote rural areas were often too ignorant of modern schooling practices or were too caught up in politics to run their own schools intelligently.

This attack on local control of schools typified the approach of educational reformers in the late nineteenth and early twentieth centuries. Vaughan, Hadley, and James E. Clark, who became territorial superintendent in 1907, agreed on the inadequacies of the locally run schools, especially in the rural districts. The shortcomings of the rural school lay in the shortness of the school term, inadequate professional preparation for teachers, the lack of uniformity in textbooks and hence in the curriculum, and the poor condition of school buildings. Since the schools suffered from limited funds, Clark believed that consolidation of rural schools would solve many of these problems. In this way school systems could afford to keep schools open for at least a five-month term, instead of the usual three-month term. As a larger administrative unit, Clark reasoned, the consolidated school would furnish "a stable and extensive basis for financing the school" that made for greater efficiency. Consolidation symbolized progress, permanency, and modernization. "The rancher has laid aside the 'little red churn,' " he argued, "and the 'little red school house' must go."[28] The ideas of Clark, Hadley, and Vaughan placed them squarely within the ranks of administrative reformers across the country who wanted to centralize control of the schools.[29]

Centralization also meant increased conformity, an important objective in the common school reformers' quest for a common culture. Certification of teachers, uniform textbooks, and graded schools all signalled adherence to one set of standards for all schools. In this context the use of Spanish as the language of instruction in the rural schools reminded educators that a common culture did not prevail in New Mexico.

Early in the territorial period, the use of Spanish in New Mexican society was widely accepted by Anglos and Hispanos alike. Anglo merchants often sought to learn Spanish to enhance their business. In 1880 the editors of the *Las Vegas Daily Optic* recommended a Spanish course at Las Vegas College to "those wishing to master 'the native tongue.' "[30] Similar instances demonstrate that before the 1880s, Anglos accepted the bilingual nature of New Mexican society and were willing to live and work within it. As the numbers of Anglos increased, however, this tolerance faded. Anglos became reluctant to learn Spanish and more insistent that only English should be taught in the schools. Hispanos, however, defended bilingualism. Writing in *El Eco del Valle* in 1908, Benigno Romero argued that with a majority of Spanish-speaking people and a common border with a Spanish-speaking nation, New Mexico should teach all its citizens to be bilingual.[31] In 1909 the editors of *El Eco* declared that "El idioma es el simbolo [sic] de la raza. . . . El pueblo que abandona la defensa de su idioma, . . . habrá perdido toda su personalidad."[32]

Reflecting the struggle over control of the schools, laws regarding the language of instruction could be interpreted either as mandating English-only instruction or legitimating bilingual instruction. In 1891 Amado Chaves, the first territorial superintendent of schools, issued an administrative ruling that only English should be used in the schools.[33] Yet in 1896 Chaves wrote an impassioned plea for the legislature to make a clear-cut ruling in favor of bilingual instruction. After calling for teachers to be well trained in Spanish, he asserted the right to use his native language:

> It is a crime against nature and humanity to want to rob the children of New Mexico of the natural advantage of the language that is theirs by right of inheritance, unjustly depriving them of the many great uses that two languages give to those who possess them. English and Spanish should walk hand in hand in the schools. . . . There is not a child in all this Territory that does not speak or understand English more or less, but at the same time this child uses and listens reverently to the sweet sounds of the mellifluous language in which his adored mother taught him his first prayer. Is this a crime?[34]

Hiram Hadley, although he too lauded the virtues of bilingualism for adults in the commercial world,[35] interpreted the school code as prohibiting Spanish in the classroom. In 1905 Hadley wrote to Leandro Lucero, superintendent of schools in San Miguel County, complaining about a letter written by a teacher under Lucero's supervision. Although "well written . . . a very nice letter," it had been written in Spanish, which led Hadley to "suppose that Mr. Sanchez, in his teaching, uses the Spanish nearly altogether in his school room." Hadley warned that there could be "no greater mistake than to have this custom pertain."[36]

Superintendent Hadley went on to expound his own interpretation of the public school law of New Mexico, which he claimed "states definitely that it is the English language that is to be taught in our public schools." Any Spanish-speaking teachers who did not abide by this law would be "standing wholly in their own light." Having chastised the county superintendent for allowing Spanish to be used by teachers in the classroom, Hadley admitted that "the law says that in districts were [sic] the only language spoken is the Spanish, the teacher must know both Spanish and English." But, according to

Hadley, this "provision is not for the purpose that the teacher shall teach the Spanish, but it is to help him to teach the English to Spanish-speaking pupils."[37]

In 1907 territorial Superintendent James E. Clark tried to implement a new policy of introducing English through the enforcement of the uniform textbook law. The state board approved the adoption of all-English textbooks, a move that Clark claimed was welcomed throughout the territory. "Almost no opposition exists to the policy of having only English taught in the elementary schools," he claimed. "No greater advantage can be given by our public schools to the children of Spanish-American parents than a thorough training in English. Both parents and children appreciate this and the all-English elementary public school is becoming more and more popular in the outlying districts where the demand has been made heretofore for instruction in the Spanish language with the use of the Spanish text-books."[38] His enthusiastic assertion of the universal appeal of English textbooks does not match Fabiola Cabeza de Baca's recollection that she happily used bilingual primary readers while teaching in a rural school in 1916.[39]

Clark hoped that Spanish-Americans would not lose Spanish in gaining the English language, and that they would "go out from the schools doubly equipped to meet the needs of a business, social, political, or religious life." But he expected them to become literate in their native language without special instruction, and only after they had been immersed in English for several years. By the time the student mastered the fourth English reader, Clark envisioned, he would find himself "in possession of the art of reading to such an extent that he [would have] no difficulty in reading at sight a Spanish text of like grade."[40]

It was not unusual, as we have seen, for educators such as Superintendent Clark to applaud the virtues of biliteracy. Yet his opinion is also typical, in that he did not think any special instruction in Spanish was required to make students biliterate. Educators assumed that through English-only instruction Spanish-speaking children would learn English and at the same time miraculously achieve literacy in Spanish as well, simply because that was their native language. This assumption guided educators of bilingual children for several decades to come, and surprisingly little was done either to support or refute it. The tendency to take this pedagogical practice for granted is especially noteworthy given the usual insistence of so many educators of the period upon verifying theories through scientific method. At best this assumption displays an amazing self-deception that children could be capable of achieving literacy in Spanish without any actual instruction in the language. At worst it indicates a willful disregard for the continued use of Spanish. In any case the primary objective was underscored: children were to be literate in English. Spanish literacy was a secondary concern.

Annual reports from county school superintendents suggest that Hispano parents in urban centers welcomed school instruction in English more readily than Hispanos living in more isolated rural areas. In 1910, just three years after Clark initiated the English instruction policy, Bernalillo County Superintendent A. B. Stroup stated that many pupils still came to school not speaking any English but picked it up quickly. Just a short time prior to this, he said, "much opposition was made to the abandoning of the Spanish language, but, at the present time, nearly all the opposition has disappeared and parents are almost universally demanding that their children be taught English."[41]

Parents elsewhere displayed greater reluctance to send their children to schools where English was the sole medium of communication. The Sierra County superintendent, J. P. Parker, bemoaned the poor school attendance and the parents' lack of appreciation for the benefits of public schooling. Many of the school districts in his county contained Spanish-speaking populations, thus creating great obstacles, since "we have not teachers enough to speak both languages ... to supply such schools, and as such populations have deep-seated aversion to patronizing schools entirely English-speaking."[42]

In his frustration this county superintendent welcomed Spanish-speaking teachers and recognized the valuable role they played in bringing Spanish-speaking students into the schools. In Taos County as well, Spanish-speaking teachers helped to accustom not only the child but also the parent to the English-only school. Superintendent Isaac W. Dwire had nothing but praise for his Spanish-American teachers, whom he "would not be willing to exchange even for teachers of better scholastic accomplishments." These teachers, he claimed, were "specially adapted for teaching Spanish-American children and creating an interest and enthusiasm in the school which is felt in the home."[43]

The belief that native Spanish-speaking teachers would encourage educational achievement in largely Hispanic communities had been recognized in 1909, when the Spanish-American Normal School in El Rito was established. Hispanic leaders Veneslao Jaramillo and Solomon Luna had joined with former Territorial Governor L. Bradford Prince in campaigning for a normal school designed specifically for Spanish-speaking teachers. The legislature began the school to provide better training for teachers who would be working in Hispanic communities. While the school's founders hoped that native Spanish speakers would have a better understanding of Spanish-speaking children, they expected the graduates to teach English to their future charges.[44]

Many educators, Anglo as well as some Hispanos, insisted upon the use of English in the schools as a means of acculturation. George Burch, superintendent of the Guadalupe County schools, thought that a teacher's ability to speak Spanish might hinder a child's learning English, because the child knew he or she could use Spanish as a last resort. Burch complained that "some of the Spanish-American teachers are using the Spanish language a little too much in teaching." He recommended that districts with a large number of non-English-speaking students hire teachers without any knowledge of Spanish at all, to prevent them from lapsing into Spanish. "We need English speaking teachers," he said, "who do not use the Spanish in order to get the best results in teaching English to Spanish-speaking pupils. . . . It is a pleasure to note that some of the Spanish-American teachers are instructing the children in English and according to the school law."[45]

Besides the language of instruction, the curriculum itself could be used as a vehicle of Americanization. Expansion of the curriculum into nonacademic subjects had been used effectively in other states to Americanize immigrant children. New Mexican educators also saw the potential for curricular innovation. Joseph S. Hofer, superintendent of the Tucumcari city schools, encouraged a New Mexico Education Association audience in 1912 to give attention to the health conditions of children in the rural schools.[46] Medical inspection and health education courses, such as those proposed by Hofer, became a popular method of instilling American health standards and practices among immigrant children in the late nineteenth and early twentieth centuries.[47] Rural Hispanos practiced what many Anglos considered to be a primitive medical folklore, and because the native New Mexican diet differed so drastically from typical American cuisine, many Anglo observers deemed it unhealthy. Health courses and home economics classes promised to teach young Hispanos the standards and values of Anglo American culture.

Nationally the expansion of the curriculum into nonacademic areas extended to vocational education. Reformers claimed that vocational education contributed to democracy by providing an education for the common man. Not all students could be expected to go to college, or would benefit from college, they argued; therefore, the school should offer these students a useful training for the life ahead of them in modern industrial society.[48] Under the rubric of tailoring the curriculum to meet the needs of the child, vocational reformers claimed to know the future destiny of the student and to limit the course of study accordingly. Too often the future destiny of children was determined by their class origins. The practical benefits of vocational training appealed to many, but some New Mexico educators made the error of assuming that Hispanos needed vocational education because they could not be expected to go to college or were not capable of advanced education.

As superintendent of the Albuquerque schools from 1891 to 1896, Charles E. Hodgin encouraged the inclusion of more courses in industrial education in the curriculum. Citing statistics that seven out of every ten students would make their living by working with their hands, Hodgin argued "If this is true, why shouldn't the state give those pupils some training in that which they are to follow for life and which will make of them better citizens?"[49]

The president of the University of New Mexico joined Hodgin in his advocacy of vocational education. Dr. E. D. McQueen Gray, who also served on the Territorial Board of Education, applauded the increasingly important role of vocational instruction in the secondary school curriculum. The high school, he stated in 1911, "is the only place where the ordinary boy or girl—by which I mean those who are precluded by circumstances from receiving the benefits of further or higher formal education—can be prepared for the battle of life; and it is the duty of the high school to equip them adequately." Gray declared that "the need of the hour is not for less vocational training in the high schools, but for more."[50]

New Mexico educators welcomed the newly expanded curriculum in language reminiscent of John Dewey. According to Superintendent Clark in 1910, the new curriculum would "bridge the chasm between the community life and the school." The old course of study had not prepared students to live in the new workaday community. But "enriching" the curriculum with industrial education would remedy that situation, Clark promised. "The school will become a life center," he said, "its course of study shaped in accordance with the community activity, and the school plant equipped to aid in instructing the youth in the best method of conducting the branches of industry of the section."[51]

Some New Mexican educators had Hispanos specifically in mind when they thought of vocational education. J. C. Ross, the superintendent of the Menaul School in Albuquerque, justified his own school's emphasis on industrial education by declaring that it exactly suited the Hispanic child's needs. The typical rural Spanish-American home, "with its comparative poverty, and its entire lack of any inspiring or uplifting influences," he claimed, "gives the child a false conception of life, its responsibilities and its vital facts." Industrial training in the schools counterbalanced the negative influence of the child's poor environment, Ross believed, and brought immediate positive results, as the child would teach parents how to improve their living conditions. Beyond the home Spanish-Americans were finding work in agriculture and the machine trades, and Ross felt strongly that the school should train them in these occupations, to enable them to enter their line of work as leaders.[52]

On the eve of statehood, New Mexico possessed an educational system that paralleled in design, if not in scope, a typical modernized school system anywhere in the United States. Chronically limited by lack of funds and frustrated throughout the territorial period by the reluctance or inability of taxpayers to support a public school system, New Mexicans had done what they could to bring American education to the new territory. From the Hispano perspective, great changes had occurred since the American conquest. The Hispano population had acculturated to a new social order in many meaningful ways, even if they had not assimilated. They had embraced American politics and welcomed education. If they had not yet built a school system the equal of Massachusetts, they had gone a long way in that direction since 1850.

Yet the system did not match the expectations of educational reformers or many Anglo settlers. In part their disappointment stemmed from the schools' failure to assimilate the Spanish-speaking population of New Mexico, although reformers tended to hold Hispanos themselves responsible for stubbornly clinging to their distinct ethnic identity. From the point of view of the reformer, the educational situation was most desperate in rural areas, where Spanish-speaking New Mexicans predominated. The schools, they believed, simply did not hold students long enough to teach them. In 1903 more than half of the state's school-age population did not attend any school. School terms, rural and urban, averaged four and a half months in length, while teachers earned an average of $250 per year.[53] By 1910 enrollment had risen to 60 percent of the school-age population, although on the average only 40 percent of those attended on a regular basis. Illiteracy, which had stood at 78.5 percent of the adult population in 1870, had decreased to 24 percent in 1910, still much higher than the national average of 8 percent of the adult population for that year.[54]

Like most American educators of the period, New Mexico's school administrators believed they could improve the schools by creating a bureaucratic hierarchy of control over the educational system. The officers of this bureaucracy, headed by the superintendent of public instruction, set out on the task of consolidating the schools, building a uniform curriculum, and rationalizing the school funding system so that local districts could build schoolhouses and pay their teachers.

In 1912 New Mexico's educators had a long, uphill battle before them in their campaign to build a school system that would help to acculturate the Spanish-speaking population. But it is doubtful that the ethnic identity of Hispanos would have been erased in the territorial period even had the schools been better financed or better organized. Certainly schooling had helped non-English-speaking groups elsewhere in the country to assimilate. But in New Mexico Hispanos, while they wished to learn English and American ways, had no desire to abandon their own cultural patterns. The paradoxical outcome was that educational conditions for Hispanos suffered, but they retained their ethnic identity. Such was the price paid for cultural integrity. And the paradox would not go away with statehood. The challenge of educating Spanish-speaking children and yet retaining Hispano culture would be one of the first priorities of New Mexico educators when the state was admitted to the Union.

When New Mexico finally became a state in 1912, the authors of the state constitution had an opportunity to sanction the bilingual, bicultural school system that had developed through local practice. With much ambiguity they squandered this opportunity, capitulating to pressure from the federal government to establish an English-only educational policy. Over the territorial period congressional opponents to New Mexico statehood frequently cited the persistent use of Spanish and the lack of an adequate educational system as reasons for keeping New Mexico out of the Union. The continued use of Spanish in the schools, courts, and even the territorial legislature of New Mexico vexed many eastern politicians and editors, who viewed New Mexicans as unworthy and unqualified participants in a democracy.[55] When at last Congress did pass an Enabling Act for New Mexico in 1910, the Senate specified that only English could be used in the schools.[56]

The New Mexicans who gathered to write the state constitution in September 1910 did not give in entirely to the dictates of Washington. Instead they wrote into the law contradictory and ambiguous clauses that would confuse educational matters for decades. Of one hundred convention delegates, only thirty-two were Hispanos, even though Hispanos made up the majority of the territory's population. The Hispanic delegation persuaded the convention to guarantee to Spanish-speaking New Mexicans the rights to use their language, to vote, to maintain their religion, and to have equal access to political office, the courts, and schools.[57]

The New Mexico Constitution ensured the right of Hispanos to participate in the educational system on an equal basis with Anglos. In Article XII, Section 10, the writers of the constitution explicitly declared that no discrimination was to be made against Hispanic children, and that they would not be subjected to segregation:

> Children of Spanish descent in the State of New Mexico shall never be denied the right and privilege of admission and attendance in the public schools or other public educational institutions of the State and they shall never be classed in separate schools, but shall forever enjoy perfect equality with other children in all public schools and educational institutions of the State, and the legislature shall provide penalties for violation of this section.[58]

Several more specific clauses reinforced this general provision. Under Art. XII, Sec. 9, no religious test could be required of either pupils or teachers, which both protected Catholics in the public schools and ensured that the schools would remain secular. And the constitution included what was essentially a compulsory school attendance law, with no reference to racial or ethnic background. Art. XII, Sec. 5, provided that "Every child of school age and of sufficient physical and mental ability shall be required to attend a public or other school."[59]

On the critical issue of the language of instruction to be used in the schools, the state constitution set up a troublesome contradiction. Art. XXI, Sec. 4, read that "Provision shall be made for the establishment and maintenance of a system of public schools which shall be open to all the children of the State and free from sectarian control, and said schools shall always be conducted in English."[60] By virtue of this passage, the practice of conducting schools in Spanish, which had been common in the territorial period, would cease to be legal, and English would be the only language of instruction in the public schools.

Elsewhere the constitution threw doubt on the English-only interpretation. Art. XII, Sec. 8, which implied that Spanish could be used in the teaching of Spanish-speaking children, read:

> The legislature shall provide for the training of teachers in the normal schools or otherwise, so that they may become proficient in both the English and Spanish languages, to qualify them to teach Spanish-speaking pupils and students in public schools . . . ; and shall provide proper means and methods to facilitate the teaching of the English language and other branches of learning to such pupils and students.[61]

This section of the constitution suggested that the use of Spanish in instruction was to be encouraged if it aided the teaching of English and other subjects to children who spoke only Spanish.

The language provisions in the constitution represented an attempt to steer a middle course between the demands of the Enabling Act and the wishes of the Spanish-speaking delegates at the convention. The Hispanic delegates insisted upon retention of Spanish in legislative debates and publications, but they did not oppose English instruction in the schools, suggesting that they foresaw the addition of English, rather than the loss of Spanish, in popular usage. Hispanos favored the introduction of English in the schools because they realized the economic benefits of being conversant in the language of Anglo society. These Hispanic representatives viewed the threat of segregation as a greater concern than the question of the language of instruction.[62]

The new state constitution thus did not resolve the controversy that had prevailed over the issue of the language of instruction in the schools through the territorial period. No consensus on the question existed among New Mexico educators at the time of statehood. Some believed that it was necessary for both pedagogical and practical reasons to use Spanish to teach Spanish-speaking children. Others considered the English-only policy to be pedagogically sound, as well as legally binding. Though territorial officials had attempted to implement a consistent English-only policy and a standard curriculum, local practice often proved contrary. This pattern would continue in the early statehood period. Official policy may have placed New Mexico squarely within the national agenda of educational reform, but the desire of local educators to accommodate to the needs of Hispano children led to practices that sometimes defied national norms. This pattern of local accommodation conflicting with state or national mandates characterized New Mexico's unique version of progressive education.

2 | Preservation and Accommodation
New Mexico Education in Early Statehood

JUST AFTER New Mexico gained statehood, Santa Fe County underwent a construction boom in school buildings. In the county's forty districts outside the city of Santa Fe, thirty-seven new schoolhouses were built between 1913 and 1915. Twenty-eight districts received some state aid, while parents contributed the rest of the cash and labor for the projects. Nine districts paid for the new buildings without any assistance from the state. According to the account of County Superintendent John V. Conway, the spate of new construction came just in time to remedy some intolerable conditions in the schools.[1]

Surveying the county in 1913, Conway found schools ranging from a fine two-story sandstone building in the railroad town of Los Cerrillos to a canvas tent schoolhouse in the mining camp of San Pedro. The superintendent described a one-room schoolhouse in the village of Jocona as being in "very poor condition, lying in a swampy boggy spot, which was detrimental to the health of the children. The room was too small and unfitted for school purposes. Very poor stove, and hardly any blackboards, very poor light, and no desks to speak of."[2] At Los Cuartelos Conway commented that the school building would make a "good dance-hall but a poor school room." Elsewhere in the county, schools featured leaky roofs, poor ventilation, dry-goods boxes for desks, dirt floors, and bad lighting.[3] Assistance from the state, along with their own efforts and money, enabled the citizens of Santa Fe County to ameliorate these deplorable conditions.

Statehood gave New Mexicans more power to collect and distribute their own tax money as they saw fit. That the state government and local citizens thought it appropriate to invest in education indicates a widespread desire to take control of this vital area of their lives. Hispanos predominated in twenty-eight of Santa Fe County's forty districts. Not just in school construction but also in deciding what would be taught in the schools, Hispanos took leading roles in the educational developments of the early statehood period.

School directors in Hispano districts tended to hire Spanish-speaking teachers for their schools. Teaching in a rural district often meant living in an isolated mountain village where everyone spoke Spanish. Transportation and roads were crude at best, making commuting from a larger town a near impossibility. Because a teacher lived in the community, it was better for everyone if she spoke the same language and understood the culture. The rural teacher's salary discouraged outsiders, while it opened opportunities for Hispanas who could not command high pay but were willing to teach in a tiny village where they had family nearby. Teachers with a first-grade certificate and a normal school diploma earned a monthly salary of from $70 to $90, but a teacher with only a third-grade certificate received $50 a month. Santa Fe County's teaching corps in 1914 was overwhelmingly female and Hispana; of sixty-five teachers, thirty-one were Hispanas. Twenty-nine of those had third-grade certificates, while one had a second-grade, and one held the first-grade certificate. The next largest group consisted of Anglo women, twelve with third-grade and eight with first-grade certificates. All but a few of the Anglo women taught in all-Anglo districts. Of the fourteen male teachers, all with third-grade ratings, twelve were Hispano and two were Anglo.[4] Few Anglos taught in Spanish-speaking communities, and even fewer Hispanos taught in Anglo communities.

The prevalence of Hispanas in teaching reflected the important role that women played in the social and economic life of their communities. Even in colonial times, New Mexican women had legal rights that allowed them to control property, bring suit in court, and retain their maiden names. Anglos found New Mexican women engaged in occupations ranging from shepherds and gold panners to healers, midwives, and laundresses. Into the American period, Hispanas continued to participate in economic activities both within and outside of the home. In the first three decades of the twentieth century, as Hispano men left the villages for seasonal labor in the beet fields or mines of Colorado, women maintained the fields and homes left behind. Extended family networks helped to sustain women as they took on outside work, managed single-parent homes, or became widows.[5] Teaching became a community-sanctioned and valued occupational outlet for Hispanas.

While not all schools for Hispano children were taught by Spanish-speaking teachers, enough were that Spanish was commonly used in the classroom despite policies to the contrary. Fabiola Cabeza de Baca, who taught at a small country school near Las Vegas in 1916, conducted a bilingual school out of necessity. Her students included Spanish-speaking Hispanos and Indians as well as English-speaking Anglos, and all became conversant in the language of the others. She claimed that the bilingual primary readers that she used were "the adopted texts of that day."[6] The state Board of Education selected the textbooks, often negotiating with publishers to make the books bilingual or to include lists of Spanish words in the editions to be distributed in New Mexico schools.[7]

Officially New Mexicans remained divided on the merits of using Spanish in the instruction of Spanish-speaking children. Hispanic state legislators repeatedly introduced measures that allowed for some use of Spanish in instruction, while the State Department of Education reminded teachers of the importance of using English.[8] In 1915 House Representative A. A. Sena sponsored an "Act Concerning the Teaching of Spanish in the Public Schools." The new law allowed the teaching of Spanish as a separate subject in any elementary or secondary school where a majority of the board of education favored it. In a passage that referred to bilingual instruction, the law stated that "the books used and the instruction given in said schools shall be in the English language, . . . [but] Spanish may be used in explaining the meaning of English words to Spanish-speaking pupils who do not understand English."[9] The law affirmed the pedagogical principle that children learn best if allowed to use their native language.

The legislature specifically targeted the Hispano population in other laws aimed at training teachers for the rural schools. In 1915 the legislature decreed that fifty student teachers were to be trained in the state normal schools, with "special attention . . . to the proper fitting of teachers to teach in the Spanish-American communities of the state." The students had to be fluent in both English and Spanish and agree to teach for two years in rural districts after completing the course.[10] This measure addressed the dearth of qualified teachers in the rural areas and pointed to a recognition that rural teachers needed communicative skills in Spanish to be effective.

In 1917 the legislature went even further in trying to circumvent the proponents of English-only instruction. A new law required teachers to be able "to teach reading in Spanish and English by the bi-lingual method to all pupils in the first, second, and third grades."[11] Although this law was repealed in 1923, it indicates the strength of the Hispano community in the state legislature and their commitment to the concept of bilingual instruction in the early years of statehood. In 1919 lawmakers passed an act that required teachers in rural school districts "inhabited principally by Spanish-speaking people" to be proficient in the reading, writing, and speaking of both Spanish and English. Although all instruction still had to be in English, the law provided that it was

> the duty of the teachers in said schools to teach, in addition to the required studies in the English language, Spanish reading to Spanish speaking pupils and to such English speaking pupils as may desire to learn Spanish reading. In addition thereto, the said teachers shall teach all Spanish speaking pupils to translate their English reading lessons into the Spanish language, to the end that such pupils may better understand that which they read in English.[12]

Governor Octaviano Larrazolo, Hispanic leaders, and Anglo friends of the Hispanic community all endorsed the law, which effectively allowed the use of Spanish in teaching English to Spanish-speaking children. In a letter to the

New York Times, reprinted in the Albuquerque paper *La Bandera Americana*, Bronson Cutting defended the governor's educational policy. Cutting, a wealthy New Yorker who had come to New Mexico for his health and had become an influential leader of the Progressive wing of the New Mexico Republican Party, answered critics who charged that the new law substituted Spanish for English as the language to be taught in the schools. He distinguished between the teaching of Spanish as the object of learning and the use of Spanish to help students learn English. No one in New Mexico questioned that the teaching of English should be compulsory. What was at stake, said Cutting, was the best method for teaching English to Spanish-speaking children. If bilingualism resulted, that was an added benefit for the citizens of the state.[13] The editors of *La Bandera Americana* frequently pointed out the advantages of bilingualism for New Mexicans. Not only was Spanish necessary for communicating in Hispano villages, but it opened opportunities for commercial and political relationships with other Spanish-speaking nations.[14] Not all New Mexicans, however, were convinced of the utility of speaking both languages.

While the legislature and the governor took the lead in promoting bilingual education, the Department of Education only reluctantly implemented the laws, if at all. The state agency issued circulars to teachers and superintendents explaining the laws.[15] But state officials showed little enthusiasm for bilingual instruction. While the state did not prevent the widespread practice of bilingual teaching, it did little to guide Spanish-speaking teachers or improve their quality of teaching. And not even Governor Larrazolo condoned the use of Spanish in teaching any subjects but English.[16]

At the heart of the debate over the language of instruction was the pedagogical question of how best to teach Spanish-speaking children. The laws passed in 1915, 1917, and 1919 favored instruction in Spanish in order to enhance the child's understanding of English. The primary mission was still to teach English rather than to make the child literate in Spanish. The benefit of bilingual instruction for the child, however, came in avoiding the frustration, confusion, and even humiliation that often accompanied the English-only method. Many New Mexico educators, working on their own in their local schools, used bilingualism as a means of treating Hispano children with dignity, thus enhancing the learning process.

Local educators came up with their own ideas for bilingual teaching. One experimental plan came to the attention of the State Board of Education in 1917. Alexia Coronel taught Spanish-speaking children in the elementary grades of the Raton schools, where she had tested her own method for teaching them English. During the first year the children learned to read in Spanish, while they practiced conversational skills in English. At the end of the first year, they had a solid vocabulary in both languages and could then proceed on in the second year to learn to read in English.[17]

The state Board of Education invited Coronel to demonstrate her Method Primer and phonetic chart and appointed a committee to look into the feasibility of adopting her method. The committee could not, however, find "sufficient expert opinion on the value of the method to warrant its adoption."[18] The lack of "expert opinion" on bilingual methods would hamper efforts to reach Spanish-speaking children for years to come. Educators placed themselves in a double bind: they would not use bilingual teaching methods unless they had been sanctioned by scientific authority, yet they conducted no scientific experimentation to determine the effectiveness of such methods.

The state Board of Education adopted only part of Coronel's program, stripped of its bilingual component. The board authorized for classroom use the *Beacon Primer*, the textbook utilizing a phonetic method for teaching English that Coronel had used in Raton. In the teaching aids the Department of Education issued for use in conjunction with the *Beacon Primer*, however, no mention was made of using a bilingual instructive approach along with the book, as Coronel had done. The only advice given to teachers relating specifically to their Spanish-speaking pupils was that "If the natural language of your children is other than English, do not allow this fact in any way to serve as an excuse for unsatisfactory language work. Your problem is to teach the English effectively. Put forth every effort and be assured of gratifying results."[19]

Although the Department of Education resisted bilingual instruction, other educators in New Mexico encouraged the use of Spanish as a teaching tool. Numerous articles discussing the merits of bilingual schooling appeared in the journal of the New Mexico Education Association, indicating that many teachers in New Mexico were familiar with and practiced bilingual instruction.

In 1917-18 D. B. Morrill, of Chamberino, wrote a series of articles in the *New Mexico Journal of Education* criticizing the "Direct Method" of English instruction. Morrill had no doubt that the "first task of the teacher of the Spanish-speaking child is to teach him to use the English language."[20] He did question the method of teaching English with no resort whatsoever to the native language of the child. In Morrill's view, using the Direct Method violated the "inexorable law of pedagogy that you must utilize the knowledge the child has, the result of all his past experiences, in imparting to him other knowledge."[21]

Morrill attributed the widespread use of the Direct Method partly to the laziness of teachers in not wanting to learn Spanish, and partly to the nature of teacher preparation programs. He claimed that it was "universally true" that teachers who knew Spanish were using it in the schools with good results. But the majority of teachers, not knowing Spanish, denied its effectiveness in teaching, leading to disastrous results for the Spanish-speaking children of New Mexico. According to Morrill, 90 percent of Spanish-speaking children did not go beyond the fourth grade.[22]

The institutions in charge of preparing and supervising teachers, Morrill believed, shared the responsibility for the failure to teach the Spanish-speaking child. While educational directors selected methods, sought out skilled teachers, and found suitable textbooks for all other branches of learning, Morrill charged that "they have supposed that learning English will come incidentally and as a matter of course to the Spanish-speaking child." He examined a teaching manual and found no references to the task of teaching English to Spanish-speaking children, although it provided specific suggestions for teaching all other subjects. Morrill was astounded to find that "the teaching of English to half the pupils of the state was not mentioned." He declared that a "pupil will no more learn the English language incidentally, without special effort to teach it to him, . . . than others will learn Spanish or Latin incidentally."[23]

Morrill's disparagement of this method of English instruction and his advocacy of Spanish instruction placed him in opposition to the policy of the State Department of Education. With teachers and state legislators advocating the use of bilingual instruction, the department's position against it may seem puzzling. Its stand was, however, in line with prevailing national sentiments regarding conformity in language use and the role of the schools in Americanization.

Unfortunately, during this critical time when New Mexico's educators were debating a language policy, the United States entered a world war and ushered in a period of rabid xenophobia and conformism. During World War I New Mexicans could not help but be caught up in the general patriotic fervor and the enhanced focus on Americanization that came with it. New Mexicans, after all, responded with enthusiasm to calls for overseas armed service and domestic wartime activity. After the U.S. Bureau of Education began to send "war study courses" to the schools across the country, patriotic campaigns appeared in New Mexico. Like many states New Mexico declared "Americanization Days" to draw attention to the virtues of the American way of life, government, and language. The State Department of Education distributed Americanization materials, sending circulars to the schools that recommended the use of Theodore Roosevelt's famous pledge: "One Flag, the American Flag; one language, the language of the Declaration of Independence; one Loyalty, Loyalty to the American people."[24] A conference of teachers and administrators issued a statement to justify the suspension of German instruction in the schools, declaring "We believe that the English language should be the first means of Americanization and should be the medium of communication between all citizens."[25]

Despite these attempts to equate patriotism with the use of English, many New Mexicans argued that being true to their own culture did not preclude loyalty to America. Nestor Montoya, editor of *La Bandera Americana,* indignantly protested a pending bill in Congress that would have outlawed the publication of newspapers in any language other than English. Montoya pointed to the wartime sacrifices made by Hispanos for country and flag as evidence of their patriotism.[26]

Influential groups in the state spoke against persecution of anyone on the basis of alleged "un-Americanism." The New Mexico chapter of the American Legion, organized by Bronson Cutting, refused to condone any efforts destructive of the cultural integrity of Hispanics.[27] In 1919 the national American Legion adopted a policy that English should be declared the only language in public school instruction. Although Cutting served as chairman of the Americanism Committee of the American Legion, he did not consider this Americanization mandate to be appropriate for New Mexico. Cutting declared that "We have no anti-American propaganda, no Bolshevism, no I.W.W., no disloyalty, and no organized group of foreign born inhabitants."[28] He understood Hispanos' devotion to the Spanish language and recognized that this did not make them any less worthy as citizens.

Americanization efforts in New Mexico may have seemed mild when compared with neighboring states, but even in New Mexico state officials sometimes used intrusive measures to reach into the home to Americanize the Spanish-speaking family. Because culture was nurtured in the home, Americanizers often went beyond the boundaries of the school in an attempt to strike at the root of the "problem" of foreign habits. One method used successfully in California under the Home Teacher Act of 1915 was to send so-called child welfare experts to the homes to work with both parents and children. These emissaries worked as adjuncts of the public school system, targeting Mexican immigrant women in particular as a means of reaching the entire family. While they often emphasized health and home economics practices, they also taught English in the hope of fostering assimilation.[29]

In 1919 the New Mexico legislature authorized the establishment of a Child Welfare Service under the auspices of the State Department of Education. The Child Welfare Service aimed to promote health reform by providing prenatal, maternity, and child care to Hispano families. Montana Hastings, a child psychologist from Columbia University and one of the first of the child welfare experts, saw her mission as smoothing the rifts between parents who liked to follow the traditional ways and their children who were becoming Americanized at school. Hastings directed her efforts toward the parents, since "much of the school work is defeated because home and street influences operate in opposition to the ideals set up by the school."³⁰ As the historian George J. Sánchez has shown regarding the California program, the object was not to destroy the traditional Hispanic home but to exploit its centrality by using the family to promote assimilationist values.³¹ Visiting social workers carried Anglo American culture with them to the home, and there, intentionally or not, they disparaged traditional ethnic practices by offering American customs as a substitute. The same socialization process prevailed in the formal classrooms of the public schools.

The Child Welfare Service in New Mexico illustrates the close connection between education and social work as vehicles for Americanization. Child welfare supervisors in each district were responsible for administering standard mental tests to children about to enter school for the first time. Each supervisor received "careful training" to qualify her "to apply the standard mental tests for general segregation of first year pupils." Montana Hastings instructed supervisors to turn over the results of the tests "to the principal who will make classifications accordingly and thus save much time which is usually lost by the process of weeks of trial on the part of each first year pupil."³² The child welfare supervisor thus had a great role not only in Americanizing the Hispanic family but also in determining the educational destiny of the children.

Hastings's guidelines to child welfare supervisors indicate that New Mexico educators utilized the results of intelligence tests to place children in differentiated classes. In doing so they were participating in a regional and national trend sweeping the country in the early twenties. Studies conducted in New Mexico schools, such as that of psychologist William H. Sheldon, reinforced the perception of Spanish-speaking children as less capable intellectually than Anglo children. Sheldon, who believed that intelligence tests allowed investigators to make comparisons of different races, carried out a series of mental tests at Roswell, New Mexico, in 1923. Publishing his findings in a major educational journal, Sheldon judged the intelligence of Mexican children to be "about 85 percent of that of a normal group of white children of the same age and social environment."³³ Such conclusions, seemingly sanctioned by professional opinion and reinforced by dozens of similar studies on other non-Anglo groups, could not have failed to exert an influence on educational policymaking in New Mexico.

Other aspects of the progressive reform movement coalesced at the same time to promote conformity and standardization in the schools. Nationwide, educators advocated a standardized curriculum, arguing that in an increasingly mobile society, children who moved from one place to another would be able to enter a new school at the same point as the one they had left. For administrators the uniform curriculum made evaluations and comparisons of different schools much easier. A uniform curriculum would provide standards for promoting students from one grade to the next or for entrance into college.[34] Curricular uniformity would assist in the creation of a common culture, albeit at the cost of abandoned local traditions and inappropriate curricula for community conditions.

Although New Mexico had issued a uniform course of study as early as 1907 and had changed it frequently, the Course of Study of 1923 may have been the most significant revision. This curricular guide included few references to the special problem of teaching English to Spanish-speaking children, one of the major instructional challenges for New Mexican teachers.[35] It did, however, reflect the influence of an educational survey conducted in the state in 1920.

Across the country the widespread use of school surveys contributed to a reliance on nationally recognized standards rather than local innovations. In the course of a survey, educational "experts" examined all aspects of a school program, reported the deficiencies and problems, and offered solutions, all wrapped in the rhetorical garb of "science." So compelling was the impetus for surveys that between 1911 and 1925 hundreds were conducted, and hardly a state school system in the country was left unsurveyed.[36]

As early as 1916, the New Mexico Board of Education proposed to have outside experts survey the state's schools.[37] This plan sat on the back burner while wartime concerns preoccupied Americans, but by 1920 a survey commission had been appointed and the project was underway. Three eminent educational experts comprised the team that conducted the school survey of 1920. George D. Strayer and William C. Bagley, of Teacher's College, Columbia University, and Ellwood P. Cubberley, of Stanford University, were nationally known for their work in reforming educational administration. Unfortunately only Mr. Bagley bothered to visit New Mexico for the survey, making a hasty eight-day tour of educational institutions around the state. Cubberley and Strayer read Bagley's fifty-nine page report and acquiesced in his hurried assessment.

Bagley recommended ways that New Mexicans could streamline and economize their school system through consolidation of the higher institutions of learning. In particular he advocated the elimination of the Spanish-American Normal School at El Rito. Although he did not visit the school, he concluded that it was "not essentially different from the better class of New Mexico rural schools and that its contribution to the supply of trained teachers for the State is negligible." He believed, furthermore, that it was "a questionable policy to attempt to segregate the preparation of teachers for the Spanish-American districts from the preparation of teachers for the other parts of the State."[38] Finding solutions to local problems did not result from giving special attention to those problems, but rather by improving the overall standards of teacher preparation, according to recognized, standard criteria. While state officials refused to close the Spanish-American Normal School, they did implement the survey's recommendations concerning the quality of teacher preparation.[39]

The 1920 New Mexico school survey led to a reevaluation of the state's school laws. The survey had revealed a high degree of dissatisfaction with the state's school system, particularly stemming from the confusion caused by contradictory interpretations of school legislation. In an attempt to rationalize the system, the legislature codified the school laws in 1923. The 1923 School Code raised the minimum qualifications for teachers and gave the State Board of Education more power to establish a uniform statewide curriculum. The code made no special provision for the instruction of Spanish-speaking children. Previous laws providing for bilingual instruction disappeared. The 1923 School Code contained no mention of the language of instruction, not even that English should be used.[40] Whether intended or not, the effect of the 1923 School Code was to apply the same rules to all schools, regardless of local conditions.

Although the new law ignored Spanish-speaking children, officials in the Department of Education interpreted the code as a mandate for applying progressive policies to their special needs. This specialized attention often came in the form of identifying Hispanos as a "problem" and segregating them as a solution. Mental tests became the means of identifying "problem" children. State Superintendent Jonathan Wagner endorsed the statewide use of intelligence tests as a goal in 1920. Test results, he believed, gave school officials the "objective" data they needed to determine where students should be placed in their first year of school. Despite the constitutional injunction against segregation, New Mexico schools earmarked prospective students for segregated classrooms, citing pedagogical grounds. The practice apparently continued through the 1920s, for in 1930 State Superintendent Atanasio Montoya spoke of "a decided tendency" of several years standing "to find out and recognize individual differences among pupils." These efforts, he believed, had led to a "much-needed differentiation in courses of study and homogenous grouping of students."[41]

The question of how to teach Spanish-speaking children thus created a tremendous dilemma for New Mexican educators. Through the 1920s the State Department of Education grappled with the challenge, providing what direction it could to teachers. In 1921 the New Mexico Course of Study offered little specific help to teachers of Spanish-speaking children. The guidelines suggested that all lessons should teach language and "every exercise is an exercise in English." Teachers were encouraged to pay more attention to oral language work than had been done in the past and to build vocabulary out of the child's own experiences. Games, stories, dramatizations, and conversation formed the basis of language instruction. Spanish-speaking children would learn a working vocabulary in English by becoming acquainted with the school environment through naming objects and learning to follow directions.[42]

On the local level, practices continued to vary widely. Through the 1920s some local school boards insisted that teachers use the Direct Method, which entailed suppression of all use of Spanish in the schools. Some teachers even punished children for using Spanish.[43] In other districts Spanish continued to be used. Many teachers simply used the methods that came naturally to them. Josephine Córdova, just graduated from Taos High School, went to teach in the Arroyo Seco school around 1924. She did not recall any special guidance from the state on the teaching of Spanish-speaking children. Although she saw her primary task as teaching her pupils English, she used Spanish to do so. Córdova listened to the children's Spanish words and translated them into English, both verbally and in writing on the board. She never punished children for speaking Spanish.[44]

By 1930 the Course of Study included an eleven-page section devoted exclusively to teaching English to the Spanish-speaking child under segregated conditions. In a section called "Removing the Language Difficulty," the teacher found a year-long course outline for imparting a working verbal vocabulary to non-English speakers. At the end of this year of exclusively oral work, the student should have mastered a basal vocabulary of 550 words, correct pronunciation, and clear enunciation. During this course, the guide read, "There will be no text book of any sort in the hands of the pupils." Upon completion of this year of work, the student could then proceed to first grade, where she or he would learn to read. The Direct Method, or total immersion, which "is recognized by authorities as being the most efficient way to teach any language," was to be used. The child "must learn from the first to think as well as to talk in English. Activities must be provided which demand and occasion need for expression. Every lesson should be an English lesson."[45]

This course of study for non-English-speaking children rested upon recognized scientific authority and mirrored standard practice throughout the Southwest. Its premises made sense by all prevailing pedagogical standards of the time. Yet the practice of curricular differentiation entailed the segregation of Hispanic children from Anglo children, at least in the first year. Children who already spoke English did not need a year of English instruction and could proceed directly to first grade and reading lessons. Meeting the special needs of Spanish-speaking students meant separating them for a customized course and holding them back a year from their chronological age group. Thus Spanish-speaking children who had experienced the special year of English instruction would be overage for their grade throughout their school career, perhaps marked indelibly with the stigma of having been in a "special" class.

Educators in the 1920s understood the risks involved in subjecting children to humiliating experiences such as being segregated or labeled "retarded." Some educators attempted to compensate for these degrading practices, even though they defended such methods on pedagogical grounds. The work of Nina Otero-Warren reveals a more sympathetic approach to educating Spanish-speaking children. Otero-Warren saw it as purely common sense that students should not be humiliated in a learning situation. She believed it was possible to provide Hispano children a measure of dignity in school by encouraging them to take pride in their ethnic identity. As a school administrator, Otero-Warren sought a middle way in the schooling of Hispano children that would give them the tools for living in American society while preserving some of their own cultural patterns.

Otero-Warren's attitudes as well as her opportunity to create a public role for herself derived from her background as a member of an old, upper-class Hispano family. Born in 1881 in Los Lunas, New Mexico, Nina Otero was the daughter of Eloisa Luna and Manuel B. Otero. Her mother's family, the Lunas, had received a grant of land on which they founded the village in 1695. From the Otero family came many prominent settlers, jurists, and political leaders in New Mexico's history. Among these was Nina's uncle Miguel A. Otero, who served as territorial governor of New Mexico from 1897 to 1906.[46]

As a descendant of two distinguished New Mexico Hispanic families, Nina grew up with a sense of the obligations and expectations of her class. The traditional class structure of New Mexico had remained intact in many of its essential features well into the American period. At the heart of this social order was the relationship between *patrones* and *peones*. The *patrón* employed the *peones,* who lived on his land, compensating them with food and other supplies. The *patrones* also provided advice and guidance, including political persuasion under the American system, and the *peones* generally responded with a loyal devotion and obedience.[47] Participants remembered the relationship with either warm nostalgia or bitter resentment, indicating that the system worked well for some but brought oppression for others.[48] Throughout her life Nina Otero exhibited the sense of noblesse oblige characteristic of the *patrón* class.

In 1883 Nina's father, Manuel B. Otero, was shot and killed in a land dispute. In 1886 Nina's mother married A. M. Bergere, a Santa Fe businessman. As was appropriate for a young woman of her class, Nina Otero attended private schools in New Mexico and was then sent to the Academy of the Sacred Heart (later Maryville College) in St. Louis for further study. In 1908 she married Captain Rawson Warren, an officer in the U.S. Army. After an unhappy marriage lasting less than two years, Nina Otero-Warren left her husband, a fact that she disguised throughout her life by referring to herself as a widow. After the death of her mother in 1914, Nina took charge of her stepfather's household in Santa Fe, where she cared for her six sisters and two brothers.⁴⁹

In 1917 the Republican Party appointed Nina Otero-Warren county school superintendent in Santa Fe, an office she won in her own right in the 1918 election and held until 1929. As Santa Fe County superintendent, she did much to upgrade a school system that had been plagued with indebtedness, poor facilities, and erratic schedules. She balanced the county school budget, even achieving a budget surplus within five years. She insisted that all teachers in the county become certified, while she increased their salaries. She placed all the schools in the county on standard nine-month terms. Under her leadership two new four-year high schools for rural students were built, and the county's first school nurse was hired.⁵⁰ These reforms marked her as an economically minded, business-like progressive educator.

What set Nina Otero-Warren apart from the average progressive educator, however, was her emphasis on cultural preservation. She devoted much energy throughout her life to the promotion and preservation of Hispanic culture, especially the arts, folklore, and drama of traditional New Mexico. She collected Hispanic stories, plays, songs, and traditional lore, some of which were incorporated into her own book, *Old Spain in Our Southwest,* published in 1936. Her view of Hispanic culture and what should be preserved from it became the basis of the curricular accommodations she implemented for Hispanic schoolchildren.

Nina Otero-Warren reflected and defended the attitudes of her class, the *patrones* of New Mexican society. Like many Hispanos of the upper class, she shared the common popular belief in the "New Mexico legend," the idea that the original conquistadores were all of pure Spanish blood and that the Spanish-surnamed population of New Mexico descended directly from a pure Spanish lineage. No matter that this was largely a romantic fiction and that most families, even if derived from a peninsular ancestor, had intermarried at some point with the native Indian population, either Pueblo or *genízaro.*⁵¹ Otero-Warren went to great lengths to trace her own ancestry back to Spain and to compile historical sketches demonstrating the aristocratic origins of her genealogy.

Because of her class orientation, Otero-Warren idealized the social relationship between *patrones* and *peones.* In *Old Spain in Our Southwest,* she describes colonial New Mexico as composed of self-sufficient communities in which rich and poor lived together in interdependent harmony. The *peones* "were not slaves, but working people who preferred submission to the *patrón* rather than an independent chance alone."⁵² Life was a difficult but nevertheless idyllic existence, in which *ricos* and *pobres* lived "close to the soil and to nature. They cherished their traditions, inherited from Spain and adapted to their new life. Theirs was a part of the feudal age, when master and man, although separate in class, were bound together by mutual interests and a close community of human sympathy."[53] She suggested that much of this way of life still remained intact in her own time.

Otero-Warren's idealized version of the Hispano past coincided with the romanticized view of the region promoted by Anglo boosters, writers, and artists. Anglo organizations as disparate as the Spanish Colonial Arts Society and the Santa Fe Railroad promoted New Mexico as a picturesque and unspoiled premodern society. Ironically Anglos created new traditions, such as the Santa Fe Fiesta, to celebrate the formerly despised culture of Hispanic New Mexico.[54] Nina Otero-Warren supported and aided the work of the Spanish Colonial Arts Society, which was dedicated to the preservation and rejuvenation of Hispanic art. She collected folklore and arranged for the society to sponsor shows of schoolchildren's arts and crafts work.[55] Mary Austin and other Anglo friends encouraged her to write *Old Spain in Our Southwest*, and the book affirmed what the artists wished to believe was the authentic version of New Mexican history.[56]

Otero-Warren's romantic account of New Mexican life undoubtedly engendered pride in the Hispano heritage. Yet romanticizing the past denied Hispanos a complete understanding of their own history and obscured the harsh political and economic realities that they faced. And idealizing past traditions such as colonial arts and crafts stunted indigenous artistic growth by forcing artists to imitate the styles of the past. By making Hispanos appear quaint and festive, the Spanish colonial revival reinforced stereotypes and warped Anglo perceptions of Hispano culture. Yet with Hispano leaders such as Otero-Warren embracing the vision of Anglo boosters, it was highly unlikely that a realistic account of Hispano culture and history could have been promoted in the schools. The message implicit in Otero-Warren's truncated version of Hispanic culture was one of accommodation and partial assimilation. She sought to inspire ethnic pride, but not at the cost of threatening a harmonious relationship between Anglos and Hispanos.

Nina Otero-Warren used her position as Santa Fe County school superintendent to spread her message to isolated Hispanos. Her jurisdiction included a number of rural villages, such as Cundiyo, located in the Sangre de Cristo Mountains above the city. Otero-Warren visited these secluded communities as often as possible, to enjoy the warm hospitality of the local folk, whom she described as "a gentle, industrious, and intelligent people, brown-eyed and suntanned." Visiting the children in their classrooms, she wondered "how to encourage them to preserve the arts, the customs, and the traditions of this New Spain in an effort to save its charm, which is its very life."[57]

The majority of the schoolchildren of Santa Fe County came from Spanish-speaking homes and lived in small villages or on farms. It was very important to Otero-Warren that such children receive a quality education, which she defined as an American education. She counseled Hispanos that "it is to our best interests that we become educated according to the standards of [the United States]. It has, for us, its distinct advantages, its definite protection." At the same time she thought that the national curriculum should be modified to spark the interest of Hispanos and enable them to retain what was valuable of their own culture. Hispanos would be making "a definite contribution to the cultural background of this country" if the native culture were incorporated into the curriculum of the schools.[58]

In 1929 Otero-Warren introduced a new course of study for the Santa Fe County elementary schools, modifying the curriculum to encourage an appreciation of Hispanic culture. Customs and activities indigenous to a particular community were to be incorporated into the programs of its school. She encouraged teachers to "Find out what games the children's parents played" and to revive them as part of the physical education program in the school. The traditional games were even preferred to American games that typically served as vehicles for Americanization. "Where old time games best suit the community," she instructed, "they should be used instead of baseball."[59]

The rationale behind Otero-Warren's curriculum reflected the progressive ideals of John Dewey in its emphasis upon the relationship between school and community life. Each school was expected to emphasize activities that the student would meet in daily life. It was thus hoped that the traditions of every community would be carried on to the next generation through the school. Otero-Warren considered the economic activities traditionally pursued in the community to be a vital part of village life. As she wrote in the course of study, "The industries of people who have lived in this country for so long should not be allowed to disappear or become modernized." In communities where traditional weaving, pottery, tinwork, beadwork, and other crafts were still practiced, the children should be instructed in these activities by "the experts of the community."[60]

Including traditional economic activities in the curriculum of the schools aimed at more than merely preserving the traditional culture. The livelihood of the village itself might be ensured if Hispanos could find markets for traditional craft products. This had been one of the goals of the Spanish Colonial Arts Society, which helped to organize the Santa Fe Fiesta and opened an outlet store to encourage the marketing of traditional crafts. Otero-Warren supported these efforts by arranging for the artwork of schoolchildren to be exhibited at the fiesta and in the Spanish Arts shop. Spanish colonial arts, however, failed to generate a sustainable market in the 1920s or 1930s, despite the efforts of the Spanish Colonial Arts Society and later programs of the New Deal.[61]

Otero-Warren was among the first in New Mexico's educational community to define the goal of cultural preservation as an element of educational policy. Nationally, progressive educators had incorporated industrial education into the curriculum to prepare future citizens for productive lives in the industrial work force. Progressives defined the needs of these students as the skills and values required by industrial society, irrespective of their cultural background. Otero-Warren agreed with the progressive emphasis on industrial training in the schools, but believed that the answer to Hispanos' economic needs lay in their own culture rather than the industrial society of mainstream America.

Otero-Warren believed that the vitality of a culture depended not only upon the survival of time-honored customs and arts, but also upon the continued use of the native language. She thought that the teaching of Spanish in the elementary schools was "not only desirable but necessary. Bi-lingualism will bring about a closer cooperation between the home and the school. The strongest tie between the two is language."[62] She encouraged students and teachers alike to think of bilingualism as a valuable tool, and she believed that the schools had a responsibility to help Hispano children achieve fluency in both languages. In 1941 Otero-Warren supported the efforts of her friend Concha Ortiz y Pino, a member of the New Mexico House of Representatives, to pass legislation requiring the teaching of Spanish in the elementary schools.[63]

Yet Otero-Warren never went so far as to defy the dominant consensus that accommodation and a level of acculturation should be the ultimate goals for the Hispano community. She recognized that Hispanos needed to learn many skills and values from the dominant society if they were to survive. A solid grounding in the English language was the first step to learning other skills. The schools, in following a standard curriculum devised for mainstream children, made no adjustment for the special needs of Spanish-speaking children, and Otero-Warren was determined to rectify this failing. She felt strongly that it was poor instruction in English that had held back many Spanish-speaking children in school and contributed to high drop-out rates as they grew older. As she wrote in the Santa Fe County curriculum, "The greatest handicap the non-English speaking child has is the untrained teacher."[64]

To combat this problem she proposed her own method of teaching English to non-English speakers. She stressed a sympathetic approach to teaching the non-English-speaking child, urging teachers to familiarize themselves with the experiences and home life of the student. She encouraged teachers to develop "a feeling of comradeship, friendliness, and mutual belief so that the child may be freed from embarrassment and self consciousness." The Hispanic child who knows no English "is extremely sensitive and timid, though he is actuated by the same impulses and craves the same attention as all children, and responds in the same way to right teaching procedures and treatment." A poorly trained or insensitive teacher only intensifies the difficulty of learning English.[65]

Otero-Warren thought that teachers working with Spanish-speaking children ought to be fluent in Spanish themselves, and that students should not be punished for speaking Spanish in school. Few New Mexican educators favored the use of Spanish in the classroom, even though the state constitution allowed for the training of teachers in both English and Spanish to enable them to teach Spanish-speaking children. State officials in fact pressured teachers to instruct students in English and to discourage or suppress the use of Spanish in the schools. Otero-Warren succumbed to the prevailing practice and did not permit the use of Spanish in classroom instruction, but unlike many educators, she urged teachers to employ the Spanish language in school in the form of songs, plays, and games. She felt that allowing the informal use of Spanish would still impart the important message to students that their language was worthwhile.

Nina Otero-Warren's innovations offered a model for reform, but few state officials took notice. In the *Course of Study* issued by the State Department of Public Instruction for 1930, the section on teaching English to Spanish-speaking children ignored Otero-Warren's work in Santa Fe. Missing entirely from the state plan was any program for incorporating Spanish arts and crafts into the curriculum of the schools. It remained for other, more forceful educational leaders to transform these ideas into official state policy.

Nina Otero-Warren is remembered as an effective champion of Hispanic culture, as well as a humane and dedicated educator. While she often assumed the role of *patrón* in deciding what was best for Hispanos of the lower classes, she sincerely cared for the welfare of her people and did much to increase their educational opportunities. As an advocate of bilingual instruction and multicultural education, she was far ahead of her time. She was also a dedicated progressive educator, who did not believe that an American education had to result in the loss of Hispanic culture. Her work in Santa Fe did not significantly alter the wider pattern of education for Hispanos in New Mexico in the short run, but soon other educators would follow her lead.

As the 1920s came to a close, a remarkable confluence of energetic young educators emerged and began to inspire changes in state educational policy. Some of those developments were foretold at a meeting of the New Mexico Education Association in 1929. On October 30 of that year, the New Mexico Education Association met on the campus of the University of New Mexico in Albuquerque for their annual convention. After an opening invocation by Rabbi H. D. Bloom, Mayor Clyde Tingley welcomed the participants to his city. NMEA President James F. Zimmerman, of the University of New Mexico, chaired the meeting. State Superintendent of Public Instruction Atanasio

Montoya addressed the gathering, challenging the state to find more funding sources for rural schools.[66] J. R. McCollum warned against political corruption, waste, and favoritism in school administration.[67]

During the four days of the conference, the members could attend any of a number of sessions devoted to issues of interest to New Mexican educators. In the English Section, members could hear UNM folklorist Arthur Campa speak on "Collecting Folk Literature in New Mexico." The county superintendents got together to hear Dean S. P. Nanninga of the UNM College of Education talk about "The New County Superintendent." Perhaps Nanninga had in mind Santa Fe County Superintendent Nina Otero-Warren, who spoke about "The Rural School Supervisor at Work." Across campus delegates in the Vocational Section debated what was right and wrong about the National Vocational Education Act.[68]

At its final session the entire assembly heard Governor R. C. Dillon boast that "the two largest items on New Mexico's public budget are spent for schools and roads."[69] After the governor finished touting his administration, a panel addressed the question "Is the Spanish-American Child Handicapped on Account of Language Difficulties?" On the panel sat Edna Rousseau, the state's rural school supervisor; Dr. B. F. Haught, the director of the graduate school at UNM; and Dr. Loyd S. Tireman, an associate professor of education at UNM.

Rousseau reported the results of a statewide study on school performance she had recently finished. She concluded that the Spanish-American child suffered "a decided handicap because of unfamiliarity with the English language."[70] Haught rebuked Rousseau's assertions with an opinion that had prevailed throughout the previous decade: the native intelligence of the average Spanish child was lower than that of the average Anglo child. After testing children from seven to nineteen years of age, Haught reasoned that the language handicap did not exist, since IQ scores did not increase as the child became better acquainted with English. Haught chided teachers who "are inclined to think that this does not mean a genuine inferiority but [believe] that low scores are due to language difficulty encountered in taking the tests."[71] Loyd Tireman offered to resolve the contradictory messages of Rousseau and Haught. While he acknowledged that Spanish-speaking children fell below the standard of Anglos, he attributed the difference to the greater exposure of reading material in English found in Anglo homes. If the schools offered a stronger reading program and made more books available to Hispanos through the grades, he believed they would show a marked improvement in test scores.[72]

Finally the conference closed with the election of a new slate of officers for 1930. Charles B. Redick of Gallup became the new president, Raymond Huff of Clayton was elected treasurer, and young Bernalillo County teacher George Sánchez received the nod for secretary.[73]

This gathering of the NMEA in late 1929 brought together a number of educators who were vitally interested in improving education for New Mexico's children. Although motivated by different reasons and advocating different methods, James F. Zimmerman, Atanasio Montoya, Clyde Tingley, George Sánchez, S. P. Nanninga, Raymond Huff, Edna Rousseau, Arthur Campa, Nina Otero-Warren, B. F. Haught, Loyd S. Tireman, and others would focus much attention on the education of Hispanos in New Mexico in the 1930s. The issues brought up at the Albuquerque conference would challenge and divide them in the coming decade. New Mexico's perennial lack of resources, compounded by partisan favoritism, would haunt educators in the financially strapped and politically charged years of the Depression. Yet new faces and fresh ideas appeared on the scene in 1929. Educators such as Tireman and Sánchez stood ready to challenge outdated notions of Hispanic inferiority and explore new teaching methods. Zimmerman, Nanninga, Montoya, Tireman, Sánchez and others would seek creative funding sources, force changes in state policy, address the problems of rural schools, and implement new approaches to vocational education. It was an exciting time to be involved in this work, and it was a dramatic moment in the educational history of New Mexico.

During the first two decades of statehood, New Mexicans had witnessed much progress in education. From a preoccupation with the basics of building a schoolhouse for every district, educators had advanced to the more sophisticated concern of how best to teach each child. In deciding what the schools should teach, the two themes of preservation and accommodation had emerged during this period. Many wanted to preserve what they considered valuable in Hispano culture, while others wished to accommodate to American society. Nina Otero-Warren may have best epitomized New Mexico educators during this time in her desire to do both. The two themes were in evidence at the 1929 NMEA conference. What is most striking about that meeting was the prominence given the question of teaching the Spanish-speaking child at the final plenary session. Maintaining the focus on the improvement of rural schooling for Hispanos would be the greatest challenge for educators in the difficult decade ahead.

3 | George I. Sánchez in New Mexico

In 1940 George I. Sánchez made news with an attack on educational conditions for Hispanos in New Mexico. In a slim volume entitled *Forgotten People,* Sánchez bluntly faulted the Anglo-dominated territorial government, backed by the federal government, for failing to provide New Mexicans with the means necessary to make the transition from Mexican to American rule. He portrayed a history of neglect extending into the period of statehood, under which Hispanos were expected to conform to American standards but were denied the economic and educational tools that would have made acculturation possible.[1] It was a message that few Anglos in New Mexico welcomed. Even those who were sympathetic to the plight of Hispanos and who had supported and nurtured Sánchez through his young career did not want to hear another jarring analysis of conditions in New Mexico. Yet it typified his approach.

Many Anglo and Hispano leaders in New Mexico in the 1930s regarded George Sánchez as a Hispanic leader with great potential to act as a "broker" between the two cultures. They hoped that he would smooth over the issues dividing the two peoples by illuminating the positive and uncontroversial features of their shared history. But Sánchez failed to provide a view of history that would have absolved the Anglo-dominated power structure of its responsibility for the poor conditions of Hispanos. Neither did he romanticize Hispano culture or deny the need for change by Hispanos themselves. Rather he envisioned a positive course of progress based upon objective scientific reasoning and in the process antagonized both Anglos and Hispanos.

As a native Spanish-speaking New Mexican, Sánchez understood the conditions of Hispanos from the bottom up. He knew how frustrating it was to attend a school where the language was foreign and the teachers unsympathetic. He also recognized the need for his people to enter the mainstream of American life and realized the value of a good education in achieving that goal. As an educator trained at several prestigious universities, he shared a faith in science and the practices supported by scientific study. Yet he questioned certain of those practices, particularly intelligence testing as it was then used. While he made his greatest impact upon education in the Southwest as a professor at the University of Texas from 1941 through the 1960s, his early career in New Mexico reveals much about his character and commitment to his people. It also explains much about the slow progress made to improve the schools of New Mexico, especially during the difficult years of the Great Depression.

George Isidore Sánchez was born in Albuquerque, New Mexico, on 4 October 1906, but spent much of his youth in Arizona, where his father worked as a miner. George returned to Albuquerque to attend high school, graduating in 1923. He immediately went to work as a school teacher at Yrrisarri, a small village in the Sandia Mountains, east of Albuquerque, to which he commuted on horseback. The next year he taught at San Ignacio, or "Stinking Springs," another rural school outside of Albuquerque, and in 1926 he became teacher and principal of the Griegos-Candelarias School in Bernalillo County. Teaching during the school year, he attended the University of New Mexico during summer sessions, completing his baccalaureate degree in 1930.[2]

In his early career Sánchez benefited from the help of influential patrons who recognized his talent. In 1930 President James F. Zimmerman of UNM persuaded the General Education Board of the Rockefeller Foundation to award Sánchez a scholarship for graduate study at the University of Texas.[3] Zimmerman and other New Mexican educators had been courting the aid of the General Education Board for several years. The General Education Board, founded by John D. Rockefeller in 1902, existed primarily to improve educational conditions in the South, especially for African-Americans. The board's decision to send assistance to New Mexico indicated that they saw in the Hispano population a situation parallel to that of Blacks in the South. Programs sponsored by the General Education Board in the South aimed to create a productive labor force through education. That the board chose to support George Sánchez suggested that GEB officials saw in the young Hispano someone who had the leadership potential to improve the social conditions of his people. This suppport also fit in nicely with the board's precedents for meeting its mission, since it had a record of fostering the careers of promising young African-Americans through scholarships.[4] New Mexicans who sought its aid understood the GEB's commitment to the education of African-Americans and recognized that the parallels between the two populations enhanced the board's interest in New Mexico.[5]

Sánchez did not disappoint his philanthropic supporters. At Austin he completed his master's degree in educational psychology under Herschel T. Manuel, already well-known for his interest in the education of Spanish-speaking children. Manuel encouraged Sánchez to work with the Spanish-speaking population, whose school conditions were just coming under scrutiny. Nearly every observer of the educational status of Hispanic children in the late 1920s and 1930s noted the high percentage of overage pupils in this group, indicating that more Spanish-speaking children than the average were held back one or more grades.⁶ A study conducted under the auspices of the U.S. Office of Education in 1933 revealed the extent of this and the related problem of early elimination, or dropping out, among Spanish-speaking pupils. Surveying educational achievement across the Southwest, Annie Reynolds found that "for 100 Mexican children in grade 1 there are 7 in grade 8, while for 100 non-Mexican children in grade 1 there are 52 in grade 8." That amounted to an elimination rate of 93 percent for Mexican children compared to 48 percent for non-Mexican children.⁷

Even more disturbing, an array of studies on intelligence testing in the 1920s reinforced notions of inferior racial intelligence and justified low expectations for Spanish-speaking children. Discounting the cultural and class biases of IQ tests, psychologists and educators tested both Anglo and non-Anglo children across the Southwest, only to conclude that the resulting disparities should be linked to racial intelligence. By the end of the 1920s, psychometricians had successfully introduced educators to the notions that intelligence was innate, that it could be measured, and that mental test results could be used to predict a child's success in school.

The psychologist William H. Sheldon easily made the leap from assuming the validity of intelligence tests for individuals to their use in the comparison of different racial groups. Reporting on a study conducted in Roswell, New Mexico, in 1924, Sheldon stated that "it is now well established that intelligence tests enable us to compare accurately the ability of one child with another." Therefore, he argued, "it seems probable that in the same way we can reliably compare the intelligence of children of different races by means of such tests."⁸ He thought that Mexican children developed mentally on a par with white children until they reached the age of twelve, when they ceased to grow at the same rate.⁹

Similar conclusions supporting the racial inferiority of Hispanics surfaced in other studies completed around the Southwest.¹⁰ The appeal of the intelligence test for educators was that it offered a partial solution to the challenge of adapting the school to the child's needs. Using this measurement educators believed they could determine what each child was capable of doing and then offer a curriculum suited to the individual child. What happened with intelligence testing throughout the Southwest, however, was that the individual child often got lost in the focus on the group. The message that frequently emerged was that Mexicans as a group, *as a race,* had a lower intelligence level than Anglo children as a group. Certainly some teachers treated Mexican children as individuals, but the prevalence of patterns of segregation based on pedagogical principles suggests that educators often interpreted the results of intelligence testing as proving the innate inferiority of Mexicans.

In his work in New Mexico, George I. Sánchez sought to reverse these patterns. For his master's thesis he used data that he had gathered at the Griegos-Candelarias School to explore the issue of language as a factor in intelligence. "A Study of Scores of Spanish-Speaking Children on Repeated Tests" was completed in 1931 and published in the form of articles the following year.[11] Sánchez pointed out that investigators through the 1920s had conducted studies of various racial and linguistic groups, offering their results "as indicative of the superiority of Germanic heredity and of the validity of 'intelligence' tests in the measurement of inherent capacity."[12] Sánchez had administered a series of tests over three years to the same group of Spanish-speaking children at the Griegos-Candelarias School, in order to determine the validity of these assumptions. He found that intelligence scores improved with longer exposure to education and greater facility in English, "which makes it seem quite possible that school experience is an important factor in producing improvements in the abilities (or in revealing native abilities) of children of inferior environment."[13]

Sánchez admitted that the homes of most Spanish-speaking children in New Mexico offered an inferior environment in terms of socioeconomic status. Indeed his case against intelligence tests rested upon this assessment, as it was precisely this factor that the tests failed to take into account. He insisted that "inferior home environment and language limitations must be considered in interpreting the test results of Spanish-speaking children in New Mexico." Sánchez's own testing program, in which children improved their scores after exposure to a positive school environment, demonstrated that inferior intelligence was not the determining factor in these students' performance.[14]

Pointing to recent studies that had raised questions about intelligence tests, Sánchez observed that investigators faced a choice of three possible explanations for differences in test performance between groups: innate capacity, environment, or bilingualism. Psychometricians could no longer pretend that intelligence tests were unassailable, but had to recognize that "the scientific value of test results is not entirely determined by the reliability of the measure used but is conditioned by the extent to which the complex factors of heredity, environment, and language, individually and collectively, have entered into the program."[15]

While Sánchez was by no means the only educational psychologist to point out problems of intelligence testing, his arguments carried weight by virtue of their cogency and scientific logic. He did not advocate a complete repudiation of tests, but asked simply that educators not abuse them by ignoring environmental and linguistic factors. Educators could use tests profitably to advance the educational interests of individual children only if it were recognized what the tests were actually measuring. In most instances, he argued, test results reflected not the innate ability of the child, but rather the performance of the school itself, or the set of opportunities afforded by the child's home.

Too often the school failed to educate the Spanish-speaking child or to compensate for a deficient background, while blaming the child for his failure. Sánchez asked pointedly who should be held responsible for this lack of success:

> Is the fact that a child makes an inferior score on an intelligence test prima facie evidence that he is dull? Or is it a function of the test to reflect the inferior or different training and development with which the child was furnished by his home, his language, the culture of his people, and by his school? When the child fails in promotion is it *his* failure or has the school failed to use the proper whetstone in bringing out the true temper and quality of his steel?[16]

Sánchez answered that it was the school's responsibility to provide the experiences which would be measured by the test. When the school provided all the language, cultural, and informational experiences that the child needed, "then failure on his part to respond to tests of such experiences and activities may be considered his failure."[17]

In blaming the schools for failing to educate the Spanish-speaking student, Sánchez had particularly in mind the schools of New Mexico, which he knew from first-hand experience and which he was in a position to influence. Even before he had completed his master's thesis at Texas, Sánchez proposed the creation of a research position for himself in the New Mexico State Department of Education, to be funded by the General Education Board. He suggested that it be named the Division of Research and Statistics, and the functions he envisioned for it reflected the scientific bent that the title implied. The division would supervise "controlled and coordinated research projects" in the schools and carry out "testing programs and studies of test results." Effective teaching methods would be explored, including questions of using Spanish or English for beginners and the effect of preschool training upon retardation and "elimination." The division would also gather and compile data on results of experiments, making this information available to teachers and supervisors through conferences and publications. Acting as a clearinghouse for information, the division would examine literature on related projects in Texas, Arizona, California, and Mexico and "establish exchange channels with other investigators for cooperative effort."[18]

Sánchez's proposal revealed his faith, so typical of progressive educators, in the power of scientific methods to solve problems and in the persuasive impact of statistics to influence people. The directors of the General Education Board shared this faith as well and agreed to fund the division for four years, beginning in July 1931, after which time the state would assume full support of it. George Sánchez thus became director of the Division of Information and Statistics.[19]

Sánchez plunged enthusiastically into the work of gathering and disseminating information on New Mexico education. For four years he energetically amassed statistics, wrote reports and articles, and traveled around the state to meet with various school officials.[20] Educators and legislators were placed on alert that Sánchez intended to demonstrate with the conclusive evidence of statistics the inadequacy of the state's schools. In his first annual report, Sánchez revealed his zealous faith in the persuasive power of his research. Although not all that was "vital to New Mexico education" could be demonstrated "by the tabular presentation of school statistics," he believed that "any conscientious study of the present report will point to the urgency of the educational crisis which is no longer a possibility but a grim fact in New Mexico." For Sánchez the statistics clearly revealed that "Increasing school loads coupled to decreasing school revenues from an archaic taxation system cannot but lead to a tragedy in state education." He called upon the general public and legislative leaders to "realize the urgency of the situation and bend every effort to secure educational reform in the interests of the state."[21]

Believing that the educational conditions of Spanish-speaking children represented New Mexico's greatest problem, Sánchez intended to use his office to promote an understanding of issues relevant to Hispanos. Most of the work he proposed for the division, including cooperation with the San José Training School, rural and bilingual work of the state Normal University, and Pan-American projects of the University of New Mexico, related in some way to the education of Spanish-speaking students.[22]

In 1932 Sánchez undertook a major study of the age-grade status of New Mexican schoolchildren, with special emphasis on the Spanish-speaking child. He reported to Leo Favrot of the General Education Board that "this piece of research will be one of the most extensive studies of its kind every [sic] conducted in the country. We are studying the rural child, the municipal child, the child of the state as a whole and the Spanish-speaking child in each one of these different aspects."[23] The Department of Education published the results of Sánchez's survey as an Educational Research Bulletin and distributed it to teachers and legislators around the state.

The economic downturn of the 1930s squeezed the already strained financial resources of New Mexico's rural schools. Sánchez had this in mind as he wrote "The Age-Grade Status of the Rural Child in New Mexico." In it he acknowledged that he hoped the publication of these statistics would influence the impending allocation of state funds to rural schools. Decisions about the distribution of these funds, he believed, "should be guided by considerations of actual needs, as shown scientifically, rather than by arbitrary judgments." By tabulating statewide statistics of the age-grade status of New Mexico's children, Sánchez called attention to the "great amount of retardation." This, he contended, amounted to "an extremely serious condition which reflects greatly upon the efficiency of our rural public schools." Breaking down the data by county, Sánchez showed that counties having greater numbers of Spanish-speaking children had the highest rates of retardation. Monetary aid, he argued, should be apportioned "on the basis of need as shown by a well-founded general criterion. Age-grade status, undoubtedly, is a composite measure of school needs which is very well suited to state-aid purposes and which can well serve as the needed criterion."[24]

Sánchez's strategy for improving the schools of New Mexico involved amassing irrefutable objective data that could be used to persuade influential people to work for positive change. It perplexed and frustrated him that others did not see as clearly as he did the logic of his arguments, particularly because, like many social scientists, he believed that his data was free of bias in its mathematic objectivity.

In his campaign to reapportion rural aid money, however, Sánchez ran into the unscientific wall of politics. After presenting his report on age-grade status to the state Board of Education in late 1932, Sánchez told Leo Favrot that he was "somewhat chagrined to find how a professional board which expresses and accepts professional ideas will, in its formal actions, cater almost entirely to that which is expedient from a political point of view." Most exasperating to Sánchez was that the board agreed with him that rural aid money "should be apportioned in a scientific manner according to need as shown through thorough research" but still persisted in its distribution of money upon "purely arbitrary lines." For instance, Sánchez complained, the board decided to continue to finance rural supervisors for four or five "favored counties," even though they realized that "this practice discriminates against others which have an equal or greater need."[25]

Although Sánchez spoke of influencing the state Board of Education, he knew that the board had little control of the school budget under the 1923 School Code. A separate state officer, the educational budget auditor, controlled the allocation of state school funds, while the state board had responsibility for setting educational standards for teacher requirements and curriculum. The state educational budget auditor, along with local budget commissioners, fixed the budget allowances for the schools of each county, based upon requests made by local school boards. Because the state auditor was appointed by the governor, the creation of this office effectively divorced control of school funds from the state board and State Department of Education, placing the central control of budgeting and finance under the governor's authority.[26]

When Sánchez wrote to Favrot in December 1932 about his efforts to influence the board's funding practices, he certainly seemed to have overestimated the board's actual power in matters of financing. This is puzzling, since Sánchez soon demonstrated that he was fully cognizant of the structure of power in the matter of school finance and indeed had set his sights upon reforming that structure.

During 1932–33 Sánchez aligned himself against the New Mexico Taxpayers' Association in a battle for revision of the state's school fund distribution scheme. The Taxpayers' Association, a powerful citizens' lobbying group dedicated to limiting taxes, had been responsible in 1923 for the inclusion of the state budget auditor in the new School Code. The association had also supported placing a limitation upon property taxes, another feature of the 1923 School Code. Following passage of the code the Taxpayers' Association worked through the new system to minimize school spending. Representatives of the Association exerted considerable influence at local budget hearings in which the state budget auditor and local budget commissioners determined annual budgets for the schools.[27]

Sánchez urged the abolition of the county budget commissions, which he sardonically labelled the "vermiform appendix of a sadly ailing system." He thought the locally elected boards of education and the county superintendents, who had the best interests of the schools in mind, should represent the people at budget hearings. The current system, with county commissioners appointing one budget commissioner from each major party, violated all principles of "sound government, efficiency, and economy," argued Sánchez. In order to professionalize the administration of school budgets, he suggested that the office of state budget auditor be subsumed under the State Department of Education, with the auditor working alongside his own Research Division. "Budgets prepared, as now," he declared, "with one eye to the needs of the schools and the other eye to the political weathervane cannot help but be inimical to the interests of the school children and of the people of the state."[28]

Sánchez's complaint about school financing derived from a deep disagreement with the method of distributing school funds on the basis of average daily attendance (ADA), regardless of length of school term or school needs. He believed that this distribution hurt rural counties with shorter school terms and greater transportation costs, most of which also happened to be counties with high proportions of Spanish-speaking families.[29]

Governor Arthur Seligman, a Democrat elected upon a campaign pledging austerity in state government, had come out in favor of the state Taxpayers' Association's position on reducing school budgets in June 1932. The stage was set for a showdown between the two sides when Sánchez helped write and lobby for an equalization bill to change the method of distribution of school funds. The equalization bill would establish a school fund to provide a minimum foundation for all schools. Schools that could not meet minimum standards with their own resources could participate in the equalization fund on the basis of a standard allowance rate. Money for the equalization fund would be derived from new sources of revenue, including sales, corporation, and income taxes, in order to relieve the overworked property tax. This final feature of the equalization bill was recognized by all concerned as a needed reform, since the state had proved unable to finance its schools adequately simply on the basis of the property tax.[30]

The New Mexico Education Association and many officials and professors from the University of New Mexico supported the equalization bill. The American Legion, encouraged by Senator Bronson Cutting, lobbied the legislature to pass the measure, in the belief that it would help the Spanish-speaking population in the rural areas. George Sánchez provided much of the statistical information showing the unequal distribution of school funds throughout the state. Although the legislature passed the bill, Governor Seligman vetoed it, claiming that it would result in an increase in the total cost of education and would subordinate local school directors to the state Board of Education.[31]

When the dust settled from this fracas, a defeated but not entirely discouraged Sánchez wrote to Leo Favrot of the General Education Board that his forces had been able "to effect an organization which probably presented the most powerful lobby, outside of political forces of the administration, that was working with the legislature." He was again perplexed and angered that he had not won the day with his studies on taxation and school administration, especially since the legislators themselves were in agreement with the reform measures. He blamed the governor himself, who offered only "flimsy" objections to the equalization bill, for thwarting his efforts. Although the fight had been "bitter and full of controversy," and it had been "necessary to incur the antagonism of a few individuals," Sánchez felt that he had gained many friends for the cause of educational reform.[32]

Even while he battled the governor "and his political advisors," Sánchez continued to involve his office in projects around the state that he believed would improve educational conditions for Spanish-speaking children. He served on the board of the San José Training School and worked with Professor Loyd Tireman of UNM, director of the training school, to publicize the work being done there. And he agreed to cooperate with Dr. Richard Page of the Psychology Department at UNM on a "study of racial attitude scales."[33] This ill-advised venture landed Sánchez in more trouble, not only with the governor but with the public as well. As a native New Mexican, Sánchez should have foreseen the antipathy that the racial survey might arouse. Instead his progressive propensity for scientific methods got the better of him, and he treated Page's experiment as an innocuous and objective academic endeavor. It turned out to be nothing of the sort.

Richard Page had only recently arrived in New Mexico, to take a position in the Psychology Department at the University of New Mexico in 1929. He had studied at the University of Chicago with L. L. Thurstone, a pioneer in the then-innovative techniques of attitude surveys, or as they are known today, opinion polls. Page thought that a survey of racial attitudes in New Mexico would offer a "legitimate and dependable tool for determining amount and degree of prejudice between two groups."[34] The survey might have served this purpose if such techniques were commonplace and well understood, but the nature of the unfamiliar questionnaire doomed it to failure. The questionnaire contained a list of expressions ranging from very favorable to highly derogatory statements about Spanish-speaking people. The instructions directed respondents to indicate their level of agreement or disagreement with each statement.[35] Page had planned to give the survey only to mature adults, until he conferred with Sánchez, who offered to send it to high schools around the state to be administered to Anglo students.[36]

Before Sánchez's office could send out the mailing, Governor Seligman intervened to stop the survey. By taking a firm stand on the issue, Seligman could portray himself as a defender of Hispanic dignity, which was especially crucial for him at the time because of recent alleged incidents of racial discrimination at the university.[37] Seligman appointed an investigative committee to hold hearings on the racial attitudes project. In the end Page was dismissed from the university and Sánchez was reprimanded for threatening to incite racial passions by distributing the survey.[38]

Sánchez escaped further punishment because of the strong support he enjoyed among university officials and political leaders. Loyd Tireman, who served on the committee conducting the investigation, had asked Sánchez helpful leading questions during the hearing and undoubtedly influenced the committee's leniency toward him. President Zimmerman's support of Sánchez never wavered during the investigation. And perhaps most important of all, Senator Bronson Cutting personally intervened to persuade the governor to ease up on Sánchez.[39]

Sánchez's involvement with Page's racial survey typified his approach to educational matters during this period. As a scientific project that aimed at accumulating objective data, the racial survey resembled Sánchez's own methods. Following so closely upon other confrontations with the governor, the Page survey had a good chance of raising even more trouble for Sánchez, and he might have understood this more clearly than he admitted. Raising a stir often seemed to be a viable option for him. His goal was to draw attention to issues regarding Spanish-speaking people, and whether the racial survey proceeded as planned or exploded in controversy, it would at least force people to confront the issue of racism. Sánchez may have been genuinely astonished at the animosity generated by the survey and the rebuke that he received, but the source of the opposition to the study could not have come as a surprise. Describing the matter to Favrot, he claimed that "Certain political forces in the state have been waiting for an opportunity to attack the University and this Division because of our independence in educational matters."[40] One senses that George Sánchez relished the good fight.

Shortly after the Page incident subsided, Sánchez left the state again to pursue graduate studies in education. He had requested and received assurance of a leave of absence and scholarship funds from the General Education Board, prior to his involvement with the racial survey. In September 1933 he began full-time doctoral study at the University of California at Berkeley, although he returned periodically to New Mexico to supervise on-going research of the Division of Information and Statistics. Having completed preliminary coursework during summer sessions, Sánchez finished his dissertation during the 1933–34 school year, relying primarily upon research he had conducted as director of the Division. His dissertation, "The Education of Bilinguals in a State School System," focused upon the education of Spanish-speaking children in New Mexico.[41]

Sánchez's doctoral study recapitulated much of his previous work, incorporating earlier divergent studies into a single forceful argument for equal educational opportunity in New Mexico. Justifying his focus, Sánchez estimated the Spanish-speaking population of the Southwest to be in excess of two million people, a group "of large enough proportion to warrant specialized emphasis on its educational problems." Only recently had the problem of educating large numbers of non-English-speaking children begun to "receive considerable scientific attention and to raise interesting and perplexing questions as to the theory and practice of education in this country."[42]

Sánchez reviewed previous studies bearing upon the educational problems of Spanish-speaking children in the Southwest, including results of IQ tests showing a below-average level of intelligence for this group. Noting the uncertainty as to the relative influence of environmental factors on intelligence, Sánchez again stressed that "improvement in home conditions, elimination of language difficulties, and adequate educational provisions may result in establishing the measured intelligence of the Spanish-speaking child at a normal level." He cited his own published research to show that many tests, including the popular Binet tests, required knowledge of vocabulary that was unfamiliar to the bilingual child and that was not taught by the "best courses of study designed specifically for these children."[43]

Of greatest interest to Sánchez was the role of language in learning and consequently, the effect of subjecting a child to a foreign language in a school environment. He hoped to amplify concrete scientific understanding of bilingualism, even though he believed that there should be "no doubt as to the fact that failure to participate fully in the language of the school constitutes a serious factor in both the measurement of achievement and of intelligence."[44] Underlying his efforts was a desire to redirect the focus of blame for the educational failure of bilingual children from the child to the school itself. Sánchez believed that "aspects more fundamental than quantitative measures of pupil ability and achievement" had to be considered in judging the performance of children. Investigators, he pointed out,

> have sought to find in the child the cause of his educational failure. It is wholly conceivable that factors, not directly related to the child's biological heritage, might be found to contribute to this failure and that, after all, the milieu in which the child functions is as open to suspicion as is the functioning of the child.[45]

Sánchez admitted that linguistic, cultural, and socioeconomic factors all acted as handicaps to the Spanish-speaking child's educational progress, but the child should not be blamed for these circumstances. Rather the school should recognize that these factors constituted special problems to be studied and met by the most efficient means available. To blame the child was to absolve the school of its responsibility to promote the fullest development of each student. In New Mexico the educational needs were greatest in the schools that the largest numbers of Spanish-speaking children attended, yet it was precisely those districts that received the least aid and direction. This violated the generally accepted principle that "education, as a function of the state, should afford equal educational opportunities to all children and that this education should be financed by the wealth of the state."[46]

In his doctoral dissertation, Sánchez established the outline of his critique of New Mexico schools. Upon his return to the state in the spring of 1934, he again took up the fight to put his ideas into practice. He resumed his campaign for equalization of school funds, incurring the enmity of many school superintendents, who believed their districts stood to lose both money and local control if his plans were enacted. Despite the opposition of this group, Sánchez was elected president of the New Mexico Educational Association for 1934–35. He recalled that "the election for the presidency was hotly contested and amounted to a battle between liberal and conservative educational forces."[47] George Sánchez prevailed nevertheless, becoming the first Hispano to serve as president of the NMEA.

Sánchez characteristically pursued the duties of the office with energy and flair. As head of the state's largest teacher organization, he saw an opportunity to push New Mexico's teachers toward progressive reforms. He urged teachers to train themselves in the "scientific principles" of progressive pedagogy and to prepare to go out into the community to create a "total educational program," by teaching adults as well as children.[48] He invited renowned progressive educators from around the country, including Helen Heffernan, rural school supervisor for California, to speak to New Mexico teachers.[49]

George Sánchez hoped to remove the schools from political influence, even if it meant taking on the Department of Education of which he was a part. In a scathing article published in the *New Mexico Business Review* in 1934, Sánchez exposed what he believed was the mismanagement of the State Department of Education. Ideally, he asserted, education should be administered on a statewide basis "to the end that all the children of the state as a whole may secure the fullest benefit from state educational mandates. The state educational system is one system—not a hodge-podge of independent principalities in a feudal confederation." As then structured the educational administration of the state lacked the political independence and fiscal responsibility to control education in an effective manner. The state Board of Education, which was appointed by the governor, had "absolutely no direct control over school finance—the life-blood of the system and the most necessary prerequisite to effective control." The state superintendent was elected by the people, but had only minor powers. "By no stretch of the imagination," declared Sánchez,

> can it be said that the State Department of Education has the power to administer, in executive and continuous fashion, the business of state education. In fact, it might be said that the present organization of that department leaves to chance and to the exigencies of political whims the execution of even those insipid powers vested in it by law.[50]

The financial crisis of the 1930s amplified the need for sound political leadership in the state. Newly elected Governor Clyde Tingley opened his administration in 1935 with genuine concern about the condition of educational finance. With tax collections at their lowest levels ever, school boards across New Mexico found themselves unable to pay teachers' salaries or keep facilities open. Under pressure from his Board of Finance, Tingley asked the legislature to enact a sales tax to boost the school fund.[51]

In early 1935 Governor Tingley appointed George Sánchez to chair a committee of educators to prepare a plan for allocating the state school fund. The committee represented both conservative and liberal elements of New Mexico's educational scene, including John Milne, superintendent of the Albuquerque schools; S. P. Nanninga, professor of education at UNM; Vernon O. Tolle, secretary of the NMEA; Raymond Huff, superintendent of the Clayton Public Schools and president of the state Board of Education from 1931 to 1954; and H. R. Rodgers, state superintendent of public instruction. Milne, Nanninga, and Tolle shared Sánchez's aspirations for reform, while Huff and Rodgers were allied with conservative political leaders. Despite these differences the committee under Sánchez's leadership wrote a new school fund equalization bill that allocated state money on the basis of classroom units, or numbers of pupils for each county.[52]

Although Governor Tingley, a Democrat, supported the bill, it came under attack in the legislature from the Democratic Party's state chairman, John Miles. Under pressure from J. E. Owens, tax agent for the Santa Fe Railroad, and Rupert Asplund, director of the New Mexico Taxpayers' Association, the Democrats in the legislature forced a compromise on the bill, which removed supervision of the equalization fund from the state Board of Education and gave it instead to the state educational budget auditor. According to the *Santa Fe New Mexican,* the educational budget auditor, R. H. Grissom, was "known in school circles as a 'railroad man'. . . . the railroads look upon him, it is said, as one who will stand with them in the making of budgets and allocation of funds." The auditor was a direct appointee of the governor.[53] The NMEA accepted the compromise, and the bill passed the state legislature in 1935. The new equalization law, a significant step toward equity in education, remained in effect until 1941.

Like many of Sánchez's other crusades, his proposed solutions reflected typical progressive principles. He wanted to remove the schools from politics and to rationalize control over school finances. As had been the case for many other progressive educators, Sánchez ran into great opposition from entrenched political forces, taxpayers' groups, and established educators. When the time came for the state to take over the funding of the Division of Information and Statistics from the General Education Board, these sources of opposition effectively terminated Sánchez's job as director of the Division.

On 19 March 1935, George Sánchez resigned from the Department of Education, expressing his regret that the state had failed to appropriate the necessary funds for the continuation of his position.[54] In a private letter to Leo Favrot, Sánchez complained bitterly that "our failure to secure a legislative appropriation for the Division was the result of our unwillingness to bow to political forces in our program. . . . Our agitation, over a period of four years, for educational reforms has naturally tread on many toes." Sánchez could take solace, however, in the fact that "we have enacted many reforms in law and have solidified educational groups back of a progressive program."[55]

The struggle over the equalization bill left Sánchez seething at the pervasiveness of political cronyism in the state. He was not alone. Shortly after the passage of the new law in February 1935, Hispano leaders protested the practice of political appointments to the Board of Regents and administration of the Spanish American Normal School at El Rito. The Albuquerque League of United Latin-American Citizens sent a resolution to the governor and legislature calling for the appointment of "men and women that are independent and competent enough, to take the school out of politics and . . . that will consider the welfare of the children always first, and disregard all personal and political ambitions."[56]

The demands of LULAC went unheeded by the Board of Regents of the

Spanish-American Normal School, which named Joseph Grant as the new president of the school. Hispanos charged that Governor Tingley had pressured the Democrat-dominated board to name his favorite to the post instead of a qualified Hispano. Filemon T. Martinez of Albuquerque blasted the governor for claiming to be a friend of the Spanish-speaking people and yet passing over Hispano educators in favor of an Anglo political crony. "It is ridiculous," he asserted, "to see in New Mexico, in one special school, the president of the board of regents, who is not known as an educator, jump to the presidency of the school."[57]

Sánchez followed events in New Mexico from afar. After leaving the State Department of Education, he accepted an appointment from the Julius Rosenwald Fund to study school conditions in Mexico.[58] Writing from Mexico, Sánchez warned James Zimmerman that he planned to use his upcoming presidential address to the NMEA to expose political corruption in state education. Sánchez declared that "it is imperative that the Department of Education's situation be shown in its true light—Roger's and Huff's reactions notwithstanding." He suggested that the NMEA "should officially reprimand the Administration (past and present) for the prominent place given to vested interests and party politics in the management of educational institutions and in state fiscal affairs. Naturally Asplund, Joe Grant, Owens, the Governor, and others will resent my temerity." Sánchez well understood the potential repercussions that could befall him or the university if he made such an attack, but his conscience would allow no other course. "If I wink at the part played by Huff and Rogers in political 'trades,' " he told Zimmerman, "or if I skip over the evident disease that has and does afflict El Rito . . . , what prestige and influence can I have in promoting social studies? I can't afford to admit defeat of my policies simply because I was eliminated in the Dept. of Ed."[59]

In his speech before the NMEA gathering held in Albuquerque in November 1935, Sánchez refrained from naming specific individuals but nevertheless made clear what practices he abhorred. He denounced political appointments for administrative positions in the state's institutions of higher learning. "We deplore the spoils system in public affairs," he declared, "particularly when those in educational positions resort to it to the detriment of sound educational procedures."[60] Sánchez believed that administrative changes should be made only on the basis of the most reliable of progressive educational principles. He singled out for particular criticism the Board of Regents and the Office of the Superintendent of Public Instruction as offices vulnerable to political maneuvering and partisanship.[61] No one listening to his address could fail to recognize the veiled references to the El Rito situation, Superintendent Rodgers, or President Huff.

Through 1936 Sánchez worked outside his native state, conducting surveys of rural educational conditions in Mexico and the southern United States for the Julius Rosenwald Fund. In 1937 he served as an educational consultant to the Ministry of Education in Venezuela. Not until 1938 did he return to join the faculty of the University of New Mexico.[62]

Within months he was again in contention with state educational officials, when he discovered that the state Board of Education had misappropriated school funds, discriminating against counties that were "largely Spanish-American and, with one or two exceptions, are in a deplorable educational condition." The board's action violated the equalization law of 1935, which Sánchez had engineered. He admitted to Leo Favrot that he "couldn't stand by and see it happen, so I'm probably 'in for it' again."[63]

On this occasion, however, Sánchez prevailed. In December 1938 both the *Albuquerque Tribune* and *Santa Fe New Mexican* put Sánchez's charges of financial mismanagement on the front page, reporting that the state had misapplied over a million dollars in school funds.[64] A group of concerned citizens and educators invited Sánchez to speak at a public forum on January 5 in Santa Fe. After hearing Sánchez describe his "accidental findings with regard to the incorrect allocation of the equalization fund," the group voted to appoint a committee of "unpaid lobbyists" to take their concerns to the legislature.[65] The New Mexico Municipal and County School Superintendents Association, meeting in Santa Fe, made the equalization issue their main topic of discussion.[66] And after listening to a presentation from Sánchez, a delegation of angry Taos educators went down to Santa Fe to meet with the governor and legislators.[67]

A special session of the State Board of Education met to consider Sánchez's challenge. "Since Dr. Sánchez has made public a report of distribution of school funds, challenging the regularity of the action of the State Board," the board agreed to meet with him in order to get the facts straight regarding the figures he had released. After discussing the matter with Sánchez, the board "went on record unanimously in a resolution giving assurance to all counties in the state that the distribution of such fund . . . will be made in accordance with the law as set forth in Chapter 66, Session Laws of 1935."[68]

Sánchez might have remained in New Mexico after this, as it appears that his position with the University of New Mexico was secure, but his repeated conflicts with entrenched forces in the state had undermined his effectiveness. Even his old supporter James F. Zimmerman had turned down his proposals to contribute to activities directly related to the Hispano population. In an obvious slight to Sánchez, Zimmerman chose J. T. Reid to direct the Taos County Project, a Carnegie Corporation-sponsored project to study the social and educational conditions of one of New Mexico's poorest counties. Sánchez should have been the logical choice for the post, because of his past experience and his involvement in the Carnegie project that had resulted in the publication of *Forgotten People*. But the book's hard-hitting analysis antagonized many who might otherwise have supported him.[69]

Perhaps nowhere else did Sánchez highlight so clearly his paradoxical role as a cultural broker as he did in *Forgotten People*. For him the purpose of education was to assist the Hispanos to live in harmony with Anglo Americans. Ultimately, Sánchez spoke for acculturation and assimilation, although he refused to gloss over the travail of the past that had forced Hispanos to submit to a dominant Anglo culture. He neither romanticized the Hispano past nor absolved Hispanos themselves of responsibility for their current conditions.

Sánchez detailed the problems faced by Hispanos living in Taos County. Similar problems of illiteracy, over-age children, and underfunded schools could be found throughout Hispanic New Mexico. Sánchez noted that over 13 percent of the non-Indian population of Taos County was illiterate, higher than the 10.2 percent rate for the non-Indian population of the state as a whole. Sánchez estimated that 37 percent of the population of Taos had less than a third-grade education, and 63 percent had less than a sixth-grade education. Taos County, with 93 percent of its population being of Hispanic descent in 1938, reflected the educational rates for Spanish-speaking persons statewide.[70]

Sánchez had long recognized that enduring social reform depended upon factors beyond mere schooling. He believed that New Mexicans had to raise their economic levels by combining improvement in education, health practices, and civic behavior. The schools would help by providing appropriate training in vocational work, agriculture, home-making, health standards, and social practices. The paradox for Sánchez, as it was for all educators of Hispano children, was how to improve living conditions and yet preserve what was viable in Hispano culture. Sánchez accepted the inevitable loss of some cultural patterns and the acculturation to certain Anglo ways. The Taoseño, he said, "must not only produce more and better crops and manage his holdings better but he must market more intelligently, he must learn to compete in his society more effectively, he must develop business acumen and learn economic values, and he must be fitted to change his society both economically and culturally."[71]

In 1940 Sánchez accepted an offer from the University of Texas to join the Department of Intercultural Relations. He remained on the Texas faculty for the remainder of his career, becoming as forceful an advocate of educational improvement in that state as he had been in New Mexico.

Sánchez left behind a record of professional achievement and personal antagonism in New Mexico. Even President Zimmerman regretted his combativeness, although he had tried hard to keep Sánchez on the UNM faculty. In conversation with Jackson Davis of the General Education Board, Zimmerman said Sánchez was "brilliant but temperamental" and had not been "as helpful as he might have been in developing other people or in getting team work, but he is chiefly concerned with his own interests and studies which he carries out brilliantly." Zimmerman even accused Sánchez of doing "a little sabotaging on the side" when he learned that Reid would take charge of the Taos Project.[72] Davis concurred, and although the General Education Board continued to consider Sánchez worthy of their support, they also understood why New Mexico officials thought him troublesome.

Sánchez would have had to compromise his ideas and language a great deal to become perfectly acceptable to the established officials of the university or the state government. As a young man he had shown great potential to become a native leader who could contribute to the uplifting of his people, and those who supported him hoped he would grow into the role without arousing too much opposition. He became a leader, but he created too many waves by pointedly demonstrating the inequities of the existing power structure. His successes were nevertheless significant. He worked to insure a more rational means of providing financial assistance and supervision to the rural schools of New Mexico. He also helped to persuade educators in New Mexico that intelligence tests had to be used cautiously and only after considering the home environment of the child. Perhaps his greatest contribution to education in New Mexico and the Southwest was the attention he brought to his "Forgotten People" by personifying the struggle for a more humane educational approach. When he left New Mexico in 1940, education for Hispanos still suffered from tremendous shortcomings, but progress had been made. And much of the impetus for improvement had come from the tireless and ever progressive George I. Sánchez.

4 | Loyd S. Tireman
Contributions and Contradictions

DURING THE 1930S educators began to realize how poorly the progressive methods of the 1920s had served Spanish-speaking children of the Southwest. The educational conditions of Hispanics had not improved, despite the widespread use of such progressive methods as scientific testing and curricular differentiation. Nearly every observer of the educational status of Spanish-speaking children noted the high percentage of overage pupils in this group, indicating that more of these students than the average were held back one or more grades. Overageness contributed to the tendency of Spanish-speaking children to drop out of school in greater numbers than English-speaking children.[1]

A study conducted under the auspices of the U.S. Office of Education in 1933 revealed the extent of overageness and the related problem of early elimination, or dropping out, among Spanish-speaking pupils. Surveying educational achievement across the Southwest, Annie Reynolds found that in a typical rural Arizona school system, 38 percent of the Mexican children were normal age for grade, while 59 percent were overage, and only 4 percent were underage for their grade in school. Of the non-Mexican children, 67 percent were normal age for grade, with 16 percent overage and 17 percent underage. In this same school system, more Mexican children dropped out early than did non-Mexican students. The study discovered that "for 100 Mexican children in grade 1 there are 7 in grade 8, while for 100 non-Mexican children in grade 1 there are 52 in grade 8." That amounted to an elimination rate of 93 percent for Mexican children and 48 percent for non-Mexican children.[2]

Reynolds cited other examples from the five southwestern states showing that Spanish-speaking schoolchildren were not only more likely to be overage for their grade and to drop out of school early, but that they did more poorly while they were in school. The problem was not limited to rural schools, for in the Los Angeles city school system, a study of achievement in reading comprehension and vocabulary revealed that "the average achievement of Mexican children, grade for grade, is somewhat below the average achievement of white American children."[3]

Reynolds's survey suggested that these conditions persisted despite the attention that had been directed toward this group in the decade and a half prior to 1930. Educators had given increased consideration to teaching Spanish-speaking children, with the assumption that a curriculum suited to their needs would provide all the educational stimulus necessary to assure the modest success in school expected of the group. By 1930 it had become clear that Spanish-speaking children had not responded well to the programs established for them and were still falling behind and leaving school prematurely.

Having noticed that the methods used during the 1920s failed to hold Spanish-speaking children in school, progressive educators in the Southwest sought more appropriate teaching practices for those students. Retaining their faith in science, they actively sought better solutions to educational problems through scientific experimentation. In New Mexico no one better represented this experimental approach than Loyd S. Tireman, professor of education at the University of New Mexico and founder of the San José Training School. At the same time, no one better exemplified the contradictions inherent in progressive education's well-intentioned but often misguided approaches to dealing with Spanish-speaking children.

Born in Orchard, Iowa, in 1896, Loyd Tireman took his bachelor's degree in history in 1917 from Upper Iowa University in Fayette. After military service he worked as a school superintendent in various Iowa schools, while attending graduate school at the University of Iowa. By 1927 he had earned the M.A. and Ph.D. in elementary education and educational psychology. Later that year Tireman joined the faculty of the Department of Education at the University of New Mexico.[4] The young professor set out upon his career with all the vigor and purpose of a driven perfectionist. As characterized by his biographer, David L. Bachelor, Loyd Tireman was an impatient and confrontational man who enjoyed expressing his will and giving orders. He carried projects forward by the force of his personality and his own hard work. Although capable of badgering subordinates to the point of tears, he was admired by his peers and remembered for his contributions.[5] Today the Learning Materials Library of the College of Education at the University of New Mexico bears his name.

Tireman took an immediate interest in the people and culture of his newly adopted state. A newcomer to New Mexico, his attitudes about Hispanos soon came to resemble the romanticized impressions of Hispanic culture and history held by the Anglo boosters, artists, and writers who had made the Spanish colonial style fashionable in the 1920s. Unlike George Sánchez, Tireman tended to minimize certain vexatious issues of conflict, discrimination, and inequity in the history of the two peoples. Instead he nurtured a view of the New Mexican past as a history of a charming but unenlightened civilization ushered into the modern world by a progressive and benevolent Anglo society. This historical perspective shaped his approach to Hispanos and their culture in his own time.

While Tireman demonstrated a genuine sympathy for Hispanos and their culture, he also revealed a judgmental disposition toward them. In an address delivered before the Rural Conference of the Colorado State Teachers College in January 1932, Tireman expounded his view of Hispanos and their educational circumstances. He thought it wrong for educators simply to impose upon Hispanics the same methods and curricula that had worked for English-speaking children or even for other non-English-speaking groups. Implying that he well understood Hispanos, he cautioned his listeners to observe and learn their ways before determining an appropriate strategy for their schooling.[6]

Almost from the start of his career in New Mexico, Tireman devoted himself to finding ways to improve education for Spanish-speaking children. Throughout his career he insisted that sound pedagogy must rest upon solid scientific data. He began collecting data in 1928, when he directed a survey of reading in the elementary schools of New Mexico, the results of which he presented to the New Mexico Education Association in 1929 as part of a panel on educating Spanish-speaking children. With the cooperation of city and county superintendents, Tireman administered standard achievement tests in reading to elementary school students around the state. He found a distressing situation. In every grade "the median scores in both comprehension and rate are below what they should be." Then he examined the scores of English-speaking and non-English-speaking students separately, discovering that "the English-speaking pupils were practically up to the normal in comprehension but considerably below the normal in rate." The Spanish-speaking children, however, had scored below normal in both categories. Another alarming pattern emerged from the data: the differences between the English-speaking and Spanish-speaking children increased with length of time in school.[7]

The decreasing scores for Spanish-speaking children compared to the English-speaking students as they progressed through the grades led Tireman to conclude that environment rather than heredity accounted for the discrepancy. Children of English-speaking homes had access to more books and were encouraged to read more often than children in Spanish-speaking homes. By not giving enough attention to silent reading, New Mexico's schools had failed to account for the impoverished background of Hispano students. The methods of instruction in the early grades had resulted in "lack of interest, effort, and practice in reading." Teachers needed to be trained in the techniques of teaching silent reading, he declared.[8]

In his emphasis upon silent reading, Tireman stood at odds with prevailing opinion about teaching adaptations for Spanish-speaking children. Most educators in the Southwest, and in New Mexico as well, stressed oral work in language activities. The common method of reading instruction, as Tireman pointed out, was for the students to stand one by one, each reading out loud several paragraphs in front of the class.[9] With the focus upon the acquisition of spoken English, this method had seemed appropriate. While continuing to stress spoken English, the school could encourage better thinking habits in other academic areas through a silent reading program.

Tireman was not one to follow an educational trend if he believed it was misdirected. In many of New Mexico's mountain counties, the median length of time that children spent in first grade was four years. One county had 1600 students in the first grade and 400 in the second grade. Tireman refused to believe the consensus view that "this slow scholastic progress is due to mentality; that whereas the average I.Q. of the Anglo is 100, the average I.Q. for the Spanish-speaking people of the Southwest is 80." He declared it was unfair to label individual non-English-speaking students as mentally inferior when they failed to comprehend geography, history, or arithmetic written in English. He pointed out that intelligence tests were written in English and employed Anglo concepts. He doubted that most Ph.D.s, who were supposed to know German or French, would score higher than 80 if they took an intelligence test written in either of those languages.[10] Tireman did not reject intelligence tests, but like George Sánchez, he believed teachers should use tests cautiously. For Tireman poor test results by a Hispano child ought to alert the teacher to the deficiencies in the child's home life, not necessarily in the individual child. The school then had a responsibility to compensate for a poor home environment.[11]

Tireman's drive to find his own methods for improving the educational achievement of Spanish-speaking children led him to the idea of creating an experimental school for that explicit purpose. President James F. Zimmerman of UNM supported Tireman's plans, but he knew that neither the state nor the university was financially able to undertake any extensive programs for the public schools. Confident that the General Education Board of the Rockefeller Foundation would be willing to assist them, Zimmerman acted as an intermediary between New Mexico officials and the board. New Mexico educators, including four of Zimmerman's predecessors, had looked to the General Education Board as a source of funds as early as 1905. The GEB, founded in 1902 by John D. Rockefeller, had focused primarily on improving education for Blacks in Southern schools.[12] New Mexico educators themselves drew parallels between the work done by the GEB in the south and New Mexico's needs. In some of the earliest correspondence about Tireman's plan, Albuquerque Superintendent John Milne and state Superintendent Atanasio Montoya requested from the GEB "that the services rendered secondary and elementary departments of education in southern states be extended to our State."[13]

In early 1930 Zimmerman arranged for GEB field agents Jackson Davis and Leo Favrot to visit New Mexico to meet with Loyd Tireman, Atanasio Montoya, John Milne, and Dean S. P. Nanninga of the School of Education. The New Mexicans argued that the state's circumstances compared with those found in the South, thus justifying an extension of GEB philanthropy to New Mexico. The Spanish-speaking population had "special difficulties because of the poor home back-ground, high illiteracy, low economic level and standard of living, and language difficulties—all operating to bring about a high rate of retardation." What Zimmerman and Tireman proposed was to take over a school in a Spanish-American community near Albuquerque and "operate it with trained teachers as a demonstration school, showing the possibilities of the Spanish-American group, and work out special adaptations in the school curriculum as may be found to best meet the special needs of this group."[14]

Zimmerman and Tireman worked with Albuquerque school officials and interested persons around the state to elicit support for the experimental school. Mary Austin joined the Board of Directors of the school and also convinced her friend Senator Bronson Cutting to endorse the school. From his personal fortune, Cutting pledged five thousand dollars a year for two years for the school, promising to extend that grant if the work proceeded satisfactorily. The Bernalillo County Board of Education allotted $22,520 for the school and, most importantly, turned over the operation of the San José School south of Albuquerque to the university. At these signs of local support, the GEB agreed on 24 May 1930 to give twelve thousand dollars a year for five years to the University of New Mexico for the purpose of conducting an experimental school.[15]

Leo M. Favrot became the chief liaison between the GEB and New Mexico, visiting the state often to observe projects first hand. Hailing from Louisiana, Favrot served as southern field agent for the GEB out of New Orleans. He became a good friend not only of Tireman, but of George Sánchez as well. After the visit to Albuquerque in 1931, Favrot summed up the purpose of the San José School. "Primarily, your school's mission, as our Board understands it," he said,

> is to discover the cause leading to retardation and withdrawal of the Spanish-American children in the schools of New Mexico and to undertake to provide remedial measures for this evil by making experimental adjustments of curricula offerings, by establishing relationships with the parents and homes of the children, by measuring whatever is measurable in the progress of the children, and by engaging in activities calculated to promote the wider interest of the pupils as well as to conserve such native aptitudes, interests and abilities as seem particularly worthwhile. The school, of course, must serve as a demonstration school for teachers in service who come to study the methods pursued there.[16]

Loyd Tireman became director of the school and a seventeen-member Board of Directors was appointed to oversee the operation. Zimmerman, Cutting, Austin, Nanninga, and Montoya served as board members along with Albuquerque Mayor Clyde Tingley, attorney Gilbert Espinosa, and Camilo Padilla, editor of *Revista Ilustrada*. After the first meeting of the board, Zimmerman happily reported that many prominent members of the Spanish-speaking community had agreed to participate and approved of the undertaking. These leaders, he said, "expressed the belief that this institution would render a service which had been delayed for one hundred and fifty years, to the Spanish-American children of New Mexico."[17]

As director of the school Tireman intended to "provide a laboratory in which certain essential data concerning the Spanish-American school pupil can be secured ... on a scientific basis." Better educational leadership could be trained for the rural areas if educators knew more about teaching Hispano children. For instance he believed that educators would benefit from knowing as conclusively as possible whether the poor achievement of the Spanish-speaking child was due to low intelligence or poor teaching. To discover if the intelligence quotient of these children could be raised, Tireman planned to conduct a "most careful and scientific program," giving each child a Binet mental test and administering a number of group intelligence and educational tests. He would experiment with various pedagogical techniques, including a program of silent reading, to determine the effect upon the intelligence quotient of Spanish-speaking children.[18]

The San José School, a county school located in the San José barrio on the southern edge of Albuquerque, encompassed grades one through eight. When Tireman's program began in the fall of 1930, 524 pupils enrolled, most of them from Spanish-speaking homes.[19] From the beginning Tireman hoped to enlist the support and participation of the community, realizing that parent involvement was a key to the school's and the students' success. He held a series of community meetings to explain to parents the purpose of the school. By October of the first school term, he felt that his strategy of community involvement was working, as reflected in a 40 percent increase in enrollment over the previous year. Even more encouraging was the fact that much of this increase was in the upper four grades, and that the "large, over-aged boys and girls, who last year were very irregular in attendance, have been unusually prompt and faithful."[20]

For Tireman the results of the San José testing program would be crucial in proving the viability of his methods. The tests, repeatedly administered over a period of years, would give the San José teachers an objective check on the progress of the pupils. The staff administered both standardized group tests and individual tests intended to measure general achievement, reading ability, and intelligence. Group testing began during the opening week of the 1930–31 school year and was repeated at the end of the first year and the close of each of the succeeding four years. The same tests were given to two control groups at separate schools with Spanish-speaking pupils, the Atrisco School, located within a few miles of San José, and Santa Barbara, in the northern part of the state. A total of nearly five thousand Spanish-speaking children in the three schools were tested.[21]

Test results from the first year revealed that up to 75 percent of the San José School population scored well below normal on Stanford Achievement examinations and Gates reading tests. On the Pintner-Cunningham Primary Mental Test and National Intelligence Test, the two tests used for measuring intelligence, the San José students scored below normal in mental age in each grade. In no case, the examiners reported, "did twenty-five per cent of the pupils in a grade earn a mental age equal to the grade norm."[22] These results mirrored test scores achieved by Spanish-speaking children throughout the Southwest during the 1920s and represented the very problem that Tireman wished to address. With data demonstrating his starting point, he set out to see what could be done to improve educational performance among these children.

Following the first phase of testing and evaluation, the staff effected a "slow and careful re-classification" of pupils. Although very few students actually changed classes, an "Opportunity Room" was established for "anyone who was a misfit in the grade in which he was originally enrolled." Students who were either overage or underage for their grade could transfer to the Opportunity Room, where they received individualized instruction suited to their needs under teacher Flora Andrews. Since the upper grades had the highest amount of overageness, only fourth-graders and up could attend the Opportunity Room during the first year. Several of these students showed improvement during the year and returned to regular classes.[23]

Tireman hoped to eliminate overageness in the school by giving as much individualized attention to weaker students as possible. In the lower grades the teachers divided their classes into three groups, each of which received work appropriate to its ability. The second grade teacher, Jennie Gonzales, gave pre-primary work to her slowest section rather than take them out of the second grade and place them with younger students of like ability. Tireman realized that many of these students would not pass at the end of the year, but "it seemed better to give them the instruction for which they were fitted, and to gradually have the school better classified, than to make quick and violent re-classification."[24]

Tireman's intensive silent reading program early on became an integral part of the San José curriculum. Beginning with the first grade, silent reading received more emphasis than any other aspect of work. Yet reading depended upon acquisition of a vocabulary and an understanding of concepts in English. Tireman felt that too many English-speaking teachers underestimated the difficulty of this task for children from Spanish-speaking homes, many of them of low economic status. These children lacked the richness of experience in terms of ideas, concepts, and words that children in English-speaking homes acquired as a matter of course. When Spanish-speaking children entered school, they were already four to five years behind their English-speaking counterparts in absorbing ideas and vocabulary expressed in English. Tireman thought the school should compensate for the inadequacies of the home environment by creating as many experiences as possible that would expose children to new concepts and ideas. The school initiated junior prefirst and prefirst classes for children who could speak no English, where teachers Newell Dixon and Vera Wood emphasized the acquisition of English concepts and vocabulary.[25]

At San José Tireman and the staff made a concerted effort to determine what a child needed to know before beginning to read. Marie M. Hughes, who served the San José School as field-worker, teacher, and principal, identified a number of prerequisites for learning to read, including experience in ideas, command of simple English sentences, a good vocabulary, accurate enunciation and pronunciation, and a genuine desire to read. Tireman believed that English-speaking homes were more likely to have provided these prerequisites, and so it fell to the school to provide these experiences for the children of limited backgrounds.[26]

In setting up the San José curriculum, Tireman and his staff consciously attempted to avoid segregated situations that might make the individual child feel inferior. By allowing slower students to remain in their age groups while receiving special instruction, for instance, they hoped to prevent those students from feeling slighted. Attention to individual potential seemed to be Tireman's strength. His weakness, however, and what could not be avoided in his approach, was a lack of regard for the cultural milieu in which the child was raised. Tireman based his pedagogy upon the presumption that the home of the Hispano child was inherently flawed. Only that which he chose to value from Hispanic culture would enter the schools, and the school would compensate for what he perceived as the failures of the Hispano community.

Tireman made decisions first on pedagogical grounds and only secondarily out of cultural considerations. Yet he did explore methods that could have reinforced Hispano ethnicity, had they been carried through. He willingly experimented with any teaching technique that promised a means of improving skills in English. Teaching Spanish to Spanish-speaking children in the early elementary grades was widely discouraged in the schools of the Southwest, yet

Tireman wondered if pupils would learn English more easily if they concurrently studied Spanish. At a December 1931 meeting of the San José Board of Directors, Tireman proposed to begin teaching Spanish at the start of the 1932–33 school year, and the board approved the plan.[27]

The fall 1932 curriculum at San José included instruction in the Spanish language for thirty minutes daily in the first five grades. Spanish was an elective for the last three grades of the school.[28] Tireman and San José teachers Mela Sedillo Brewster and Lolita Pooler justified this innovation on both cultural and pedagogical grounds. Studying Spanish would be beneficial for Spanish-speaking children, because it would "awaken in them an appreciation of their lingual heritage." Teaching Spanish in the schools would also give English-speaking children "an opportunity for cultural development." Bilingual instruction offered "a competitive field in which group advantages and disadvantages are more or less equalized and in which group barriers can be effectively broken down." More importantly, however, they hoped it would help Hispano children to acquire English more easily, by turning a flaw into a benefit. Tireman, Brewster, and Pooler believed that "the bi-lingual tendencies that now operate as an educational handicap to Spanish-American children in general, can be transformed into an educational asset by the simple process of teaching Spanish along with English in the lower grades."[29]

While Tireman's interest in bilingual instruction was remarkable for his time, his need to have scientific proof of the validity of his methods eventually led him to reject it. Initially he was so enthusiastic about bilingual education that he toured Europe in 1933 to observe teaching methods in other countries where two or more languages were spoken. Visiting Wales, Belgium, Luxembourg, Switzerland, and Spain, he found that in the first few years of schooling the mother tongue was used as the language of instruction. The Europeans encouraged him to pursue the same policy, but Tireman found little concrete data to justify the method. "I shall never be satisfied," he wrote Leo Favrot from Luxembourg, "concerning the use of the mother tongue for the first few years, till I try it out and *measure results carefully.*"[30]

When he returned to New Mexico, Tireman seemed to have rejected the European methods when he reported his findings to the San José board. He concluded that they were "in no way superior to the ones that are known in this country and in many cases were quite inferior." Although children in bilingual countries of Europe were able to speak two languages fluently by the age of ten or twelve, Tireman attributed this partly to the proximity of various national groups to one another and the toleration of persistent use of their respective languages. These conditions did not exist in New Mexico, according to Tireman.[31] He seemed to overlook the proximity of Spanish-speaking New Mexicans to English-speaking New Mexicans, and he missed an opportunity to encourage tolerance by many Anglos for the continuing use of Spanish. Tireman himself, despite his often-stated assertions about the benefits of bilingualism, showed in practice a deep-seated intolerance for the use of Spanish.

Yet if he could have shown the viability of bilingual instruction by scientific proof, he probably would have advocated its use. It is important to understand what he wanted to prove, however. For Tireman bilingual instruction would have been worthwhile only if it contributed to better acquisition of English. The overriding goal was not to preserve ethnic identity or to make students feel more at ease in an unfamiliar classroom environment so that they would stay in school longer. Tireman's goal was not even to improve achievement in overall academic performance. Bilingual instruction would be counted a success only if it resulted in a measurable improvement in English language ability.

To determine quantifiably if children could benefit from bilingual teaching, Tireman integrated Spanish language instruction into the San José curriculum. After taking Spanish lessons for a year, San José students in the sixth through eighth grades performed above the norm on standardized tests in Spanish.[32] Yet the teaching of Spanish in the lower grades appeared to retard the learning of English. Both the first and second grades had been divided into two groups, with one group in each grade receiving Spanish instruction for forty-five minutes daily. The children in the first grade who received the Spanish lessons had not done as well on reading tests in English as the control group who had had no Spanish. As a result Spanish instruction was dropped from the first grade and reintroduced in the third and fourth grades.[33] The priority of English acquisition over all other concerns is clearly demonstrated in this decision. In the early grades, where it would have made the youngest children feel more comfortable to have contact with their native tongue, bilingual instruction was rejected because it slowed their learning of English.

Tireman's unswerving focus on English achievement remained constant even in the light of contradictory evidence from other academic subject areas. As an example, he found that Spanish-speaking children "uniformly perform better on arithmetic computation tests than on tests involving reading skills."[34] He attributed this pattern to the fact that the Spanish-speaking child was usually overage for his or her grade. Tireman surmised that "During this added year he will have been exposed to many arithmetical conceptions, while they will have been in Spanish and will not be helpful as far as the English language is concerned, they will have formed the arithmetical background quite as truly as though they were in English."[35] By implication then, Tireman admitted that in some subjects children learned just as well or better in their native language and, incidentally, that they could learn something in their communities. Since, however, this learning occurred in other academic areas and failed to contribute to better English skills, it did not prove the viability of bilingual instruction.

Tireman did not believe that the San José program had demonstrated beyond a doubt the worth of bilingual instruction, so he did not advocate its use in the schools. He admitted that the evidence was inconclusive and that it was still "an open question whether the system of instructing in English from the beginning is the correct one to employ in this state." He acknowledged that teaching only in English had contributed to the elimination of many Spanish-speaking children from school before the eighth grade. He even expressed regret that Hispano children lost their own language when they went to school. "Spanish is the second most widely used language in the world," he pointed out, "and it seems a great pity that children who have the natural advantages of speaking this language as their mother tongue should be deprived of their advantage until they get into high school, there to study Spanish as a foreign tongue."[36] Yet Tireman's own logic and common sense did not outweigh the results of the tests run in the experiment at San José. He continued to condone policies that discouraged the use of Spanish in the schools, even urging teachers to prevent students from using Spanish on the playgrounds.[37]

And yet simply by expressing an interest in bilingualism and by experimenting with it at San José, Tireman became a pioneer in bilingual instruction. So overwhelming was the consensus for English-only instruction that even Tireman's limited excursion into the potential of bilingualism represented a significant departure from prevailing practice in the United States. In a study of southwestern education, Annie Reynolds of the U.S. Office of Education drew attention to the innovation. The proposal to teach beginning children in Spanish was "contrary to the prevailing viewpoint that foreign-language-speaking children should be placed as early as may be into school, and insofar as it is possible, speak English only during the entire school day." As far as Reynolds could determine, the bilingual experiment at the San José Training School was "the first instance of an expression of interest in an experiment with a foreign language in teaching pupils of foreign speech in a public school in the United States."[38]

Because the San José experimental school had been scheduled to last only five years, Tireman began in 1934 to justify extension of the program. As the school entered its fourth year, he saw much progress, even if he could not always amass the concrete data he wanted to prove conclusively that his methods were working. In September 1934 he reported that the teachers had commented after the opening of school that "each year the children that we receive seem to be younger. In other words, the 'over-ageness' is being cared for to a large extent."[39]

A month later Tireman wrote Favrot that they needed three more years to validate their work according to professional standards. Already they had brought many of the children up to normal levels as indicated by test scores. Without further follow-up they would not know if these results were "just a freak or whether these children can be kept up to the normal." Three more years of work might make the difference between professional acceptance or scorn. "I should feel," he admitted, "professionally speaking, that education in general would have a perfect right to put a great big question mark after all of our statements in regard to the performance of the Spanish speaking child."[40]

Although the San José Training School was viewed favorably by the Bernalillo County School Board, the state Department of Education, and UNM, none of these agencies could afford to maintain the school without outside help. Consequently James F. Zimmerman again appealed to the General Education Board to extend its support of the school for another three years. He noted that the San José children demonstrated substantial improvement, but "the limit of their achievement has not yet been reached." He also thought that the experiment in bilingual education appeared promising. Yet these programs needed further work and observation, for it would be unwise "to make positive statements regarding the ability of Spanish-speaking children unless every precaution has been taken to guard against error."[41] The GEB, recognizing both the worth and the need exhibited by the San José Training School, agreed to contribute $27,000 for a three-year extension of the project.[42]

Tireman continued to look for the statistical evidence he needed to demonstrate without doubt that the San José project was a success. By 1936 he had accumulated "considerable data," but was reluctant to publish it, even though "the I.Q.'s of the younger children are going higher each year of our work." While performance was improving steadily, scores were still not up to the norm of English-speaking children. "No one knows," he said, "whether this will continue as they become older or whether there will be a downward slant to the curve." If he published his data now, he would have to say that "on the basis of present evidence the Spanish speaking children are definitely inferior to the English speaking children." Because the number of cases was so small, "any scientist would be skeptical of the results." Even more important, he admitted,

> if we published such an announcement we might lose much support in the state. San José is an intangible but potent force in New Mexico for the continuous study of the Spanish speaking child. We must allow nothing to jeopardize this influence, especially since we hope to continue in the wider field of curriculum reorganization.[43]

Tireman knew that there was much to lose with bad publicity, for the San José project had gained widespread repute for its innovations. Ironically the success of the school in attracting students undermined Tireman's carefully planned testing program. As word of San José spread in the Spanish-speaking community, enrollment in the school increased to the point that the school rooms overflowed, and Tireman claimed that the scientific control of the experiment had been compromised.[44]

Nevertheless he later used the data accumulated from the San José experiment to argue that the schools of New Mexico should adopt the project's methods. Writing in 1948 Tireman contended that the San José program enabled students in the first two grades to improve their reading ability in comparison to the two control schools. Other questions remained unresolved, however, and needed more attention. He could not explain why the San José students achieved test scores above normal up to the third grade but fell below norms in all grades after the third. He thought the extra year of prefirst training offered at San José, while it helped the child in the first two grades, did not serve as a great advantage as the child grew older. Rather, he believed, the home environment of Spanish-speaking children failed to acquaint the maturing child with the necessary vocabulary for comprehending the reading material encountered in the upper grades.[45]

Tireman's belief that Hispano homes offered limited learning experiences coexisted with his commitment to making the school a vital part of the community. Paradoxically his view of the home environment as flawed did not prevent him from looking to the community as a source for curricular enhancements for the school. It did, however, contribute to his tendency to pick and choose among those attributes that, according to his own measure, had value and those that needed changing. The school's involvement with the community was a two-way street, through which the school could guide the community to make improvements, while the community could contribute local variations to the curriculum.

Like many progressives following the lead of John Dewey, Loyd S. Tireman hoped to create a new role for the school by addressing the needs of the community in which the school was found. Just as Dewey had advocated that the school should be part of the life of the community, Tireman and his associates sought ways to integrate community needs and interests into the school's activities. According to David Bachelor, this propensity in Tireman was reinforced by observations he made during a visit to a Mexican village in the summer of 1930. Mexican officials had tried to reconcile school and community by presenting a relevant curriculum that would help villagers improve their everyday lives. Mexican children learned practical lessons, such as how to raise rabbits for food or to take care of personal hygiene, designed to upgrade the standard of living in the villages.[46]

As with much of the progressive agenda, the high-minded intentions of the community school movement often masked little-examined assumptions about cultural superiority. The idealism and good intentions of helping a community meet its own needs seem undeniable. Often, however, progressives defined the needs of a particular community as missing elements that would bring the community into conformity with national standards. From territorial times Anglo educators had tended to assume that village needs should be determined by what was necessary to help Hispanos acculturate and assimilate into Anglo society. Tireman's emphasis upon English acquisition certainly placed him among these educators. Beyond speaking English, what did it mean for Hispano villagers to become acculturated or assimilated? For Loyd Tireman the answer seemed to be whatever would enable Hispanos to continue to live in their villages without being taken advantage of economically or politically, while meeting reasonable standards of health and without becoming public charges. Unlike urban progressives who saw the role of education as imparting the skills necessary for immigrants to enter the industrial workforce, New Mexican educators did not view the Hispano population as a potential urban industrial workforce or even as a source of labor for agribusiness.[47]

Tireman's philosophy of the community school began with the assumption that the curriculum should prepare the rural students of New Mexico for everyday life in their own communities. He strongly believed that "if New Mexico has problems which differ from the problems of New England, then the curriculum of the common school should be designed to aid New Mexico in the solution of its problems."[48] The San José experiments represented a repudiation of New Mexico's curriculum, which had largely been modeled upon schools designed for English-speaking children who were expected to go on to college. Instead the San José teachers set out to determine what Hispano children needed in order to live successfully in their own rural villages.

Based upon physical examinations of the students, the San José staff decided that Hispano homes lacked modern health and hygiene practices. It became a high priority of the school to give attention to the physical and mental welfare of the individual child. School nurse Virginia Johnson examined every child enrolled in the school and found that nearly 250 students needed medical attention in the first year. A home visitation campaign was started, in which the nurse visited parents in an attempt to persuade them to seek medical care for their children and to promote better health standards generally.[49]

All teachers at San José kept diaries, where they recorded comments about the academic progress, emotional behavior, evidence of leadership, or other observations about the performance of each student.[50] The teachers' diaries revealed much preoccupation with health, cleanliness, and family background. Ann Jones, the second grade teacher in 1936–37, detailed a long battle with one girl's impetigo sores and the extraction of two rotten teeth. She also commented at length about meetings with parents, noting their general appearance, color of skin, apparent physical injuries or sickness, and whether they spoke English or Spanish. Comparing two boys she wrote that

> Bonnie Garcia does well considering his home environment. He lives in that awfully bleak adobe house at the corner of Broadway and John. I have never been in but the door is often wide open . . . and from a distance it looks as barren inside as it is without. . . . Joe Tartaglio is the product of just the opposite type of Spanish home. It is neat and well-cared for and so are the members of it.[51]

Tireman believed that the attention given to the welfare of the child would generate more interest on the part of parents in the work of the school. He attributed the increased attendance at San José to the parents' faith in the school. If the parents were not "impressed with the work of the school they would not encourage their children to continue, often at financial sacrifice," he said. Many parents told him that they were trying to use more English at home to help with their children's education. Tireman saw these developments as signs that the San José School was succeeding in its aim of bringing the school and community into harmony.[52] One wonders, however, how many parents felt shamed when confronted with the polite but firm criticism of a visiting nurse, urging them to keep their home up to standards of Anglo society.

In an attempt to meet the economic needs of the community, the San José Training School implemented a vocational program based upon traditional arts and crafts work. This approach, in which the children learned traditional New Mexican arts of tinwork, weaving, dying, and tanning, resembled the arts and crafts curriculum begun in Santa Fe County by Nina Otero-Warren. San José board member Mary Austin, enthusiastic about the prospects of the vocational program, offered to publicize and interpret the school's efforts. Tireman, grateful for her assistance, hoped the well-known writer would help the school establish a solid reputation.[53] Austin had settled in Santa Fe in 1924 and was a devoted champion of American Indian culture and Spanish colonial art. She became a leader in the movement to conserve the region's native arts and handicrafts before her death in 1934.[54]

For Austin the beauty of the San José School was that it recognized the intrinsic worth of native New Mexican culture and sought to mold its curriculum to fit that culture. It was absurd, she thought, to educate Spanish-speaking children with a system that "goes on taking for granted that every public school child can and should take on the intellectual pattern of the orthodox university graduate." The Spanish and Indian ancestors of New Mexicans had never "acquired the habit of receiving their education from the printed page," and she did not think their descendants should be expected to do so now. Hispanos were capable of learning through doing, she asserted, because "the

Spanish speaking peon derives from both lines of his descent the capacity to make things requiring a high degree of artisan skill, and to make them beautifully and well." With proper instruction, she said, "the despised peon class could become the superior hand-craftsmen of the western world."[55]

Austin envisioned a role for the school in the restoration of community life and preservation of traditional culture. She believed that arts and crafts were part of the "normal activities of rural community life" in New Mexico, which the schools should foster. For too long the schools drew children away from the work of the community, to the point that the "best of the Colonial period" had been lost. Also lost was the element of community entertainment in New Mexican villages, and for much of this Austin blamed the school. By severing the school from the community, an indifferent middle-class American society had almost exterminated "all that is dramatic, entertaining, poetic, and generally cultural in the social life of the native New Mexican village."[56]

The movement to revive the traditional colonial arts and crafts in the 1920s and 1930s was driven by the Anglo artists and writers of Santa Fe and Taos, as well as by a few urban Hispanics in positions of authority in schools or government. Viewing a Hispanic arts revival as an antidote to modern mechanization, they wanted native artists and craftsmen to rely entirely upon traditional methods and patterns. They went so far as to provide "good" examples of colonial art for the local people to emulate, as if Hispanic artisans should not or could not create an authentic modern style. They condemned work that utilized modern materials, such as that of the Chimayo weavers who used commercial dyes to increase their margin of profit.[57] During the Depression years, New Deal reformers created programs to use arts and crafts manufacture as the basis of a revitalization of the village economy.[58]

Through these efforts Austin and others hoped to restore village life to what they thought it ought to be. In fact their highly romanticized and fully revived village economy never materialized. While many Hispanic villagers did pursue crafts work during the Depression years, most moved on to other opportunities when the economy improved. The efforts of Austin and others in the preservation movement were striking in their contradictions. On the one hand the sympathy shown for Hispanos and their culture was laudable, and certainly their position compares favorably with the cultural genocide inherent in the worst extremes of Americanization. Yet these mostly Anglo observers wished to impose their own vision of Hispano culture and to determine what in it should be valued or not.

Loyd Tireman apparently did not object to Austin's ideas about Hispano culture, and he allowed her to publicize the project in her own way. He also welcomed the advice of Camilo Padilla, editor of *La Revista Ilustrada*, who sat on the San José board and urged the inclusion of Spanish plays in the school's curriculum. As a member of the Spanish Arts Society, Padilla had collaborated with Austin and others in translating traditional plays such as "Los Pastores" and "El Niño Perdido."[59] Although they did not play decisive roles in the direction of the San José School, intellectuals connected with the Spanish colonial arts revival nevertheless influenced the nature of some of the important programs within the San José curriculum.

While Tireman believed that the primary goal of the arts and crafts program was to facilitate overall learning by "stimulating the mental processes of these pupils," he shared Austin's sentiment that the curriculum should awaken in students an appreciation of what was valuable in their own culture.[60] And he saw it as the duty of the school and the educators in charge to decide what were the valuable elements. The arts and crafts program became part of the larger vocational curriculum at San José. Traditional Hispanic crafts joined carpentry, home economics, and other vocational courses that the teachers believed would help their students make a living. Tireman himself claimed no original innovations in vocational or crafts teaching, but he encouraged the work of others, especially Brice H. Sewell. Sewell did the hands-on work of directing the crafts and vocational program.[61] Later the State Department of Education adopted much of the vocational program begun at San José and hired Sewell to run it as the state supervisor of trade and industrial education.

As San José practices and personnel became more popular with state officials, the school itself became the favorite of parents. Enrollment increased each year until it grew too unwieldy to be conducted as an experimental project any longer. After the 1936–37 school year, San José was returned to the control of the county school board, and the original demonstration project came to an end.[62] The influence of San José would continue to be felt statewide through the teachers trained there, revised state curriculum standards, and other demonstration schools, particularly the Nambé Community School.

The long-term impact of the San José experiment depended upon continued cooperation between the State Department of Education and the San José staff. UNM faculty had initiated the San José project and took a continuing interest in the school. The experiment represented the university's commitment, often expressed by President James Zimmerman, to assume a leadership role in the state's public education. It was in the university's best interest to work with the state offices. State recognition of the training school and any other programs connected with the university made future financial support from the legislature more likely. The state agency offered a centralized structure through which to reach educators throughout the state. The Department of Education itself needed the fresh ideas and dynamic energy coming from the university. If the students of New Mexico were to realize any benefit from the innovations of San José or any other research undertaking, the combined efforts of reformers and state officials would be crucial.

The San José project was a public relations success, which helped to spark the interest of the politically minded officials in the state Office of Education. The school generated a great deal of excitement and praise in educational circles in the mid-1930s. Teachers from around the state came to visit and participate in demonstrations. Staff members, including Loyd Tireman, Principal Harlan Sininger, Jennie Gonzales, Marie Hughes, Brice Sewell, and others also traveled around the state to speak at conferences and workshops.[63] Even the U.S. Bureau of Education noted the remarkable experiment taking place in the Albuquerque suburb of San José, praising the school in its first circular ever devoted entirely to the education of Spanish-speaking children in the Southwest.[64] New Mexico educators attested to the positive influence of the school. President Donald W. MacKay of Eastern New Mexico Junior College thought San José had lessened the "great apathy toward the terrible conditions in the rural schools" and had made more people aware of the need for improving the elementary schools of the state.[65]

The cooperation between the Department of Education and UNM faculty in the case of the San José Training School suggested that administrative and pedagogical reform were finally being merged in New Mexico. Further evidence of the increased coordination of state officials and innovators came with the initiation of a statewide curriculum revision project. In 1934 the state Board of Education assigned a committee to investigate the curricular needs of the state. On the recommendation of this committee, State Superintendent H. R. Rodgers appointed a commission to study the state's curriculum in 1935. Following the suggestion of James Zimmerman and the New Mexico Education Association, Rodgers requested funds from the General Education Board to carry out a statewide curriculum revision. The GEB agreed to consider a proposal, particularly if Loyd Tireman directed the project. After Tireman agreed and wrote the proposal, the GEB allocated $18,000 for a three-year curriculum revision project, beginning in 1936.[66]

Loyd Tireman came to dominate the curriculum revision project and even to consider it his own. His proposal persuaded GEB officials to provide the funds for the project. He was placed in charge of it, as stipulated in the grant from the GEB. Tireman named the Advisory Council for the project and chose his San José coworker Marie Hughes to head the Curriculum Laboratory, where most of the work would be done. The project closely tied curriculum revision to the work of the San José Training School. The purpose of the project, Tireman stated, was to insure "that the contributions of San José could be woven into the schools of the state in a more extensive way than otherwise we can ever do."[67]

In the curricular revisions that followed, many of the principles of the San José School did become part of official state policy. The initial curricular work of 1936–39 was done by the Curriculum Laboratory under the auspices of the University of New Mexico, with Hughes serving as director. Hughes worked with teachers to develop steps for incorporating the San José curriculum into the local schools.⁶⁸

Recognizing the tradition of local innovation, Hughes and Tireman called upon each county to conduct experiments in curricular reform and to report the results to the university. Hughes and "Field Worker" Mary Watson evaluated curriculum materials at the UNM laboratory before testing them at laboratory schools in Valencia and Torrance Counties. Successful ideas were disseminated around the state, in the form of bulletins on "Handwriting Instruction," "Activities for the Non-Recitation Period," "Equipment and Materials," "Experiences in Elementary Classrooms," and a "Soil Conservation Unit." The laboratory also distributed an "Annotated Bibliography of Professional Magazines."⁶⁹

Teachers and administrators around the state welcomed the State Program for the Improvement of Instruction. Director of Rural Education Ulrich Beeson hoped the program would bring backward rural schools up to the level of more progressive city schools. He reported that in 1937–38, all of the rural county supervisors "were attempting to carry on with their teachers the improvement of instruction in cooperation with the Curriculum Laboratory" and had used the materials sent out by the project.⁷⁰ Director of Secondary Education L. W. Clark hoped that the program might be expanded to include the high school curriculum in addition to the elementary schools.⁷¹

Expansion and continuation of curriculum revision depended upon the state taking over control of the project. From the start the state Board of Education, the GEB, and the university had expected that the State Department of Education would eventually assume responsibility for the work and would issue a revised elementary school course of study for the entire state. As the work of the Curriculum Laboratory was winding down in 1939, Tireman hesitated to turn it over to the Department of Education under newly elected State Superintendent Grace Corrigan. To Leo Favrot of the GEB, Tireman expressed fear that the state agency "would only make a fizzle of the undertaking." He implied that Corrigan lacked administrative ability and should not be granted further GEB funds.⁷² A few weeks after Tireman's letter, Corrigan reported to Favrot that the state would take over curriculum revision, merging that activity with rural supervision and teacher training under one divisional head. She asked the GEB to extend its funding to the state so the work on curriculum revision could continue. The GEB rejected Corrigan's request.⁷³ Tireman's influence could work not only to facilitate educational progress but also to derail it.

Despite the setback a new course of study for the social sciences resulted from the curriculum revision project. The new curriculum that emerged from the joint efforts of Tireman, his university associates, and the State Department of Education reflected the progressive principles advanced at San José.

Teachers were encouraged to involve pupils in planning, to provide opportunity for creative expression, and to account for individual differences.[74] In 1944 Superintendent Georgia Lusk expanded upon this work by issuing a new Elementary School Curriculum. In a major section devoted to "Teaching Bilingual Children," the San José vocabulary and reading programs were outlined for teachers. None of the curricular guidelines, however, advised a program of bilingual instruction for beginners.[75]

Loyd Tireman's contribution to the curricular revision project was, like most of his career, a contradictory blend of energetic direction and disappointment. On the one hand he masterfully coordinated a statewide project that brought together some of the most innovative teachers and pedagogical techniques available in the state at the time. And then in a moment of peevishness, he undermined the entire project as it was about to be taken over by the state. He evidently could not let the project go forward under the direction of someone else. His influence also accounts in part for the failure of the state to implement bilingual instruction. Had he supported bilingual instruction more forcefully, there would have been a better chance that the new curriculum would have included it. As it was, Tireman claimed that no conclusive scientific data had emerged to prove that bilingual instruction assisted children in learning English. On that ground he rejected it, dismissing his own and others' arguments that bilingual instruction helped students adjust to the school environment and reinforced their pride in their own ethnic identity.

Any assessment of the work of Loyd S. Tireman must take into account the contradictions of the man and his message. A quintessential progressive, Tireman possessed an absolute faith in scientific methods and quantifiable proof. As far as Tireman was concerned, if something could not be measured, it could not be proven. This dependence upon scientific data partly explains the greatest contradiction in his thinking—the gap between his professed regard for Hispano culture and the Spanish language on the one hand, and his ultimate rejection of bilingual instruction and certain aspects of Hispano culture on the other. Tireman's faith in science explains his methods but not his goals. Like many other progressives, he was an assimilationist who believed that Hispanos would benefit from becoming more like Anglo Americans. Yet at the same time, he argued for the preservation of Hispanos' unique identity.

In some ways Loyd Tireman's innovations promised positive reinforcement of Hispanic culture within the schools. By emphasizing traditional arts and crafts, singing Spanish folk songs, and teaching Spanish in the upper grades, the San José School did impart the message that Hispanic culture had its worthwhile aspects. These ideas, so similar to those of Nina Otero-Warren in Santa Fe, represented a dramatic improvement over the efforts of some Americanizers, who seemed bent upon eliminating all vestiges of Hispanic influence. Yet the San José approach also selectively romanticized Hispano culture, while denying Hispanos a true understanding of the political and economic realities of their own history. By and large Anglos, not Hispanos themselves, determined what was valuable and what should be preserved from the culture. Loyd Tireman, acting on sincere intentions, participated in this process of cultural selectivity.

Underlying these beliefs was the assumption that Anglo culture was superior in many ways to Hispano culture. This is not to suggest that Tireman consciously articulated them. What he did as much as what he said revealed these attitudes, although they went largely unexamined. Nor is the point to flail Tireman for failing to recognize his own culturally engrained biases. Rather it is important for later observers to understand why progressive educators such as Tireman failed to achieve their goals of a more democratic and harmonious society. Whether intended or not, their ideas and actions reinforced notions of Anglo superiority, disparaged Hispano culture, and denied Hispanos a means of addressing their own self-defined grievances. Frustration and anger were the consequences of those policies, as Hispanos ultimately asserted their claim to their own history, language, and ethnicity.

5 | Prospects for Enduring Reform
The Community School Ideal

THE DECADE OF the 1930s seemed an inauspicious time for educational innovation of any sort. Across New Mexico decreasing tax revenues had forced counties to curtail spending for schools. Teachers found their salaries reduced or temporarily suspended. School districts cut back terms to a few months or closed altogether. Yet educators seemed determined to make the schools better suited to meeting the needs of students in times of crisis. Timely philanthropic assistance and the advent of the New Deal programs provided New Mexicans with opportunities to pursue bold new directions. Although federal funds and philanthropy came with strings attached, such resources enabled New Mexican educators to launch unique regional programs to meet the challenges of the 1930s.

Fortuitously the aims of New Mexican reformers coincided with the agendas of both the New Deal and philanthropic organizations such as the General Education Board. Under the New Deal the Roosevelt administration sought to bring impoverished and neglected sectors of the population up to a minimal level of prosperity and productivity. Sharing this goal, the GEB had primarily focused its efforts on southern Blacks but included New Mexico Hispanos as a comparable group. The GEB and the New Deal hoped to revive community life and allow people to remain on the land and in their native villages. Both considered education as critical in achieving these goals, even though neither wanted to become directly involved in supporting day-to-day school operations. The GEB funded experimental programs such as the San José Training School but fully expected state and local government to assume support for them in the long run. The New Deal, to be considered in the next chapter, entered the educational field even more circuitously, by creating relief programs that offered educational services.[1]

With limited resources available in the state, all New Mexico educators stood to benefit from outside assistance. Pedagogical progressives, however, probably received the greatest boost, since their goals of school reform seldom attracted more traditional forms of support. Reformers such as George I. Sánchez and Loyd S. Tireman, as we have seen, were able to challenge the status quo and to pursue new ventures in pedagogy partly as a result of GEB funding. Nationally a wave of disillusionment with business-oriented panaceas gave impetus to more far-reaching progressive ideas. By 1932 educators were more willing to consider George S. Counts's bold challenge: "Dare the schools build a new social order?"[2] Counts and others demanded that the schools reconstruct American society from the bottom up.

John Dewey had envisioned social reconstruction resulting from the interaction of community life and the schools. Believing that the school should be a focal point of community activity, he urged educators to find in the surrounding environment the substance of school curricula. Whatever interested the community and affected its livelihood should become part of what was taught in school. The school itself, Dewey thought, should be organized as a community, so students would learn by actively participating in democratic decision-making and cooperative projects. Teachers should use this busy, dynamic school as a tool for eliminating the bad habits and wrong thinking that caused social evils. Thus the schools would contribute to an improved democratic society.[3]

Numerous New Mexico educators shared Dewey's ideal of the community school. The directors of the San José Training School had attempted to involve the community in planning and conducting the school from the start. Loyd Tireman happily reported the participation of parents in school activities and was gratified that "many homes are making a distinct effort to speak English as an aid to the education of their children." At San José he had begun "to bring the community and the school into harmony, to vitalize the school curriculum by inclusion of life situations, to remove the school from a sequestered and isolated position and to make it the center of interest and effort of all the group."[4]

Not all New Mexico schools, unfortunately, were like San José. Tireman knew that most Hispanos in New Mexico lived in villages where conditions differed dramatically from those in the cities. In meeting the needs of the Hispano community, he would first have to understand the attributes and weaknesses of the culture. In a paper presented to the Rural Conference of the Colorado State Teachers College in 1932, Tireman revealed his assessment of the Spanish-speaking people of New Mexico. He urged others to "see through the clouded vision of intolerance and prejudice" to find the good qualities in different cultures. The Spanish-speaking people of New Mexico, he believed, could be justly proud of their heritage and had much to offer Anglo civilization. Hispanos were justified in rejecting as undesirable many Anglo customs. For instance the Spanish-speaking people excelled in courtesy and simply could not understand "the Anglo's abruptness, his haste to be getting somewhere, his indifference to the little attentions of life, and his lack of time to talk." If Anglo civilization could be considered an economic one, Tireman thought, then the Hispanic civilization was a spiritual one. Planning for the future, as an Anglo was wont to do, did not suit a person who "considers the task he is doing more important than the proposed one." To Tireman this represented "a spiritual tranquility unknown to most Anglos."[5]

Tireman counted other cultural distinctions among the attributes of Spanish-speaking people. Anyone close to Hispanos, he said, recognized their "beauty-loving tendencies." In folklore, music, and colonial arts such as woodwork, tin, and leather, they possessed a rich heritage. And he lamented that "this delightful and cultural contribution of the Spanish-speaking people has never received its proper place in the ordinary affairs of our daily life in the Southwest."[6] Like other Anglos who considered themselves friends of the Hispanos, Tireman chose to praise those aspects of their culture that seemed the most innocuous and posed the least threat to the established socioeconomic patterns of American life. What he chose to emphasize as valuable in Hispano culture tended to reinforce the view of Hispanos as exotic, romantic, and non-threatening.

Yet Tireman believed the school should attempt to eradicate those cultural attributes that he did not consider positive. For instance he thought that Hispanos showed a tendency to idealize and follow colorful individuals. He feared that Hispanos could easily be led to the dangerous extreme of *caciquismo,* which characterized political life in Latin American countries. The school had to assume the responsibility for teaching students "how to differentiate between the good and the bad in public leadership."[7] Even after he had been in the state twenty years, Tireman continued to judge Hispanic culture by the standards of Anglo society, generalizing that "For centuries the social life in Spanish-speaking countries has crushed the initiative of the common man. His thinking about the general affairs of the state has been done by others." Tireman envisioned the school eradicating this alleged fault in Hispanos as well as alleviating other perceived shortcomings such as divergent health practices, nutrition, land management, and superstitious beliefs. According to Tireman the school should "correct existing evils in the community."[8]

Tireman expressed dismay at the degree to which New Mexico's small villages remained *Hispanicized.* He lamented that in the isolated mountain villages where so many Hispanos resided, the people still used Spanish in everyday speech and preferred to build their houses out of adobe in the traditional architectural style. Although the people were hospitable and kept their yards clean and attractive, "the situation is entirely non-English; the speech, the customs, the very habits of thinking are non-English." The same circumstances prevailed in the rural schools where the teacher was "commonly a Spanish-American girl with perhaps one year at a normal school. The law requires her to teach in English, and most comply, but the English is not pure, and her grammatical mistakes are many." With little equipment, few library books or textbooks, and short terms, the Hispano children received very poor schooling. Furthermore, he complained, "All natural conversation outside of the school is in Spanish, and indeed, when the children whisper behind their books, they do so in Spanish."[9]

In building his community school ideal, Tireman's sense of what was valuable or detrimental in Hispano culture translated into curricular practice. He encouraged the development of what he considered natural talents for arts and crafts. He sought to improve health and land management practices, to nurture civic responsibility, and to teach English skills. Tireman also recognized that Hispana teachers, often poorly trained, composed the core of the teaching ranks in the rural villages, and much of his work was directed toward improving their qualifications. But in noting their inadequate training and resources, he failed to grasp their significance as community leaders, role models, and members of family networks.

In oral history interviews with women who had taught in rural schools in the 1930s, Erlinda Gonzales-Berry found that although they worked under challenging circumstances, the teachers were assisted by supportive communities. Anita Dominguez Chávez offered some insight into the less-than-ideal conditions encountered in the rural schools. She began teaching in 1930 at El Valle in Taos County, where she and one other teacher had charge of grades one through six. The "little ones" who were learning English demanded the most attention. But Dominguez Chávez did more than just teach. She had to light the fire to warm the building in the morning, to cook for the children, and to sweep the floors, as well as to supervise extracurricular activities such as school plays. When she began teaching, she had only a high school diploma and no special training. She continued to teach after her marriage and proudly recalled that she and her husband sent their own three children through college on their teachers' salaries.[10]

Many teachers in the rural Hispanic districts were Hispanas who had grown up close to the schools where they worked. Like Dominguez Chávez most did not have advanced training when they began teaching. Yet their devotion to teaching and to improving their own credentials was apparent. Dominguez Chávez and many others attended college during the summers to obtain degrees and higher certification. Their parents and husbands supported these efforts, suggesting that teaching was a valued and necessary occupation even for married women. The experience of Mary Sanchez bears this out. Her father placed great emphasis on education, overcoming doubts about non-Catholic instruction in sending her to Albuquerque to board at the Harwood School for a time. After graduating from Albuquerque High School in 1925, Sanchez enrolled at the University of New Mexico for one semester before receiving an offer to teach in the Valencia County schools. Her father wanted her to finish her degree, but nevertheless respected her decision to take the job and helped her find adequate housing in Valencia County. There Mary met her future husband and married, with the understanding that she would continue to teach and go to college. Her husband drove her to Albuquerque to attend night school and summer classes. Mary eventually received her B.A. degree and continued teaching even after she had her daughter in 1930.[11]

Dora Vásquez Chacón found support and mutual respect from the people in the community where she taught. Born in 1908 in Ocate, Mora County, Vásquez attended a Presbyterian mission school as a child. She took her first teaching job in Loma Parda, which she described as "sort of a placita that the people lived on both sides of the street." Isolated in the deep part of a canyon, Loma Parda could be reached only by crossing a river with no bridge. When the high spring waters were running, the road was impassable. Vásquez agreed to take the position only because she had a cousin living in the village, with whom she could live. She remembered her first day of teaching:

> You had those cowbells to ring and I stood at the door, ringing that bell and my knees were just shaking. I didn't know how I am going to get started. And there was nothing in my schoolroom like I say, there was nothing. I had a few papers and pencils and that was about all. There was an old man, Don Cosme, eh, Se de Vaca, that lived across from, it wasn't a school house, it was a rented room that they rented for us to have school. He lived across the street and he looked at me and he told his wife, "Oh that teacher is too young. *Es una muchachita, muy jovencita. Los muchachos van hacer sopa con ella.*"[12]

Even though a few of the older boys did come to school only "just to check and see *la maestra,*" Vásquez persevered and became a respected member of the community. The villagers came to rely upon her to translate and write letters, advise them on business matters, and find assistance for the sick and hungry. Teaching in the winter and attending normal school during the summer, Vásquez eventually finished her college degree. After her marriage she and her husband both taught school in Socorro and Valencia Counties.[13]

The experiences of these teachers indicate the central role played by Hispanic women in schooling in the 1920s and 1930s. The most successful efforts for improving education for Hispanos would be those that enhanced the already accepted role for Hispanic women teachers in the local communities. Meeting the teachers' needs for greater access to advanced training was a key element in addressing community needs. The San José directors understood and appealed to the community support and intense desire for improving teacher qualifications. Writing to President James F. Zimmerman, Loyd Tireman reported receiving many letters "in which the writer has regretted that she could not come to San Jose for the Training School Course during the school year, but would like to come during the summer months." Indicating that nearly all of these teachers were Spanish American, Tireman asserted that providing them with an opportunity for summer training would be the best way of improving rural education for Hispanos.[14]

The San José staff sought various ways to expose rural teachers to new ideas and advanced teaching methods. In 1930, when the program began, the San José School provided scholarships for teachers to stay for three months. The visiting teachers, who had to be employed in rural schools with Spanish-speaking pupils, both observed and took an active part in the instruction. The San José board created five scholarships for native Spanish-speaking teachers with two years experience to attend the College of Education at the University of New Mexico. Yet another means of reaching the rural teacher was the dissemination of training school bulletins containing practical suggestions to aid teachers.[15]

The first year of the teacher training program proved disappointing, mainly because of the disparity between the environment of San José and the schools from which the teachers came. The quality of the San José School, with two rooms for each grade, far exceeded the poor one- or two-room schools where most visiting teachers worked. Some teachers who visited San José found it frustrating to return to their spartan schoolhouses after experiencing the rich environment of the training school. One trainee bought her own materials to reproduce a useful hectograph she had learned about at San José because her district could not afford the extra expense.[16]

The San José staff experimented with various solutions to the problems posed by rural teaching. They reorganized the Opportunity Room, allowing any student who was overage or otherwise having serious problems in learning to be admitted to this special class. The class then resembled conditions in a one-room country school, where the rural school teacher could observe the type of instruction and organization necessary to make such a school work.[17]

Restructuring the Opportunity Room to approximate a one-room rural school still did not provide the same set of conditions as those present in an actual country school. Consequently the San José Board of Directors asked the state Board of Education to allow Tireman to establish another demonstration school at Cedro, a small village in the mountains east of Albuquerque.[18] Jennie Gonzales, a native of Gallup and a UNM graduate who had taught at San José, took charge of the one-room school at Cedro in the fall of 1932. This tiny village of seven stone houses huddled in a clearing in the Cibola National Forest typified the isolated and largely self-sufficient communities of Hispanic New Mexico. The villagers raised cattle on ranches located quite a distance from the village and grew corn, beans, pumpkins, and other vegetables for subsistence.[19]

Gonzales found the villagers kind and hospitable but lacking in enthusiasm for the school. Parents needed their children's help in the seasonal chores of ranching and farming and only grudgingly consented to send them to school during the fall harvest. Gonzales sought to counter this resistance by involving herself in activities vital to the community. Appealing to traditional as well as practical concerns, she organized a production of the Christmas play "Los Pastores" and encouraged the installation of a hydraulic pump so the villagers would no longer have to carry water up a steep hill. The good teacher, she believed, did not "shut herself in and expect the four walls of her school room to contain only her ideas but makes them so elastic that they embrace all the village."[20]

Jennie Gonzales certainly did not confine herself within the walls of the schoolhouse. She gave freely of her time in response to the needs of the villagers, to the point that the parents came to see her role as a "mixture of doctor, nurse, politician, and what have you." Gonzales considered it her duty to provide opportunities that the community lacked as a result of its isolated circumstances. She went to much trouble to install a radio in her home and invited her little pupils to listen to it. "All came eager and full of awe," she recalled. "Only one child had heard a radio before. Their eyes sparkled with pleasure and excitement." She also taught them the game of baseball, which they had never played before. And she went into the homes to instruct women on modern health practices and nutrition. Gonzales helped to deliver babies and tried to persuade villagers to improve their diet.[21]

Gonzales knew that the problems she confronted at Cedro faced rural educators throughout the state, and the solutions could be found only by understanding the communities in which they served. She believed that "every red-blooded teacher aspires to make her school the center of the community's life." The teacher must be willing and able to "draw from her community all that it can contribute toward a better understanding between home and school." Gonzales advised other rural teachers not "to try to teach the three R's as something separate from the every day life of those who compose your school."[22] In 1935 she had a wider opportunity to offer advice to rural teachers when State Superintendent H. R. Rodgers appointed her state Rural School Supervisor.[23]

While Gonzales established the demonstration school at Cedro, the San José School initiated other extensions to assist teachers in the rural areas. In July 1932 Marie M. Hughes joined the San José staff as "field worker," whose duties were to visit those teachers who had received training at San José, to interview potential scholarship candidates, and to assist county school superintendents in improving classroom teaching. For more efficient dissemination of information, certain centrally located schools in each county were designated as "key schools." Hughes held workshops and demonstrations for San José cadets and other rural teachers at these schools.[24]

In her first year as field worker for the San José project, Hughes discovered how slow and frustrating progress in New Mexican education could be. In observing former San José teacher trainees, or cadets, at work, Hughes found that they did not perform up to the standards the San José directors expected of them. Under pressure from principals and other teachers, they easily slipped back into the old teaching procedures and habits. The lack of equipment and materials made progressive teaching difficult in many isolated communities. For instance reading charts played an important role in the San José methods, but some rural teachers were unable to acquire chart paper and ink. Recognizing the problem, Hughes suggested that cadets at San José be furnished with such basic materials before they returned to their rural schools.[25]

The accomplishments of the field worker in supervising teachers in their own districts favorably impressed State Department of Education officials, including State Superintendent Georgia Lusk, who persuaded the legislature to appropriate funds for this aspect of the school's work.[26] The Department of Education gradually took over the work of rural supervision, first by sending out materials Marie Hughes and state Rural Supervisor Grace Corrigan jointly prepared in 1933.[27] The department adopted the use of key schools and increased the number of its own rural supervisors in 1934, enabling the San José School to discontinue its program. Grace Corrigan noted the improvement wrought by a better organized plan for the seven rural supervisors. "The benefits accruing from this plan are especially noticeable in better program, better preparation of teaching materials on the part of teachers and better use and understanding of English on the part of the pupils."[28]

Rural supervision and teacher-training institutes served a vital role in improving teaching methods in the rural schools. In keeping with New Mexico's time-honored pattern of local initiative, however, many teachers and school administrators came up with their own ideas for improvement. Almost universal consensus existed on the need for Hispano children to learn English. Differences of opinion focused on the best methods to teach English and whether or not students should also be literate in Spanish. Although the San José experimental program was the best publicized, numerous other educators tried out bilingual methods. In 1930 a summer program conducted at the New Mexico State Agricultural College in Las Cruces brought praise from State Superintendent of Education Atanasio Montoya, who declared it the first attempt in the state to attempt to meet the needs of non-English-speaking children.[29]

Virginia Gonzáles, a Taos native with a year of college training, began teaching at El Prado in the Taos County schools in the early 1930s. County Rural Supervisor Ruth Miller-Martinez instructed Gonzáles to teach the children English in "whichever way you can do it best." After she found that her children could read English but did not understand what they were reading, Gonzáles worked on vocabulary by teaching them the English words for ordinary things in their environment. "I started taking them outside and they liked it so," she recalled. "This is the sky, the sky is blue, this is a tree, the tree has leaves, the trees are green . . . and so on and so forth." Although the school maintained a rule that no Spanish was to be spoken on the school grounds, Gonzáles used Spanish when needed to explain something and she did not punish children for speaking Spanish. Supervisor Miller-Martinez invited Gonzáles to present a demonstration on her teaching methods at a county teachers' convention.[30]

In 1938 Miller-Martinez issued a pamphlet to teachers in which she encouraged bilingual instruction. Less than 3 percent of the thirty-five hundred children enrolled in the elementary schools of Taos County spoke English, she pointed out. This situation was nothing new, she added, "*nor is it to be deplored.*"[31] New Mexico had two official languages, and in her view it was "quite evident that it was the intention of the framers of the Constitution of the State of New Mexico to insure the continuance and usefulness of the Spanish language as well as the English language."[32] She intended to do her part in carrying out that mandate.

Miller-Martinez admitted that most teachers in New Mexico used the "Do not speak Spanish method" that they had been taught in college and which most experts advocated. Her observations of the undesirable affects of the method on children led her to reject it. "A feeling of uncertainty and inferiority, with lack of responsiveness, is developed in the child forbidden the use of his mother-tongue," she explained. "Spanish speaking children become ashamed of their language, their music, their customs, their handicrafts and other home industries. . . . These human aspects, or human elements, are not considered in the research studies relating to bilingual children." In Taos County, therefore, teachers were encouraged to use the bilingual method of teaching in Spanish concurrently with instruction in English.[33]

Miller-Martinez and County Superintendent Lionides Pacheco held a conference in September 1938 to instruct Taos County teachers in the bilingual method. They invited several educators from around the state, including Nina Otero-Warren and Dr. F. M. Kercheville, of the University of New Mexico, to conduct workshops. Otero-Warren and Kercheville stressed the importance of continuing the use of Spanish in New Mexico and urged teachers to become fluent in both English and Spanish.[34] The teachers apparently agreed with them; early in 1939 the Taos County Teachers' Association passed a resolution calling for an experimental school to facilitate the teaching of Spanish in the grade schools. They also resolved that teachers should be required to pass written and oral examinations in both Spanish and English in order to teach.[35] The teachers' resolutions, along with Ruth Miller-Martinez's recommendations, were submitted to the state Curriculum Revision Committee. These suggestions did not, however, appear in the state's revised course of study.

The ultimate failure of university faculty, local educators, and state officials to work in tandem negated more than one commendable endeavor in educational reform. The Nambé Community School, one of the most promising school ventures ever attempted in New Mexico, also fell victim to the cross-purposes of its designers, the local people whom it touched, and the state.

In May 1937 an opportunity arose for Loyd Tireman to direct a demonstration school in Nambé, a small Hispanic village just north of Santa Fe. Cyrus McCormick, a wealthy Chicago businessman who maintained a home in Nambé, offered to give the directors of the San José project three thousand dollars annually for five years if they would set up an experimental school in Nambé.[36] The General Education Board provided another eight thousand dollars for the project, again giving Tireman a chance to work out his ideas in an actual demonstration school.[37] In addition to building upon the curriculum and methods developed at San José, Tireman hoped "to carry out a demonstration, for the school people of New Mexico, of a desirable school-community relationship." The Nambé School would serve as the focus of social and educational activities for the village and would act as a resource center for health and agricultural assistance.[38]

With the Sangre de Cristo Mountains to the east and the shallow Nambé River winding past fields and adobes and old cottonwood trees, the tiny village of Nambé seemed frozen in time, impervious to modern American life. Mr. and Mrs. Cyrus McCormick liked the rustic valley enough to buy 85 acres of land and build a fine house there, making theirs the largest estate in Nambé. The McCormicks' neighbors were mostly dirt farmers, although they had grazed stock on Pueblo Indian lands until the Indians of nearby Nambé Pueblo forced them to stop. The Nambé villagers, who had divided and subdivided their plots of land down to an average of 4 or 5 acres, also shared precious water with the Pueblo Indians. Growing wheat, corn, onions, chile, and other vegetables, the farmers of Nambé eked out a bare subsistence from the land.[39]

The property the McCormicks had purchased included the site of the old Nambé School, and in payment they gave a new piece of land and one thousand dollars to build a new one. With the McCormicks furnishing cash for materials and the villagers providing labor, the new building was completed in 1933. Still the McCormicks wanted the school to be more than just a new building, and after hearing about the San José project, they approached the University of New Mexico about the possibility of structuring the school not only to teach children but to help the villagers to improve their living conditions. McCormick wanted Loyd Tireman to direct the school. After securing commitments from the university, the Santa Fe County School Board, and the General Education Board, McCormick called a mass meeting of the Nambé villagers to ask their approval of the new plan. After several days and many individual conferences to explain the purpose of the experiment, the majority of the citizens of Nambé voted in favor of the proposal, "though a few were frankly skeptical."[40] The Nambé parents' willingness to try a new educational approach stemmed in large part from their dissatisfaction with the current academic curriculum.[41]

McCormick recognized that the Nambé villagers were willing to do much to help with the school, which reinforced his own desire to assist them. "We have esteemed it a privilege to collaborate in the Nambé Demonstration School project," he wrote Tireman, "it has been a program of self help because the people, in spite of their small resources, are so willing to give dances, plays and small sums of money to finance playground equipment, library books, school repair and other things."[42]

For Tireman the community's attitude augured well for his plans to integrate the school into the life of the community. Echoing John Dewey, Tireman declared that "A school should be the center of the community. It should be sensitive to the needs of the community and in cooperation with the parents plan a program that will make the best use of all available resources." New Mexico needed such schools, he believed, in order to interest the pupils in attending school. "Through participating in planning, executing, and evaluating their work," Tireman said, "they will learn to think and to use the facts and tools of learning. They should find the school a vital place in which it is good to live."[43]

Tireman planned to keep the curriculum flexible, in order to allow the needs and resources of the community itself to determine what would be taught. Only in regard to "the basic skills of the three R's" and the use of English would the Nambé School stress the conventional subjects of the American academic curriculum. Tireman intended to emphasize an intensive reading program, so that students would develop a love of reading. He hoped that their own individual reading tastes would lead them to acquire some of the traditional knowledge that the school's unorthodox curriculum would omit. He hoped as well that every child would leave the school able to "read as well as speak Spanish," although no plans were made to provide bilingual instruction.[44]

Mary Watson, a native of Logan, New Mexico, and a former state elementary education supervisor, became principal of the school. Watson and Tireman believed that the teachers of the community school must reside within the community, learning the needs of the villagers first-hand. In the five years that Nambé operated as a demonstration school, twenty-one persons taught on the faculty. All but one of the staff came from outside of Nambé; Cordelia Ortiz was the only teacher who had been raised in the village and had family there. All but one of the teachers were women, and only eight were native Hispanas.[45]

The Nambé staff found that the village shared problems typical of the small rural communities of New Mexico. Although infant mortality, social relationships, craft work, recreation, and command of oral English all needed attention, they decided that the greatest of Nambé's needs were health and land management. Their emphasis on health may have been encouraged by the McCormicks' support for the Nambé public health nursing project. Until 1940 Florence McCormick paid the salary of the district nurse, Maria Casias, who also served as the school nurse.[46]

The Nambé teachers primarily integrated health and other nonacademic subjects into the curriculum through activities. For instance when the third grade class showed an interest in the activities of the school nurse, they invited her to speak to them and then produced a class chart telling of her work. Miss Casias, the children wrote,

> goes to our houses. She tells our mothers how to keep the babies well. She tells them what kind of food to give the babies. She tells them to put the food where the flies will not get on it. She tells them to put netting over the babies to keep off the flies. . . .
> Miss Casias tells our fathers where to put the toilets and the wells. She tells them to put screens on the wells, so that the flies cannot get in. She tells them not to put the wells near the toilets.[47]

The fourth and fifth graders learned about land management through a project entitled "The Study of Irrigation, Water, the Land, and Man." With this project the Nambé directors hoped to "contribute to the daily life of the children and also lead them out to other parts of the unknown world." After classroom lessons on all aspects of water, irrigation, and soil erosion, the class went on field trips to the Nambé River and ditches, seeing for themselves the condition of the arroyos and hillsides around the village. They saw their fathers draw water from the ditches to irrigate the fields. They listened as their teacher told them how the water flowed down the river into the Rio Grande and from there to the Gulf of Mexico. In a single project they gained lessons in natural science, soil conservation, agriculture, geography, and even social relationships.[48]

The school's soil conservation program went even further, with the upper classes landscaping the Nambé School grounds. The students of the land management classes planted nearly three hundred trees and built a series of small terraces to serve as laboratory plots for drought-resistant plants. The adults of the village, although some had been highly skeptical of these projects at the outset, became "admiring co-workers" in the endeavor. Villagers went to work on their own eroded gullies and hillsides, using soil conservation methods demonstrated at the school.[49]

While health education and land management took center stage in the Nambé curriculum, the school did not neglect the acquisition of English. The staff initiated both a nursery and a prefirst class, similar to the one at the San José Training School. In these settings small children learned basic concepts and vocabulary to get them started in English. As they entered first grade, their teachers stressed oral expression in English. On the playground teachers monitored their language, to prevent them from speaking Spanish.[50]

As he had done at San José, Tireman required the teachers to keep diaries of their impressions of the children and their families, which he reviewed on a regular basis. After prefirst teacher Cordelia Ortiz described an abused child who misbehaved in school, Tireman wrote in the margin that such comments were not what he wanted and asked her to report what she had found in the community that would help the school curriculum. Ortiz, a Nambé native whose father had sent her to schools in Santa Fe, then wrote an entry that struck Tireman as a "good idea." Under the heading of "History of Nambé" she wrote:

> My own father had documents proving his ownership of his greatest part of his land, but had to call Agapito Hererra as a witness for a small piece of land. Most of the people had no idea about that they needed any kind of document about a land purchased or a business agreement. I believe the school could help those people by teaching the older pupils in school, and they in turn take it home.[51]

Recognizing the problems of the village was only the first step in bringing the school and community together for a common purpose. In order to gain the trust and participation of the townspeople, the teachers invited parents and other visitors to come often to the school. In the fall of 1937 the schoolchildren hosted a fair for the villagers. Ortiz reported that the village people reached an understanding of some of the teaching methods employed at the school through their visit. When they saw all the toys in her room, she explained to them "how much vocabulary the children could learn through toys, and they said no wonder they learn so quickly to speak English." Ortiz felt that the school had made a real breakthrough in reaching the people during this fair. "The health play and talk was the best lesson for the people," she said.

> They certainly realized the importance of a good modern well and toilet. The wells and toilets made by the children was a very good contrast of good and bad health habits. Years before when the nurse used to give talks on cleanliness, diseases, etc. the people thought she was criticizing them, so they started to hate her, and now that we put it through the school they took it in the right way. . . . The people saw with their own eyes that the children were developing health habits in school.[52]

As teacher of the prefirst class, Ortiz had the responsibility of teaching basic English to her children, most of whom spoke only Spanish when they entered school. She began by teaching simple sentences that the children would need for everyday conduct in school and proceeded to teach vocabulary based upon the objects around the school and playground. She took her pupils on walks around the village, "so as to carry good conversations," teaching them words for everything they saw and wanted to discuss. By the end of October, she was amazed at how much English the children were using. "I think it is very interesting," she wrote in her diary, "to see the children speaking English, after hearing them speak nothing but Spanish when they start school." Ortiz did not use English exclusively, however, but led the children in singing songs in Spanish. One day a villager told her that some of the people did not like "the idea of having the pupils sing so many Spanish songs, since we were emphasizing so much in 'English.' They like to sing them, but they also like to have their children sing English Songs." To this Tireman responded, "We can't please everyone. Some attention must be given to Spanish songs."[53]

The interaction of school and community seemed evident in every aspect of the school's program. The school nurse and teachers went into the homes of the children to encourage better health standards, discuss problems, or simply to visit. The parents went to the school for a wide variety of activities and organized a Parent-Teacher Association that held dances and bake sales in order to buy equipment for the school. When electricity was installed in the school building, it was the PTA that paid the $25 for electric lights. "The school buildings became the center for community functions," wrote Tireman and Watson, "but they came to mean more than mere community meeting places." Villagers came to the school for help and advice, particularly as they realized that the school people would aid them in getting assistance or employment with the NYA, WPA, and other agencies. Tireman and Watson noted that the "school became the link between the people and the channels of living from which they had been isolated for so long, and the people began to make use of the existing opportunities."[54]

Through the efforts of the McCormicks, Loyd Tireman, Mary Watson, Cordelia Ortiz, Maria Casias, and other teachers, the village of Nambé opened the door to the outside world. While the entire community benefited from the Nambé School, the children's educational achievement held the most promise. At the start of its fourth year, the Nambé program had made considerable progress in increasing rates of attendance and promotion. In 1938 only six students completed the eighth grade and went on to high school in Pojoaque. In 1940 fifteen finished the eighth grade, and twenty-seven were expected to finish the highest grade in 1941. Few Nambé students, however, completed high school, and for this Tireman blamed the traditional academic curriculum offered at Pojoaque. It was useless, he felt, to reform the elementary curriculum only to have students go on to a high school that offered no courses in agriculture or home economics.[55]

The Nambé experiment came to an end in the spring of 1942, under confusing circumstances. Funding from the General Education Board ran out and was not renewed. Cyrus McCormick appeared ready to extend his support of the project, if the community desired its continuation. In a town meeting, however, the citizens of Nambé voted to terminate the experimental program and to return the school to the administration of the Santa Fe County Schools.[56] The parents of Nambé's students expressed dissatisfaction with the curriculum, complaining that the school did not enforce discipline and did not prepare students to go on to high school. It seemed to them that with the school's emphasis on health education and land management, the basics of reading, writing, and arithmetic had been neglected.[57]

Some teachers shared the parents' concerns. Frank Angel wrote in his diary that he wondered if the school was adequately preparing the students for high school. Tireman bluntly responded that "This school will not worry very much about high school."[58] Indeed it had never been the Nambé School's goal to prepare students to go on to high school or college. Tireman and Watson stated clearly that their plans for the school were based upon the assumption that the majority of the people of Nambé would remain in the village and that "our job is not to prepare these children for college but to live happier and more efficiently in this community."[59] In summing up the lessons learned, they claimed that "Our study at Nambé suggests that if the rural schools would give less attention to college preparatory courses and more attention to the problems of their community, that children would not drop out in large numbers at an early age and thus be deprived of needed training."[60] Clearly, however, parents did not agree with Tireman that schooling should not lead to higher education.

The school had experienced internal staffing problems that probably contributed to its failure to meet the high expectations of parents. The turnover rate for teachers was quite high; a few stayed only six months, while fifteen stayed two years or less. Only Mary Watson and Cordelia Ortiz remained at the school throughout the entire five years. All but Ortiz came from outside Nambé, yet were expected to live in and interact with the community. Many of the teachers rented rooms in the homes of villagers. The experience of sharing their lives with the community may not have turned out to be as harmonious and productive as the school directors had hoped. And finally it could not have been easy to work for Loyd Tireman, who was demanding and abrasive with his subordinates, especially women.[61]

When it came to Nambé, Tireman seemed to have forgotten that for several decades native Hispanas, whose families were woven into the fabric of the community, had served as the backbone of the rural schools of New Mexico. Lacking degrees and training, they had nevertheless managed to do what Tireman had hoped his teachers could have done at Nambé: understand the aspirations of the villagers and earn their respect. In bringing so many outsiders to Nambé, he ignored one of the vital traditions in the life of the community.

Tireman placed some of the blame for the termination of the Nambé School on the State Department of Education. It was clear that Tireman and Superintendent Grace Corrigan did not agree on the virtues of basing the school curriculum on community needs. Tireman still resented Corrigan's taking control of the curriculum revision project away from the Education Department at UNM. Jackson Davis, of the General Education Board, found that Corrigan's action had resulted in "a little jealousy and LST was somewhat hesitant to speak of it." After visiting the Department of Education, Davis agreed with Tireman that the "staff of the Department do not have the professional ability and spirit to make this work effective."[62] Corrigan, who served as state superintendent of education until 1943, showed little inclination to incorporate ideas from the Nambé project into the state's school system. Although Tireman complained about the superintendent's lack of interest in Nambé, he too had lost interest well before the project ended. In an interview with a GEB staffer in July 1940, Tireman admitted disillusionment with the experiment and predicted that "his own work will be finished there in one more year."[63]

The Nambé project, with its emphasis upon community involvement, had promised to improve not only children's school performance but also the community's standard of living. The results were mixed at best. Enrollment at the school increased, and more students went on to high school. Villagers learned about health practices and soil conservation. The school's successes were balanced, however, by disappointing failures. The Nambé directors had not convinced state officials of the viability of the community school model or bilingual instruction. They had alienated some parents and teachers. And they had not found a way to draw upon the strengths of the Hispano community.

The community school ideal sought by Tireman and others rested upon an admirable notion: the school should become a part of the community and meet the needs of the people it served. In some ways New Mexico's school reformers accomplished those lofty goals by involving parents in school activities and in structuring curricula to reflect the livelihoods pursued in a particular community. Schools helped to break down some of the isolation of rural areas and brought needed information about health and soil conservation. But the schools did not substantially change the economic prospects of either adults or the younger generation, and perhaps it was unrealistic to hope that they might. Outside the schoolhouse door, other educational programs proliferated in the 1930s that even more explicitly aimed at improving the economic conditions of Hispanos.

6 | The New Deal and Education in New Mexico

THE GREAT DEPRESSION triggered immense social and economic distresses in New Mexico, as it did across the nation. Like other Americans New Mexicans suffered from widespread unemployment, the collapse of agricultural prices and markets, and the ravages of drought. They welcomed federal aid through New Deal agencies, although they sometimes found these programs intrusive and inadequate for their needs. For better or worse the New Deal brought immense and long-lasting changes to New Mexico. As Suzanne Forrest, Sandra Schackel, and Sarah Deutsch have shown, New Mexico's New Deal focused particular attention on improving the lives of Hispanos while preserving their traditional way of life. These well-intentioned programs, however, failed to relieve the stagnation of the regional economy and did not effectively enable Hispanos to control or direct their own cultural destiny.[1]

Education became a vital part of the federal response almost by accident. The New Dealers did not set out to reform the nation's schools or to forge a federal educational policy. Rather the New Deal espoused a larger social goal of insuring opportunities for all citizens to enjoy a minimal standard of living. Education became an avenue for empowering people without directly involving the federal government in the public schools. New Deal agencies created alternative institutions peripheral to the schools, through which educational benefits were channeled to people at the bottom of the socioeconomic ladder. The New Dealers did not wish to challenge local and state control over schools, but at the same time they wanted to reach marginalized groups such as southern Blacks, who traditionally had not benefited from mainstream schools. In doing so the New Deal agencies often antagonized professional educators on the local and state levels.[2]

Such animosity between federal bureaucrats and state school personnel did not develop in New Mexico, for a variety of reasons. Unlike educators in other states, those in New Mexico found ways to integrate their goals with those of the New Deal. They worked well with the federal agencies because they shared a common commitment to improving the standard of living of underprivileged groups. New Mexicans had also demonstrated a willingness to experiment with new methods of reaching the unique population of Hispanos in their midst. The decentralized nature of New Deal programs, with authority for running programs dispersed to the states, allowed for variation and local influence, which in New Mexico often translated into increased attention to Hispano needs.[3]

In the early 1930s New Mexico educators began to realize the extent of the economic downturn, as they watched tax revenues shrink and budgets decrease. At the same time enrollment in schools increased each year. Many of the new pupils were Hispanos. In 1930-31, 73,821 Hispano children attended school on a regular basis, out of a total school population of 144,234. Two years later the total number of students in school had risen to 153,793, while the number of Hispanos had increased to 80,989. By 1938 the total number of students in school reached 180,680.[4] No New Mexico county actually closed all its schools during the 1930s, but hardship hit in other ways. Across the state construction of new school buildings ceased, school boards shortened terms and cut back staff, superintendents saw their budgets reduced, and teachers had to make do with less equipment.[5]

Federal relief funds began to reach New Mexico in 1933, under the Federal Emergency Relief Administration (FERA). New Mexicans who had experienced crop failures or unemployment received emergency loans from federal money matched by state funds. Although never enough to offset losses caused by drought, grasshoppers, or layoffs from the Santa Fe Railway, FERA helped people face hard times. Even this slight infusion of money helped the schools, by enabling people to keep up with their taxes.[6] Rural schools also benefited from direct grants in 1933, 1934, and 1935.[7]

Despite some favoritism shown for registered Democrats, many New Mexicans found work with New Deal projects, and numerous public works projects aiding the schools were completed.[8] In June 1935 Governor Clyde Tingley announced that he would seek funds from the Public Works Administration (PWA) and Works Progress Administration (WPA) for school construction in the rural districts of the state. In July he traveled to Washington to discuss New Mexico's needs with Rexford G. Tugwell and Will Alexander in the Roosevelt administration.[9] Upon his return to Santa Fe, the governor announced confidently that hundreds of school buildings would be built in New Mexico, using federal funds for labor. Local counties would have to supply the building materials, but using uniform plans of construction and locally produced adobe bricks and vigas, the governor predicted, the costs would be manageable.[10]

Tingley called upon the county school superintendents to conduct surveys of existing conditions in their counties and to submit requests for new or remodeled school buildings. The county superintendents' surveys revealed the impoverished conditions of the rural schools. Mrs. Philip Sánchez, Mora County superintendent, called public meetings in as many districts as she could, to determine what the local citizens thought about their schools. Hardly a single schoolhouse in the county sufficed to meet the needs of the number of pupils attending. Most were too small, nearly all had lighting and heating problems, and some had no access to fresh water. But even though the citizenry recognized the need for new schools, no one had extra money to build them. Most people favored the consolidation of districts containing one-and two-room dilapidated schools into larger districts, where funds could be pooled and students would have a better chance to attend a high school.[11]

Taos County Superintendent Floyd Santisteven, although apparently he did not call meetings to elicit public support, also submitted a compelling survey of existing conditions. Like Mora County residents, Santisteven saw consolidation of districts as the solution to lack of funds. He recommended the construction of a new high school in Taos to accommodate students from Talpa, Arroyo Seco, and Arroyo Hondo. Other district schools suffered a range of maladies from uneven floors to lack of toilets. He made a modest plea for a new roof on the one-room adobe building in Los Cordovas, after reporting that "During the heavy rains last Spring this building took the prize for being able to let the rain in more easily than any other in the County." Throughout the county more children attended school than could be comfortably seated, and little money existed to remedy the situation.[12]

The WPA construction projects brought new consolidated schools to Taos and Mora Counties and throughout the state. Between 1935 and the end of 1939, the WPA provided labor for the construction of 257 new and 56 remodeled school buildings, 23 gymnasiums, 6 libraries, and 9 auditoriums. Wages paid to WPA workers to build roads, bridges, hospitals, stadiums, fairgrounds, parks, playgrounds, and assorted other public facilities also helped the schools by making it possible for more people to pay their taxes.[13]

The WPA school construction program clearly benefited New Mexicans, both Hispano and Anglo. Less certain was the degree of success achieved by other educational programs fostered by the WPA, the Civilian Conservation Corps (CCC), and the National Youth Administration (NYA). The broad mandate given to the WPA by President Roosevelt allowed it to enter almost any economic activity in the country; it had authority to carry on "small useful projects designed to assure a maximum of employment in all localities." Under the Emergency Education Program, the state WPA administrator was instructed to appoint an outstanding educator from within the state and "to utilize the leadership of the State and local public school authorities and avoid establishing a dual system or separate educational program."[14] Projects eligible for WPA funding included literacy classes, workers' education, vocational training, native arts and crafts, home nursing, recreation, home economics, agriculture, general adult education, parent education, service to transient or work camps, and nursery schools.[15] The WPA mandate seemed ideally suited to the goals of those New Mexican educators wanting to focus on the needs of the Hispano population.

The New Mexico WPA Educational Program attempted to address the problem of illiteracy in the state. Working with the CCC, FERA, NYA, and interested parties from within the state, the WPA conducted numerous adult education programs. Unemployed teachers were given jobs teaching night classes under FERA's Emergency Education Program. Many of these married women teachers had been among the first fired as school districts cut back on staff. FERA teachers such as Thelma London Lyon, of Yrisarri, taught English reading and writing to both Anglo and Hispano adults.[16] Educational activities became a part of the daily lives of CCC workers in the thirty-eight camps located in New Mexico. Besides their work of building trails and parks, CCC enrollees could attend classes in English, mathematics, and civics.[17]

Dautin W. Rockey, who advised teachers in CCC camps in northern New Mexico, found a high degree of illiteracy in English among the mostly Hispano workers. Even those who had completed the seventh or eighth grade had not retained enough reading skills to enable them to comprehend an English language newspaper. To meet this problem Rockey recommended the preparation of adult reading material specifically tailored for this population. He asked for short narratives and informational articles "of adult appeal" that provided a functioning vocabulary of words needed to understand road signs, ballots, and popular scientific literature. Cognates and Spanish words commonly used in English, such as mesa, adobe, and pueblo, should be liberally sprinkled throughout these texts. And the literature "must not be preachy although they must not glorify any anti-social or immoral situation or act."[18] In providing useful skills that broadened the individual's occupational opportunities, the CCC classes may have been the most successful of all the New Deal educational programs.

Nina Otero-Warren had an opportunity to apply her ideas on education when she was appointed assistant regional director of women's activities for the WPA in 1935. In this capacity she coordinated educational programs for "foreign-speaking groups," primarily Hispanic women. A year later she became state supervisor for literacy, and in 1937 she was appointed state supervisor of education, both positions in the Education Division of the WPA. Otero-Warren set up literacy classes for workers in CCC camps and established adult education programs throughout the state. She organized teachers' work conferences, where she stressed that instructors must allow adult learners to preserve their self-respect by using appropriate materials and vocabulary from adult experiences. Adults who did not speak English should be taught first in their native language, while they gradually learned English. Because she wanted her teachers to be bilingual, Otero-Warren enlisted the help of UNM Professors F. M. Kercheville and J. T. Reid to train instructors in proper Spanish pronunciation and usage. She had to obtain special permission from WPA officials in Washington to provide this bilingual instruction for adults.[19]

In 1936 Otero-Warren's program employed 23 teachers working with 460 students. The peak of activity was reached in 1937–38, with 52 teachers and 1,976 students. From 1936 to 1939 a total of 4,383 adults received instruction through the WPA literacy program. Otero-Warren proudly reported that "the majority of these students are bi-lingual and can now read and write both Spanish and English with equal facility and correctness."[20]

Although limited in scope, the WPA literacy programs encouraged academic training among Hispano adults. With improved skills these individuals were prepared to seek better opportunities outside of the stagnant village economy. They also gained an appreciation of education that they would impart to their children. As important as literacy training was for the few who received it, New Deal programs providing academic instruction were dwarfed by those offering vocational training. A number of educators inside and out of the New Deal believed that Hispanos would benefit more from vocational training than they would from academics or college preparatory studies. Educators and New Deal administrators alike envisioned a future for Hispanos in which they would continue to live in their small villages, where agriculture and tourism represented the most promising economic opportunities. The vocational programs of the New Deal did not aim to prepare Hispanos for much beyond village life.

Cultural imperatives sometimes seemed to overshadow the need for realistic economic opportunities. Suzanne Forrest has argued that New Deal efforts in northern New Mexico aimed to preserve the Hispanic villages by promoting traditional arts and crafts. The participation of so many individuals from the Spanish colonial arts movement helps to account for this inclination toward preservation of the idealized close-knit villages that so inspired the antimodernists of that movement.[21] But nearly everyone involved with New Deal programs in New Mexico emphasized the importance of maintaining the state's distinct character, while accepting huge federal projects. WPA State Administrator Lea Rowland declared that New Mexico's unique features must be protected "from the kind of progress that would exploit them commercially and result in their ruination." It would not do to "put our Indians in a cage and place them on exhibition. We don't want to destroy the evidences of the first European settlements on this whole continent."[22]

The emphasis on cultural preservation among the state's New Dealers meshed well with the attitudes expressed by professional educators in the state system. The State Department of Education already had embraced a vocational program that aimed to enhance traditional arts and crafts work within Hispano communities. The state agency adopted the vocational curriculum of the San José Training School in 1932, when Brice H. Sewell was hired as the state supervisor of trade and industrial education to administer programs funded through the federal Smith-Hughes Act. Throughout the 1930s Sewell worked in cooperative ventures with New Deal programs to implement statewide vocational training programs.

A sculptor by training, Brice Sewell came to New Mexico in 1930 from St. Louis, where he had attended the School of Fine Arts at Washington University for four years. Although he had not received an academic degree, he was hired as an instructor by the UNM Art Department and became involved with the San José Training School. Personable and energetic, Sewell impressed President James Zimmerman with his ability "to interest the native people in these various arts and crafts and in the excellent work he has done . . . in the San Jose Training School."[23] Mary Austin also noted Sewell's San José work in her recommendation for his appointment to the position of state supervisor. "Mr. Sewell has been in charge of the handicrafts in connection with extension work in the University," she reported to Governor Arthur Seligman, "and I have had him closely under my eye in that capacity. I think he is admirably fitted for that work, and that he realizes . . . the need for rehabilitating native culture along with the most successful vocational training."[24]

Sewell well understood the need to design a vocational policy specifically for New Mexican conditions. Nationally educators had viewed vocational education as a means of training workers for industry. In New Mexico, Sewell noted, little manufacturing existed, and so a standard vocational program intended to create an industrial workforce would be inappropriate. Sewell favored the creation of small, local industries such as tanneries or brick-making enterprises, which would use resources available within the state.[25]

Sewell thought that New Mexican students would profit more from vocational education than from a standard academic curriculum. The high number of students who did not complete high school, he claimed, demonstrated the lack of attraction the school held for students. In his view the standard academic curriculum gave students who graduated from high school "the idea that work was something to be avoided and that if a boy obtained an education he would not have to work hard for a living." But New Mexico's students needed to return to the old idea that "work was pleasure and pleasure was work."[26] Not only had the academic curriculum failed to meet the employment needs of the rural community, but it actually drove students to abandon education at an early age, as they found no practical purpose to what they were learning. Local educators should determine what livelihoods were available in a particular community and prepare the students for that work.

Guided by the belief that the resources available in a particular community should determine the vocational trades taught, Sewell urged the development of "village hand-craft industries which utilize local raw materials and convert them into finished products." The state vocational program included training in the established trades of carpentry, woodworking, auto mechanics, welding, machine shop practice, weaving, beauty culture, tanning, spinning, and commercial needlework. What was to be taught in a particular school depended upon "what is demanded by the community and is deemed practical from the standpoint of giving a fair assurance of the students' being able to follow and earn a livelihood from the trade."[27] Many of these vocational activities reinforced Hispano culture, while some training opened up employment possibilities for graduates in nontraditional areas.

With a long tradition of providing vocational training, the schools of New Mexico greeted Sewell's ideas with enthusiasm. Nor was it difficult to convince school directors to incorporate native handicrafts in their vocational programs. At Santa Cruz High School, in Santa Fe County, the Vocational Department offered "weaving, spinning, dyeing, canning, and all kinds of wool work." Second grade pupils under teacher Sister M. Sienna carried on a wool project of their own, the results of which were "remarkable, especially in vocabulary building and self-expression by Spanish speaking children."[28] Española High School proudly advertised the "special features" of its vocational program, including weaving, knitting, and Spanish embroidery, all taught by Celina Vigil, and woodworking and tanning offered by A. Martínez. The Vocational Department was "glad to arrange for the filling of any orders in weaving, woodworking or tanning products."[29]

Sewell welcomed the assistance of federal agencies in his campaign for vocational training. The WPA paid the salaries of some vocational teachers in the public schools, while the NYA provided work-study jobs for students from isolated villages so they could attend vocational classes.[30] To continue receiving aid under the Federal Department of Vocational Education, the state had to demonstrate that students were finding employment with their skills. In 1938 some federal aid was lost for weaving classes, because there were "few new weavers needed for the weaving industry in the state and the opportunities for self-employment would be limited, to a great extent, to an avocational basis."[31] The lack of outlets and dependence upon a seasonal tourist trade posed the greatest drawback to Sewell's plans.

When Sewell thought of students needing employment in the future, for the most part he had boys in mind. Few if any educators of the time thought of the curriculum as gender-neutral, and when Sewell and his associates turned their attention to girls, they thought in terms of the practical needs of women in sex-typed roles. Although Brice Sewell did not often address the issue of vocational education for girls, he encouraged programs in cosmetology, needlework, nursing, and midwifery for them.[32] Most of the direction for vocational training for girls in the 1930s came from Zelpha Bates, who became state supervisor of home economics education in 1932. From the start Bates's work encompassed both public school and adult education aimed at enabling people to live more frugally under depressed economic conditions. The home economics program stressed sewing, canning and food preservation, nutrition, and consumer buying.[33] Even more than the vocational courses designed for boys, the home economics programs brought the public school teacher in contact with the parents at home.

Bates's goals for training in home economics paralleled those of Sewell and the New Deal leaders, who believed that education should help New Mexicans live independent lives in their own communities. She counted as a success one community that had been largely dependent upon the Red Cross for charitable donations, but which achieved self-sufficiency as the result of an adult education program in homemaking, canning, and sewing. Adult education, she declared, must address the "actual problems which women are facing daily in their efforts to keep their families nourished and clothed and preserve the family morale in the face of almost overwhelming difficulties." To discover what actual problems existed in the homes of students, Bates urged home economics teachers to visit the homes, meet the parents, and encourage them to participate in the adult programs.[34]

Brice Sewell also contributed to adult education in his capacity as state supervisor. Along with other state officials, Sewell worked with FERA and the WPA to implement a statewide plan to establish a vocational school for adults in every county. In May 1935 representatives of all the agencies involved met in Taos to dedicate the first such school, to be completed using state and FERA funds. The school, called the Taos Cultural Center, offered courses ranging from agriculture to crafts, music, and dancing. Sewell spoke at the opening ceremony along with Maude Kemp, director of the Social Service Division of the New Mexico ERA, Albuquerque attorney W. A. Keleher, State Superintendent of Schools H. R. Rodgers, State Director of Emergency Education Raymond Huff, Taos County Superintendent Floyd Santisteven, Taos Crafts President L. P. Martínez, UNM professor Dr. Loyd S. Tireman, and Dr. George I. Sánchez, president of the NMEA.[35] Such an assembly testifies to the wide consensus among both relief administrators and professional educators in the state concerning the need for vocational training adapted to community needs.

At the State Conference on Adult Education held in June 1935, Sewell explained the rationale behind the new vocational schools. Adult education, he argued, should not merely give people jobs, but should share something from the culture surrounding the school. All communities had their unique local geology, folklore, or knowledge in the archives. "Through this program of adult education we could make all these things functional," he said. "As I see it, vocational schools now are growing into something more—centers of culture and interest." Interesting courses such as music, Spanish, and dancing would draw people into the school and inspire in them a desire to learn more.[36]

Sewell pointed to the northern counties where Hispanos predominated as examples of communities in need of specialized vocational programs. The average farm in that section consisted of less than 4 acres, which produced barely enough for a family to subsist on. Sewell suggested that families could supplement their income with production of native handicrafts, which could be sold at local tourist markets. Sewell helped to launch one such successful venture in Chupadero, in Santa Fe County. With the help of County Superintendent Manuel Lujan, Sewell's department held community meetings to interest residents in a new vocational school. The villagers constructed a building, and the state paid the teachers. Adults learned tanning, woodworking, spinning, harness and saddlemaking, and weaving. Chupadero residents sold twenty-eight thousand dollars worth of crafts at a Santa Fe market in 1935.[37] Fostering vocational programs with state and federal support would help villagers achieve self-sufficiency.

Much of the vocational agenda promoted by Brice Sewell shared similar goals with the Spanish Colonial Arts revival movement. Not only Sewell but also others within the state educational hierarchy had close ties with the various organizations and individuals associated with the revival.

Among the organizations working to revive Spanish colonial traditions was La Sociedad Folklórica, organized by Cleofas Martínez Jaramillo in 1935. Jaramillo began recording Hispano folklore in the early 1930s, having "caught the fever from our famous 'cinco pintores' and author Mary Austin."[38] As Genaro Padilla has suggested, Jaramillo founded La Sociedad not merely to rescue the disappearing heritage of her people, but also to recover some control over a preservation movement largely directed by Anglo romantics. Joining Jaramillo on the executive committee of La Sociedad were Margaret Abreu and Aurora Lucero-White, both of whom worked for the State Department of Education.[39]

While La Sociedad Folklórica encouraged people to make colonial-style costumes for the Santa Fe Fiesta, Lucero-White promoted cultural revival in her official role as assistant state superintendent of schools from 1932 to 1934. A former San Miguel County superintendent and member of the state Board of Education, she had long been active in collecting and publishing Spanish folklore.[40] As assistant state superintendent, Lucero-White instituted a "folk-cultural" program to encourage the use of folk dramas, folk customs, and folk festivals in school curricula. She sent packets of songs, plays, and other materials to teachers, along with instructions for their use. Lucero-White hoped that "the whole repertoire will become a permanent feature of the State's folk-cultural program, thus insuring the preservation of a vast and rich traditional heritage reminiscent of the Spanish-colonial epoch."[41]

If anyone had the expertise to instruct teachers on how to use folklore materials, it was Lucero-White. After searching throughout New Mexico for old manuscripts, she carefully researched every play and *canción,* comparing conflicting versions in an attempt to restore the text to the original. She spoke of Hispanos' devotion to folklore in glowing terms:

> Hence it can be said ... that the manuscripts of the Pastores in counties of Hispanic origin must be very extensive and we do not believe that there is a community of any size ... where these plays have not been presented within the memory of the present generation, proving conclusively that they have enjoyed great popularity in past generations among Spanish-speaking people and that there must be a profound and intrinsic reason for a universality which no other classical works including those of Lope, Calderon and Shakespeare, have ever enjoyed.[42]

Many schools incorporated Spanish colonial folklore into their student activities. In December 1938 Pojoaque High School presented "La Aparición de Nuestra Señora de Guadalupe al Indio Juan Diego" for a village fiesta. Aurora Lucero-White welcomed the event as a chance for the young people to become acquainted with the "traditional mystery folk plays." She predicted that the play would ignite the villagers' interest in other "folk materials such as ballads, corridos, songs and cuentos, and, of course, priceless folk ways." As a result of the school's folklore program, "the lovely old traditional folk ways will come to again hold sway, adding to the picturesqueness of the already incomparable beauty of the landscape."[43]

The best known organization devoted to cultural preservation, the Spanish Colonial Arts Society, had languished after the deaths of founders Mary Austin and Frank Applegate. In 1938 a group headed by Leonora Curtin, Kenneth Chapman, and Mary Wheelwright revived the society. Artists joined local and state educators in a lively discussion at an organizational meeting held in Curtin's home. Carmen Espinosa, Sewell's assistant in the State Department of Vocational Education, encouraged the society to preserve all phases of the culture of the Spanish-speaking people, not just the colonial aspects. Nina Otero-Warren and Superintendent R. P. Sweeney of the Santa Fe city schools agreed that the educators would welcome the inclusion of native arts and crafts in the curriculum. Reporting on present efforts to preserve, revive, and adapt crafts to modern conditions, Leonora Curtin told the members about the founding of the Native Market in Santa Fe, where artisans could sell their work. With Brice Sewell and the government providing the training for the artists, Curtin predicted, the society would assist the craftsmen in finding markets.[44]

Brice Sewell and his state office were not officially affiliated with the Spanish Colonial Arts Society, but the group's objectives coincided well with his own goals for village self-sufficiency. For the villagers to have stable markets, the area's tourist industry needed all the local boosterism that could be mustered. Neither the boosters nor Sewell, however, seemed to have questioned the long-term viability of tourist markets or the consequences of commercializing traditional arts and crafts. The Depression decade was not a time for long-term planning, and Brice Sewell had too many projects going to oversee the efforts being made by allies such as the Society.

Whether he actually attended many events of the Society or not, Sewell absorbed the language and vision of the arts revival movement. Describing a new vocational school being built with WPA funds in Los Lunas, he reported that the new structure would use the "fine old examples of Spanish Colonial architecture found in the Los Lunas region," including old windows, doors, and vigas that community residents had donated. He hoped that "the building will serve as an inspiration to the younger people in reminding them of past architectural and cultural glories that form the heritage of the Spanish-speaking peoples of New Mexico."[45]

Hardly a New Deal program failed to incorporate the revival of traditional culture as a goal, and those programs that touched the schools in any way thus carried the cultural agenda into the curriculum. The Federal Music Project in New Mexico, under the direction of Helen Chandler Ryan, hoped to revive and preserve traditional songs and musical instruments from New Mexico's past. In this endeavor, as with so many vocational projects, the local schools collaborated with the federal project or took over activities when they could afford to do so. Ryan received assistance from the Hispanic Institute of New Mexico as well as from UNM Professors Arturo Campa and Loyd Tireman in planning her campaign to recover old songs and dances. Folklorists hired by the project collected and recorded songs, taught community groups to sing and perform dances, and prepared teaching materials for distribution to schools.[46]

The Music Project supervised music teachers who were working in the schools and being paid by the WPA Education Program. The most popular work of the extension program came from the Visiting Rural Music Teachers. Five music instructors were placed in rural schools that had never had music instruction before. FMP Assistant Director Bruno David Ussher reported to the federal headquarters that "Practically every County School Superintendent is begging for music teachers through Federal Music Project."[47] The Santa Fe Board of Education took over the salary of the music teacher who had started a music program in the schools there under the auspices of the project.[48]

The music programs engendered some revealing responses from the Anglo community, suggesting that contradictory social and racial attitudes about Hispanos compelled school people to support music in the curriculum rather than any educational rationale. The president of the Bernalillo Women's Club, Mrs. Alec Brown, wrote to Ussher to thank the WPA for the "splendid work" being done by Helen Chandler Ryan in the state music program. Club members felt that "this musical program has been more effective in raising the cultural standards of homes in this vicinity—where we have a majority of Spanish-American inhabitants—than any previous efforts in that direction."[49] T. P.

Gallagher of the Santa Fe Northwestern Railway wrote Ussher to report the wonderful effect the music program was having on his employees, many of whom were "Spanish Americans who, by nature, are music lovers." One then wonders about the "nature" of the rest of his workers, as Gallagher observes that since the beginning of "the WPA set-up some of my employees who had theretofore exhibited little or no appreciation for music, are now displaying a marked interest in the same."[50] Ironically the music program appealed to opposing stereotypes of Hispanos as natural music lovers and as lacking high cultural standards.

The blending of educational, economic, and cultural objectives, as well as the cooperative interaction of people and agencies devoted to those goals, is illustrated by the work of the National Youth Administration (NYA) in New Mexico. Under the direction of Thomas L. Popejoy, the NYA committed its resources to the improvement of economic and educational conditions for Hispanos.[51] The NYA Student Aid Program enabled hundreds of high school and college students to work at jobs building baseball fields and playgrounds, running community softball leagues, landscaping schools, and making furniture. Boys greatly outnumbered girls in these projects, but as the "New Mexico Youthogram" reported, girls were just as willing to work as their male classmates. "Not to be outdone by the boys, the NYA girls on the YWCA project in Albuquerque recently donned slacks, and assisted by Miss Bette Vette, painted doors and trimming at the Atrisco School. Mr. Chavez, school principal was immensely pleased by their interest and versatility."[52]

The NYA sponsored educational and vocational projects throughout the state for both adults and school-age youth. In many such ventures other New Deal agencies or public schools joined in providing staff or materials. Most of these projects involved some type of traditional crafts activity. In Las Cruces twelve high school boys trained by the NYA opened a woodworking shop and produced hand-carved Spanish furniture for sale.[53] The Clayton Board of Education sponsored a rug-making project for the vocational classes in Mora, with the NYA providing the services of weaving instructor Agnes Vigil. In Santa Fe young people trained by the NYA found work and an outlet for their wares at the Native Market. Santa Fe County NYA Supervisor May B. Kenney reported that four out of six girls trained in the NYA Housekeeping Project had gotten jobs as waitresses at the Native Market. Another girl trained by the NYA sewing project had sold two *colchas* (embroidered spreads) to a woman from New York. And a young man trained by the NYA in wrought iron work was employed at the Native Market on a commission basis.[54] Kenney, who lived with her sister Nina Otero-Warren in the Bergere family household, may have used her sister's contacts with the operators of the Native Market to secure opportunities for NYA youth.[55]

In Las Vegas the NYA established a community center called "El Centro

Cultural" in 1936. A local citizen, Louis C. Ilfeld, donated the building, the NYA provided material and labor to remodel it, and the New Mexico Normal University paid for the lights and heat. The NYA hired Virginia Mainz as the director to oversee the classes, health clinic, club meetings, recreation, and entertainment in the fourteen-room house. The state Emergency Education Program supplied instructors in Spanish, English, sewing, cooking, music, folk dancing, weaving, carpentry, and woodworking. An average of eighty people a day, both adults and youth, visited the center.[56]

The NYA joined the WPA and other federally supported programs in contributing to dozens of community-based projects throughout New Mexico during the 1930s and early 1940s. These efforts did not achieve the economic objectives sought by the participants, however. Only the onset of war and the introduction of massive defense projects would bring new employment opportunities for New Mexicans. But the New Deal projects did leave a great imprint on educational and cultural patterns. Vocational training based upon traditional arts and crafts, which had begun to filter into the schools with the San José Training School's experimental curriculum, became an institutionalized part of the school program across the state. The New Deal programs both drew inspiration from and reinforced the Spanish colonial arts movement. The growing dependence of northern New Mexican villages upon a seasonal tourist industry received a boost from the New Deal emphasis upon cultural rejuvenation. If Hispano culture had not previously achieved status as a unique and valuable island within the national community, it had established its place as such by the end of the 1930s. In the transitional period between the New Deal and World War II, some official recognition of the usefulness of the New Mexico New Deal occurred.

With war looming in 1940, the nature of New Deal programs changed. Officials in Washington encouraged state agencies to incorporate patriotism and defense readiness in their educational programs.[57] New Mexicans whose expertise had been in bilingual training now found themselves in demand for their teaching skills. Under the shadow of impending war, the Roosevelt administration could not allow its Good Neighbor policy with Latin America to falter. The WPA launched programs to strengthen ties with Spanish-speaking territories and nations. In Puerto Rico the WPA worked to improve the public school system. In the U.S. armed services the WPA sought to teach Spanish to servicemen who were to be stationed in Spanish-speaking countries.

Because of her experience with rural schools, bilingualism, and adult education, Nina Otero-Warren became involved in both WPA projects. In 1941 she was named special consultant on education for the WPA in Puerto Rico. She began her work by familiarizing herself with the history and conditions of Puerto Rico. She found that over half of the island's children did not attend schools, due to a lack of facilities in the rural areas. Those children who did attend school were taught in Spanish until the fifth grade, while learning English as a second language. This educational system had resulted in a high rate of adult illiteracy. She also discovered that the existing WPA adult education program was not only impractical for the needs of adult students, but was humiliating to them as well. In her work Otero-Warren set up training sessions for teachers, in which they received "the proper instruction on adult psychology, and training in the preparation of adult centered materials to meet the needs of the people."[58] Otero-Warren also introduced her bilingual method of instruction, which stressed the advantages of bilingualism rather than treating it as a handicap. Although she spent only five months in Puerto Rico, she was credited with reinvigorating a demoralized adult education program. Over a thousand teachers participated in her training sessions, many of them expressing deep gratitude for her fresh ideas and enthusiasm.

Hoping to facilitate friendly relations with Latin America during the war, the WPA initiated its Air Corps Spanish Project in 1941, to give members of the Army Air Forces conversational fluency in Spanish.[59] Federal WPA officials looked to New Mexico to provide bilingual teachers to go to air bases throughout the country to teach Spanish. Isabel Lancaster Eckles, Director of the WPA Service Division in New Mexico, called upon Nina Otero-Warren and Mamie Meadors to recruit Spanish teachers and conduct a training conference for them. Otero-Warren may have grown weary of these assignments by then, for she jokingly told Eckles to tell the WPA that she wanted "a salary of $10,000 and your promise that you will bury her in the National Cemetery!"[60] Forgoing any guarantee of an Arlington interment, Otero-Warren conducted the conference.

The war brought a halt to the WPA, NYA, CCC, and a host of other New Deal programs. Without actually taking over the public schools or dictating educational policy, the New Deal had made immense changes in the schools of New Mexico, thus opening more opportunities for Hispanos. The number of new facilities alone came as a great boon for education in this impoverished state. School curricula at the end of the Depression decade reinforced and validated Hispano culture, although primarily through vocational training. All efforts were undertaken with a genuine intention of improving the economic and educational opportunities of Hispanos. Working in tandem with state and local educators, as well as with private citizens interested in the same agenda, the New Deal used relief, public works, schools, and adult education to improve conditions for Hispanos. In contrast to the southern states, where state and local officials often fought tooth and nail to obstruct programs intended to help Blacks, in New Mexico nearly all involved with relief and educational efforts wanted to do something for Hispanos.

As with so many other educational efforts in New Mexico, however, the New Deal programs were often based upon Anglos' notions of what would be good for Hispanos. Hispanos may have shared many of the same goals as those stated in the New Deal, but in a real sense they had no other choices before them. Economic options had been limited long before the New Deal, when the cash-based capitalist economy had replaced the land-based subsistence economy of colonial New Mexico. Only the introduction of new industries would have provided Hispanos with jobs to enable them to continue to exist at a decent standard of living in the villages. When such industry did arrive during World War II, the educational system constructed in the 1920s and 1930s and reinforced by the New Deal left Hispanos unprepared to participate at any level above service and construction jobs. New Mexico educators did not prepare Hispanos for high-paying engineering or scientific jobs in the defense industry, but then they could hardly have been expected to anticipate the need. They might, however, have made better efforts to provide at least a portion of the school population with opportunities for higher academic advancement. Some voices in the Hispano community had expressed interest in a higher level of education but had been largely ignored. Early in the decade, *La Bandera Americana* and *La Revista Popular* had called upon rural schools to provide classes that would prepare more Hispanos for college. The editors saw a need in the villages for more Hispano teachers, doctors, dentists, and pharmacists. The schools had a duty, they argued, to prepare village natives to enter colleges so they could pursue these professions.[61] The educators, both Anglo and Hispano, who directed the schools in New Mexico saw different needs in the villages, and in the 1930s they found willing partners in the agencies of the New Deal.

Conclusion

BETWEEN THE WORLD wars a pattern of common teaching practices developed in the schooling of Spanish-speaking children across the Southwest.[1] In the crucial function of teaching English, the direct method became the preferred technique, with its corollary of suppressing the use of Spanish. Incorporating activity lessons in the curriculum became a vital part of the overall strategy for teaching English, American values, and habits of health, cleanliness, and conduct. Nonacademic subject areas such as music, physical education, manual training, and art replaced traditional fundamentals.

Many of these innovations characterized progressive educational changes in general. Progressive curricula for English-speaking White children placed more emphasis upon nonacademic subjects and utilized activities and projects geared to the child's interests. Yet there was a qualitative difference in the attitudes and approaches to teaching non-English-speaking, non-White children. Some educators readily accepted racial stereotypes about the supposed talents and interests of Hispano, African American, or Native American children. One senses that they did not expect as much *intellectually* from these youngsters; occasionally they declared outright that they did not.

The tendency of progressive educators to vary expectations according to race or ethnic group did not go unnoticed by perceptive observers across the country. At the turn of the century, W. E. B. DuBois explored the roots of southern race relations in his book *The Souls of Black Folk*. The first African American to receive a Ph.D. at Harvard, DuBois joined the faculty of Atlanta University in 1897 and immediately began to assess the lives of Blacks in Georgia. African Americans in the Deep South had not greatly improved their economic circumstances in the four decades since slavery. DuBois found many reasons to account for this lack of progress, one of which was the system of industrial training that had become the sole option for the education of southern Blacks.

DuBois condemned a school system that would leave an entire population suited only for menial labor. He questioned the accommodationist approach of Booker T. Washington and his White allies, who reasoned that Blacks should be properly trained only for the economic opportunities they could be expected to have in life. DuBois believed that Whites had encouraged industrial training because they knew a liberal arts education would breed ambition and broaden the horizons of Blacks. The message of southern Whites was clearly that "an education that encourages aspiration, that sets the loftiest of ideals and seeks as an end culture and character rather than bread-winning, is the privilege of white men and the danger and delusion of black."[2]

DuBois did not object to industrial education in itself; he realized that most men in Georgia in the early 1900s, both Black and White, would work with their hands. DuBois wanted African Americans to have open for them the same option, no matter how small it might be for Whites as well as Blacks, to become teachers, doctors, or scholars. If a "Talented Tenth" of White boys could hope to grow up to be doctors or scholars, then so should a "Talented Tenth" of Black boys. If they did not, there would be no hope for the improvement of conditions for African Americans.[3]

DuBois's challenge struck at the heart of the problem of equal educational opportunity in the United States. More so even than equal facilities or equal spending per pupil, the opportunity to pursue training for any livelihood may be the true measure of educational equity in America. For DuBois the pinnacle of individual intellectual success was to become a scholar, and he wanted a Black child to have as great a chance to become a scholar as any White child did. No matter that scholars such as DuBois had limited employment possibilities, or that only a few talented and disciplined individuals of any race could persevere through the years of hard study required to become a scholar of DuBois's stature. Only when all children knew that such a life was an option for them would there be true equal educational opportunity. A moving passage in *The Souls of Black Folk* evokes the deeply felt, almost religious significance that DuBois attached to the chance to experience the life of the mind:

> I sit with Shakespeare and he winces not. Across the color line I move arm in arm with Balzac and Dumas, where smiling men and welcoming women glide in gilded halls. From out the caves of evening that swing between the strong-limbed earth and the tracery of the stars, I summon Aristotle and Aurelius and what soul I will, and they come all graciously with no scorn nor condescension. So, wed with Truth, I dwell above the Veil. Is this the life you grudge us, O knightly America? Is this the life you long to change into the dull red hideousness of Georgia? Are you so afraid lest peering from this high Pisgah, between Philistine and Amalekite, we sight the Promised Land?[4]

Progressive educators of DuBois's generation and beyond did not share his definition of equal educational opportunity. John Dewey, a genuine champion of democracy and equality, thought it was appropriate for different groups in society to receive a different type of education, depending upon their prospects for employment in life.[5] The progressives considered vocational training as a means of meeting the needs of children and the community within which they lived. The pressure to retain students in school also pushed educators to adopt vocationalism as a course of study they thought was easier and more likely to keep students' attention than academics.[6] Loyd Tireman in New Mexico agreed, as did Nina Otero-Warren, George I. Sánchez, Brice H. Sewell, and a host of other educators. Their objective of improving retention rates for Hispano children was laudable, but the policy resulted in a loss of emphasis on academic training. The progressives' goal of meeting the needs of individual children was also lost, since small rural schools could not afford to offer customized curricular tracks for individual students. The statewide emphasis on vocationalism reflected a set of decisions made about Hispanos as a group and a policy that was administered on a group basis, not an individual one.

This is not meant to imply that New Mexico educators should have tried to turn all of their young charges into classical scholars. Obviously DuBois used the example of the scholar to suggest to educators that no limits should be imposed upon children's dreams, no matter how impractical or unobtainable they might seem. Several decades later the equivalent to DuBois's classical scholar might have been the nuclear physicist, a professional who actually did have a reasonable chance for employment in New Mexico in the 1940s or 1950s. The school system of the 1930s, however, made it no more probable that New Mexico would produce great Hispano nuclear physicists than that Georgia would have produced great Black classical scholars in the 1900s. New Mexico educators had no way of knowing that a demand for nuclear physicists would arise, but they might have thought a bit harder about the need for native doctors, dentists, lawyers, engineers, and other professionals.

That they did not succeed in opening the full range of possibilities for New Mexico's children should give us pause as we contemplate the challenge of equal educational opportunity in today's society. Educators in New Mexico were motivated by the best of intentions to improve education for Hispanos. The work of Tireman, Sánchez, Otero-Warren, Sewell, and others succeeded in rationalizing school administration, equalizing school funds, and focusing greater attention on issues of bilingualism and biculturalism. They encouraged equal treatment and respect for Hispanos at every opportunity. And yet they failed to deal with the full implications of a class-based and gender-based education. Their policies did not solve the economic problems faced by Hispanos and did not prevent further educational failure and economic dislocation for Hispanos.

What is surprising is that Tireman and Sánchez did not seem to recognize how limiting the emphasis on vocationalism would be. They knew the record of Black education in the South and all that was implied by that. DuBois's viewpoint was within the available pool of ideas at the time; he wrote prolifically until his death in 1963, although he was asked to leave Atlanta University in 1944 because he had become so radical in his politics. Unlike the ideas of Booker T. Washington, however, DuBois's ideas were not emulated widely. Tireman and Sánchez visited Tuskegee, not Atlanta. New Mexicans enlisted the help of the General Education Board, perhaps the most significant private organization in the shaping of southern Black education along the lines envisioned by Washington. Leo M. Favrot, southern field agent for the GEB, mentored both Tireman and Sánchez. The parallels between the South and New Mexico were not exact, of course, but enough similarity existed that the GEB agreed to work in New Mexico on that basis.

That New Mexican educators emphasized vocational training over academic preparation does not mean that they purposefully sought to keep Hispanos in a state of second-class citizenship. The greatest distinction between New Mexico and the South may have been that southern educators understood that, whether they wanted to or not, to educate Blacks beyond their "place" in society was to put Black lives in danger. While violence between Hispanos and Anglos did occur in New Mexico, members of both groups welcomed social interaction, intermarriage, and assimilation. The cost incurred by Hispanos in becoming educated and rising to the middle class came from the pressure to erase their ethnic distinctiveness. Finding a way to avoid that cultural loss while still offering equal educational opportunities was the great challenge to New Mexico educators. To their credit, they accepted the challenge. Unfortunately for Hispanos, they achieved only limited success in finding the solution.

Hispanos consistently favored both equal educational opportunity and cultural preservation. They accepted the American capitalist system and wanted good jobs and careers within it. They valued education and the wide range of opportunities it opened. But they also wanted to retain their own culture. To them the issue of the language of the schools should not have been an either-or question. Hispanos wanted to learn English. At the same time they wanted the right to use Spanish in their own homes and communities and in some public proceedings. Although many people discussed this issue during the century between the conquest and World War II, and even though many local educators found viable bilingual teaching methods, official policy never sanctioned bilingualism. The use of Spanish in the schools was reluctantly tolerated, but never encouraged, except in a few experimental programs.

The best known experiment in bilingual instruction, conducted at the San José Training School, reveals the contradictions that undermined progressive education efforts in New Mexico. Progressives such as Loyd Tireman wanted to address the specific needs of individual children, and they saw scientific testing as an objective tool for determining what students needed. Yet in using group tests and results, they necessarily made decisions for groups based on averages, not individual performances. What is more significant about the specific program at San José, however, is that the criteria used for determining the viability of bilingual instruction was not the overall academic performance of children, but their acquisition of English. And despite the progressive rhetoric about solid scientific evidence, Tireman rejected bilingual instruction on the basis of one study in a school with a high rate of pupil turnover.

After dismissing bilingual instruction as undesirable, Tireman seemed determined to compensate for the resulting cultural loss by focusing more on community needs. The desperate plight of the northern Hispanic villages during the Depression reinforced Tireman's resolve at the same time that New Deal agencies caught the same inspiration. The ubiquitous campaign of the 1930s to save the village by reinvigorating Hispano culture stands out as one of the most remarkable and ironic social engineering efforts in American history. A group of intellectual and social elites, both Hispano and Anglo, took it upon themselves to rescue from pending oblivion the formerly despised cultural heritage of an impoverished and increasingly powerless segment of the population. Clearly these efforts helped to save many of the treasures of Hispano culture and brought to Hispanos greater respect and admiration for their traditions. Yet the events of the 1930s proved how fragile Hispanic culture appeared during the Depression. Many Hispanos realized that their culture needed help from the same dominant society that only a generation before had been trying to eradicate it. They accepted as a given that the dominant culture should therefore help to determine the cultural destiny of Hispanos. This capitulation was made most evident by the type of cultural revival fostered in the 1930s. The artists of Santa Fe and an Anglo-driven market determined that colonial arts would be the emphasis of this revival. Instead of encouraging new styles or unleashing the Hispanic artist to respond honestly to the Depression, the schools and the New Dealers taught Hispanos the old styles of a glorious past.

The very emphasis on arts, crafts, and music reflected common stereotyping of Hispanos as a racial type gifted in these natural talents. Transforming school curricula to nurture these assumed abilities amounted to an abandonment of the expectation of academic ability. It also reassured Anglos that this was a harmless, unambitious people who did not pose a threat in the competitive economy. Indeed the cultural agenda of the 1930s signaled that the most frightening specters of this foreign element within the common culture had been tamed. The more threatening aspects of Hispanos' heritage—their communal landholding and water-use patterns and their bitter recollections of conquest, loss of land, and countless humiliations—could be swept under the rug. Instead Hispanos and Anglos alike were urged to look back to the time before the American conquest and cultivate the innocuous and highly romanticized Spanish period that had been vanquished in 1846. The great celebration of the 1940s, planned for years in advance, was the Coronado Cuarto Centennial, not the anniversary of the Treaty of Guadalupe Hidalgo.

Yet for all the grand fiestas, all the fine work of cultural preservation, and all the lofty rhetoric about the glorious past, the complete historical record and the real economic conditions remained to be reckoned with. Several decades later young activists, self-consciously labeling themselves Chicanos to identify with their denigrated Indian and *mestizo* heritage, demanded to know why the schools had not addressed the history of conquest. Knowing first-hand the frustration and humiliation of attending a school where they did not understand the teacher's language, they demanded bilingual instruction in the elementary grades. The time had passed when an educational elite could dictate curricula based on its own preconceptions of what schools should teach.

The ninety years from 1850 to 1940 demonstrate how persistent in the American mind has been the notion that culture can be determined from above, and that the schools are a viable tool for determining culture. The myth that Hispanos did not value education came about not because Hispanos actively resisted schools in the territorial period—they did not—but because the schools they were struggling to build and staff did not acculturate them to American standards. The administrative centralizers in the 1910s and 1920s thought they could Americanize Hispanos if they could only build a bureaucratic apparatus that would enforce standard courses of study and teacher certification. The resulting central bureaucracy proved inadequate to counter local initiative and control. During the 1930s New Deal cultural imperatives temporarily preoccupied the Hispano community and actually did some good in preserving past traditions, but they did not alter Hispanos' own self-directed cultural development for the future. Ultimately in a free society, any efforts to legislate, dictate, direct, or plan the evolution of culture through education must take into account the customs, interests, and hopes of those being educated.

Notes

Introduction

1. "The Proposed State of Lincoln," *Santa Fe Daily New Mexican*, 10 February 1870.
2. In this study the term *Hispano* is used to refer to persons of Hispanic descent living in New Mexico whose roots there go back to the colonial period. The term was widely used by Hispanos themselves from the territorial period through the 1930s. The terms *Spanish American* or *Spanish* have also been used by New Mexicans, but rarely have they embraced the term Mexicans or Mexican American, unless they have immigrated to New Mexico from Mexico in the twentieth century. The term *Chicano* was not used widely until after the 1960s, and for a time it was used only to refer to militant activists in the Chicano civil rights movements. Now the term is more widely used to designate anyone of Mexican descent.
3. Elliott West, *Growing Up with the Country: Childhood on the Far Western Frontier* (Albuquerque: University of New Mexico Press, 1989), 179-210.
4. Lawrence A. Cremin, *American Education: The National Experience, 1783-1876* (New York: Harper & Row, 1980), 103-13; Rush Welter, *Popular Education and Democratic Thought in America* (New York: Columbia University Press, 1962), 24-36; Merle Curti, *The Social Ideas of American Educators* (Totowa, NJ: Littlefield, Adams & Co., 1978), 34-49; Robert L. Church and Michael W. Sedlak, *Education in the United States: An Interpretive History* (New York: Free Press, 1976), 55, 79, 84-85; and Carl E. Kaestle, *Pillars of the Republic: Common Schools and American Society, 1780-1860* (New York: Hill and Wang, 1983), 3-12.
5. Kaestle, *Pillars of the Republic*, 8-18; and David Nasaw, *Schooled to Order: A Social History of Public Schooling in the United States* (New York: Oxford University Press, 1979), 33-43.
6. Kaestle, *Pillars of the Republic*, 75-82.
7. Reginald Horsman, *Race and Manifest Destiny: The Origin of American Racial Anglo-Saxonism* (Cambridge, MA: Harvard University Press, 1981), 229-31.
8. Josiah Gregg, *Commerce of the Prairies*, (Ann Arbor: University Microfilms, 1966), 1:198.
9. Christine M. Van Ness and John R. Van Ness, "W. W. H. Davis: Neglected Figure of New Mexico's Early Territorial Period," *Journal of the West* 16(July 1977):68.
10. W. W. H. Davis, *El Gringo: New Mexico and Her People* (Lincoln: University of Nebraska Press, 1982; originally published 1857), 193.
11. Ibid., 195.
12. Richard L. Nostrand, *The Hispano Homeland* (Norman: University of Oklahoma Press, 1992); and Donald W. Meinig, *The Southwest: Three Peoples in Geographical Change, 1600-1970* (New York: Oxford University Press, 1971).
13. Ramón A. Gutiérrez, *When Jesus Came, the Corn Mothers Went Away : Marriage, Sexuality, and Power in New Mexico, 1500-1846* (Stanford, CA: Stanford University Press,

1991), 77, 81; and Bernardo P. Gallegos, *Literacy, Education, and Society in New Mexico, 1693-1821* (Albuquerque: University of New Mexico Press, 1992), 63, 92.

14. Gallegos, *Literacy,* 29-30, 37, 53.

15. W. G. Ritch, "A Survey of the Development of Education in New Mexico," 1880, Reel 6, #1916, William Gillet Ritch Papers, microfilm, Center for Southwest Research, Zimmerman Library, University of New Mexico, Albuquerque (hereafter referred to as UNM). Original collection at Huntington Library, University of California at Los Angeles, Los Angeles, California.

16. Warren Beck, *New Mexico: A History of Four Centuries* (Norman: University of Oklahoma Press,1962), 208-9; and E. L. Drake and T. F. Bledsoe, "American Guide—New Mexico; Introductory Essay—Education in New Mexico" (Federal Writers' Project, 1937), 1, manuscript in WPA Files #151, New Mexico State Records Center and Archives, Santa Fe (hereafter NMSRCA).

17. David J. Weber, " 'Scarce More Than Apes.' Historical Roots of Anglo American Stereotypes of Mexicans in the Border Region," in *New Spain's Far Northern Frontier: Essays on Spain in the American West, 1540-1821,* ed. David J. Weber (Albuquerque: University of New Mexico Press, 1979), 298-300; and Horsman, *Race and Manifest Destiny,* 210-11.

18. Susan E. Keefe and Amado M. Padilla, *Chicano Ethnicity* (Albuquerque: University of New Mexico Press, 1987), 13-14.

19. Frances Leon Swadesh, *Los Primeros Pobladores: Hispanic Americans of the Ute Frontier* (University of Notre Dame Press, 1974), 159-82; Roberto R. Bacalski-Martínez, "Aspects of Mexican American Cultural Heritage," and Reyes Ramos, "The Mexican American: Am I Who They Say I Am?" in Arnulfo D. Trejo ed., *The Chicano As We See Ourselves* ed. (Tucson: University of Arizona Press, 1979), 19-21, 49-65.

20. *Annual Report of the Commissioner of Education Made to the Secretary of the Interior for the Year 1870* (Washington, DC: U.S. Government Printing Office, 1870), 326.

21. Hubert Howe Bancroft, *History of Arizona and New Mexico, 1530-1888* (Albuquerque: Horn & Wallace, 1962), 643.

22. Wayne E. Fuller, "Country Schoolteaching on the Sod-House Frontier," *Arizona and the West* 17 (Summer 1975):121-23.

23. James E. Clark, "New Mexico's Educational Policy," *New Mexico Journal of Education* 7(February 1911):15.

24. William G. Ritch, "A Survey of the Development of Education in New Mexico," Reel 6 #1916, Ritch Papers, microfilm, UNM.

25. Cremin, *American Education: The National Experience,* 178.

26. For overviews of the Progressive movement see Robert Wiebe, *The Search for Order, 1877-1920* (New York: Hill and Wang, 1967); Richard Hofstadter, *The Age of Reform* (New York: Vintage Books, 1955); Robert M. Crunden, *Ministers of Reform: The Progressives' Achievement in American Civilization, 1889-1920* (New York: Basic Books, 1982); Herbert H. Gutman, "Work, Culture and Society in Industrializing America, 1815-1919, in Herbert H. Gutman, ed., *Work, Culture and Society in Industrializing America* (New York: Vintage, 1977).

27. Lawrence A. Cremin, *The Transformation of the School: Progressivism in American Education, 1876-1957* (New York: Vintage Books, 1961), 66-75; Robert A. Carlson, *The Americanization Syndrome: A Quest for Conformity* (London: Croom Helm, 1987), 90; and Paula Fass, *Outside In: Minorities and the Transformation of American Education* (New York: Oxford University Press, 1989), 5, 13-20.

28. Cremin, *Transformation,* 115-17; Robert M. Crunden, *From Self to Society, 1919-1941* (Englewood Cliffs, NJ: Prentice Hall, 1972), 8-9, 60-61; and Lawrence A. Cremin,

American Education: The Metropolitan Experience, 1876-1980 (New York: Harper & Row, 1988), 164-69.

29. John Dewey, *The School and Society* (Chicago: University of Chicago Press, 1900), 8-11.

30. Ibid., 14.

31. Ibid., 15-17, 26.

32. John Dewey, *Democracy and Education: An Introduction to the Philosophy of Education* (New York: The Macmillan Co., 1916), 101-2.

33. David Tyack, *The One Best System: A History of American Urban Education* (Cambridge, MA: Harvard University Press, 1974), 14, 28-30, 66-71; Walter Feinberg, *Reason and Rhetoric: The Intellectual Foundations of 20th Century Liberal Educational Policy* (New York: John Wiley & Sons, 1975), 69-73.

34. Tyack, *The One Best System*, 39-40, 43-45, 180-181; Raymond E. Callahan, *Education and the Cult of Efficiency: A Study of the Social Forces That Have Shaped the Administration of the Public Schools* (Chicago: University of Chicago Press, 1962), 96-99; Hamilton Cravens, *The Triumph of Evolution: American Scientists and the Heredity-Environment Controversy, 1900-1941* (University of Pennsylvania Press, 1978), 63-66, 75-76; and Ellen Condliffe Lagemann, "The Plural Worlds of Educational Research," *History of Education Quarterly* 29(Summer, 1989), 211-21.

35. Fass, *Outside In*, 118-34; and David Tyack, Robert Lowe, and Elisabeth Hansot, *Public Schools in Hard Times: The Great Depression and Recent Years* (Cambridge, MA: Harvard University Press, 1984).

36. The educational history of Hispanos in New Mexico is considered so unique that most scholars do not even bring it into discussions of Hispanic education. Studies devoted entirely to or with chapters on the education of Spanish-speaking children in the Southwest include Thomas P. Carter, *Mexican Americans in School: A History of Educational Neglect* (Princeton, NJ: College Entrance Examination Board, 1970) and Herschel T. Manuel, *Spanish-Speaking Children of the Southwest: Their Education and Public Welfare* (Austin: University of Texas Press, 1965); Douglas E. Foley et al., *From Peones to Politicos: Class and Ethnicity in a South Texas Town, 1900-1987* (Austin: University of Texas Press, 1988); Mario T. Garcia, *Desert Immigrants: The Mexicans of El Paso, 1880-1920* (New Haven: Yale University Press, 1981); Mario T. Garcia, *Mexican Americans: Leadership, Ideology, and Identity, 1930-1960* (New Haven: Yale University Press, 1989); Gilbert G. Gonzalez, *Chicano Education in the Era of Segregation* (Philadelphia: Balch Institute Press, 1990); Judith Rosenberg Raftery, *Land of Fair Promise: Politics and Reform in Los Angeles Schools, 1885-1941* (Stanford, CA: Stanford University Press, 1992); Ricardo Romo, *East Los Angeles: History of a Barrio* (Austin: University of Texas Press, 1983); Guadalupe San Miguel, Jr., *"Let All of Them Take Heed": Mexican Americans and the Campaign for Educational Equality in Texas, 1910-1981* (Austin: University of Texas Press, 1987); George J. Sánchez, *Becoming Mexican American: Ethnicity, Culture and Identity in Chicano Los Angeles, 1900-1945* (New York: Oxford University Press, 1993).

Chapter 1

1. Robert W. Larson, *New Mexico's Quest for Statehood, 1846-1912* (Albuquerque: University of New Mexico Press, 1968), 193.

2. C. E. Hodgin, "Early School Laws of New Mexico," *Bulletin*, University of New Mexico, Educational series (Dec. 1906) 1:8-16; and *Annual Report of the Commissioner of Education Made to the Secretary of the Interior for the Year 1870* (Washington, DC: U.S. Government Printing Office, 1870), 327.

3. Jane C. Atkins, "Who Will Educate: The Schooling Question in Territorial New Mexico, 1846–1911," (Ph.D. diss., University of New Mexico, 1982), 327–30.

4. Hodgin, "Early School Laws of New Mexico," 18, 22–29.

5. U.S. Department of the Interior, Territorial Papers, New Mexico, 1851–1914, Record Group 48, National Archives (hereafter NA), microfilm, Reel 1: Executive Proceedings, Fr. 15–25, 213–28, 408–29.

6. Message of Gov. Lionel A. Sheldon, to the Legislature of New Mexico at Its Session Commencing January 2nd, 1882, Territorial Papers, New Mexico, Reel 1, Fr. 570, NA.

7. *Las Vegas Daily Optic,* 22 October 1883.

8. Territorial Papers, New Mexico, R. G. 48, NA, microfilm, Reel 1, Fr. 22, 42. J. B. Ralliere, a Catholic priest, was elected school commissioner for Valencia County in 1874 and 1876 and also served as county superintendent of schools.

9. Frederick Mason Bacon, "Contributions of Catholic Religious Orders to Public Education in New Mexico Since the American Occupation" (M.A. thesis, University of New Mexico, 1947), 35–36.

10. Charles D. Biebel, "Cultural Change on the Southwest Frontier: Albuquerque Schooling, 1870–1895," *New Mexico Historical Review* 55(July 1980):217.

11. W. G. Ritch, "Report of W. G. Ritch to Commissioner of Education John Eaton," 1876, Reel 5, #1743, William Gillet Ritch Papers, microfilm, Special Collections, Zimmerman Library, UNM.

12. Ritch had come to New Mexico from Wisconsin. Howard R. Lamar, *The Far Southwest, 1846–1912: A Territorial History* (New Haven: Yale University Press, 1966), 167.

13. W. G. Ritch, *Education in New Mexico: Reports of Honorable W. G. Ritch, Sec. of the Territory to the Commissioner of Education,* Washington, D.C., 1873, 1874, 1875 (n.p. 1876): 3, UNM; and *Annual Report of the Commissioner of Education for the Year 1870* (Washington, DC: U.S. Government Printing Office, 1882): 381.

14. W. G. Ritch to "Editor of the Denver Tribune," 10 March 1879, Reel 6 #1879, and W. G. Ritch to J. A. Annin, 13 September 1879, Reel 6 #1880, Ritch Papers, UNM.

15. Paul A. F. Walter, "First Meeting of the New Mexico Educational Association," *New Mexico Historical Review* 2(Jan. 1927):68–75.

16. Editorial, *Santa Fe Daily New Mexican,* 24 December 1886.

17. Howard R. Lamar, "Edmund G. Ross as Governor of New Mexico Territory: A Reappraisal," *New Mexico Historical Review* 36(July 1961):195–96, 201; and Myra Ellen Jenkins, "Early Education in New Mexico," *NEA-NM School Review* (Mid-Winter 1977):13.

18. Edmund G. Ross, "An Address," 1 March 1889, Reel 102, Fr. 277, Territorial Archives of New Mexico, NMSRCA.

19. Ralph E. Twitchell, *The Leading Facts of New Mexican History* (Cedar Falls, Iowa: The Torch Press, 1912):2:507–9; and *Compilation of the School Laws of the Territory of New Mexico* (Santa Fe: El Boletin Popular Printing Co., 1903), 3, 5.

20. Fabiola Cabeza de Baca, *We Fed Them Cactus* (Albuquerque: University of New Mexico Press, 1954), 161.

21. Twitchell, *Leading Facts,* 508.

22. Anna R. Hadley, Caroline H. Allen, and C. Frank Allen, *Hiram Hadley* (Boston: The Authors, 1924), 11, 13–14, 19, 32–34.

23. *Albuquerque Morning Democrat,* 14 April 1893, 10 May 1893, 12 May 1893.

24. Informe del Superintendente de Instrucción Pública Amado Chaves por el Año Que Termina el 31 de Diciembre de 1896 (Santa Fe: Compañía Impresora del Nuevo Mexicano,

1896), 8, in State Department of Education Papers, NMSRCA; and C. M. Light, *Course of Study for County Institutes* (Santa Fe: El Boletin Popular Printing Co., 1904), intro., 14, 18, 48, in State Department of Education Papers, NMSRCA.

25. Hiram Hadley, "Educational Conditions in New Mexico," undated manuscript, pp. 3–5, in Speeches—Concerning Education, Box 1, Folder 2, Hiram Hadley Papers MS 168, Rio Grande Historical Collections, New Mexico State University, Las Cruces (hereafter NMSU).

26. John H. Vaughan, "New Mexico's Educational Crisis," *New Mexico Journal of Education* 7(Feb. 1911):63.

27. Ibid., 67.

28. James E. Clark, "New Mexico's Educational Policy," *New Mexico Journal of Education* 7(Feb. 1911):17.

29. See James H. Madison, "John D. Rockefeller's General Education Board and the Rural School Problem in the Midwest, 1900–1930," *History of Education Quarterly* 24(1984):181–88, for a discussion of consolidation of rural schools in the Midwest.

30. Editorial, *Las Vegas Daily Optic*, 21 August 1880. The *Daily Optic* editors not only encouraged instruction in the Spanish language, but they did not mind Catholic clerics as the teachers. On 21 January 1881 their editorial informed readers that "Brother Silva, a tutor in the Las Vegas College, has consented to give lessons in Spanish to east side residents . . ."

31. Benigno Romero, "Sobre Enseñanza Español," *El Eco del Valle* (Las Cruces), 24 September 1908.

32. "Símbolo de Nuestra Raza," *El Eco del Valle*, 22 July 1909.

33. Carolyn Zeleny, "Relations between the Spanish-American and Anglo-Americans in New Mexico: A Study of Conflict and Accommodation in a Dual-Ethnic Situation" (Ph.D. diss., Yale University, 1944; reprint ed., New York: Arno Press, 1974), 274.

34. *Informe del Superintendente de Instrucción Pública Amado Chaves*, 9. Translation by author.

35. Hiram Hadley, "The Value of Education," undated manuscript, pp. 1–2, in Speeches—Concerning Education, Box 1, Folder 2, Hiram Hadley Papers MS 168, NMSU.

36. Hiram Hadley to Leandro Lucero, 3 November 1905, Territorial Archives of New Mexico, Reel 67, Frame 251, NMSRCA.

37. Ibid.

38. *Annual Reports of the Territorial Superintendent of Public Instruction to the Governor of New Mexico for the Years 1907–1908* (Santa Fe: New Mexican Printing Co., 1909): 17.

39. Cabeza de Baca, *We Fed Them Cactus*, 161.

40. Clark, "New Mexico's Educational Policy,"

41. *Annual Reports of the Territorial Superintendent of Public Instruction to the Governor of New Mexico for the Years 1909–1910* (Santa Fe: The New Mexican Printing Co., 1911), 51.

42. Ibid., 82.

43. Ibid., 88–89.

44. Guillermo Lux, *Politics and Education in Hispanic New Mexico; From the Spanish American Normal School to the Northern New Mexico Community College* (El Rito: Northern New Mexico Community College, 1984), 2–6.

45. *Annual Reports 1909–1910*, 62–63.

46. Joseph S. Hofer, "The Child as the Supreme Study in Education," *New Mexico Journal of Education* 8(Jan. 1912):14. This essay was the President's Address to the New Mexico Education Association for 1912.

47. William J. Reese, *Power and the Promise of School Reform: Grassroots Movements During the Progressive Movement* (Boston: Routledge & Kegan Paul, 1986), 209-11, 225.

48. Harvey Kantor, "Vocationalism in American Education: The Economic and Political Context, 1880-1930," in *Work, Youth and Schooling*, ed. Harvey Kantor and David B. Tyack (Stanford, CA: Stanford University Press, 1982), 14-26; Joel Spring, *Education and the Rise of the Corporate State* (Boston: Beacon Press, 1972), 66-69, 72-76; and Paul C. Violas, *The Training of the Urban Working Class: A History of Twentieth Century Education* (Chicago: Rand McNally, 1978), 124-43.

49. Hodgin quoted by Elizabeth Strong Shamberger, "A Thirty Year Educational History of Albuquerque, New Mexico," (M.A. Thesis, University of New Mexico, 1928): 157.

50. E. D. McQueen Gray, "How the Curriculum of the Secondary School Might Be Reconstructed," *University of New Mexico Bulletin, Educational Series*, 1(5)(Oct. 1911):145.

51. Annual Report of the Territorial Superintendent . . . 1909-1910, 29.

52. J. C. Ross, "Industrial Education for the Spanish-Speaking People," *New Mexico Journal of Education* 7(Feb., 1911): 20-21.

53. George I. Sánchez, *Forgotten People: A Study of New Mexicans* (Albuquerque: University of New Mexico Press, 1940), 22.

54. J. E. Seyfried, "Illiteracy Trends in New Mexico, Including comparison of Trends in New Mexico with those in Certain Other States and the United States," *University of New Mexico Bulletin, Education Series*, Vol. 8, No. 1(March, 1934):9-10.

55. Larson, *New Mexico's Quest for Statehood*, 119, 124-25, 167-68, 172-73, 180, 183, 303; and Heinz Kloss, *The American Bilingual Tradition* (Rowley, MA: Newbury House, 1977), 128.

56. Larson, *New Mexico's Quest for Statehood*, 268.

57. E. B. Fincher, "Spanish-Americans as a Political Factor in New Mexico, 1912-1950" (Ph.D. diss., New York University, 1950; reprint ed., New York: Arno Press, 1974), 163-67.

58. Zeleny, "Relations Between the Spanish-Americans and Anglo-Americans," 119, 219-20; "Constitution of New Mexico," in *The State Constitutions*, comp. and ed. by Charles Kettleborough (Indianapolis: B. F. Bowen, 1918), 959, 964-65; and Robert Arthur Moyers, "A History of Education in New Mexico" (Ph.D. diss., George Peabody College for Teachers, 1941), 491.

59. "Constitution of New Mexico," 959; and J. E. Seyfried, "Analysis and Evaluation of New Mexico State School Laws," *University of New Mexico Bulletin, Education Series*, 6(2)(Sept. 1932):10-11.

60. "Constitution of New Mexico," 965.

61. Ibid, 959.

62. Larson, *New Mexico's Quest for Statehood*, 279; and Zeleny, "Relations," 275.

Chapter 2

1. John V. Conway, Special Report to Hon. Alvan N. White, Superintendent of Public Instruction from County School Superintendent, Santa Fe County, New Mexico, 1914, in Department of Education Papers, NMSRCA.

2. Ibid., 14, 30, 32.

3. Ibid., 24, 34, 55.

4. Conway, Special Report. In the entire state in 1914, women outnumbered male teachers 1356 to 580. The state superintendent's report does not indicate the ethnicity of teachers in 1914. *Report of the State Superintendent of Public Instruction for the Biennial*

Period Ending November 30th, 1916 (Santa Fe: New Mexican Printing Co., 1916), 2. Santa Fe County's 65 teachers in 1914 represented an increase from 1912, when there were 45 total teachers. *Biennial Report of the Superintendent of Public Instruction to the Governor of New Mexico For the Years 1910–11 and 1911–12* (Santa Fe: New Mexican Printing Co., 1912), 57–58.

5. A number of studies shed light on the role of women in colonial and nineteenth-century Hispano culture. See Rosalind Z. Rock, " 'Pido y Suplico': Women and the Law in Spanish New Mexico, 1697–1763," *New Mexico Historical Review* 65(April 1990):145–59; Janet Lecompte, "The Independent Women of Hispanic New Mexico, 1821–1846," *Western Historical Quarterly* 22(Jan. 1981):20–22; Deena J. González, "La Tules of Image and Reality: Euro-American Attitudes and Legend Formation on a Spanish-Mexican Frontier," in *Unequal Sisters: A Multicultural Reader in U.S. Women's History*, 2d ed., ed. Vicki L. Ruiz and Ellen Carol DuBois (New York: Routledge, 1994), 58–61; Beverley Trulio, "Anglo-American Attitudes toward New Mexican Women," *Journal of the West* 12(1973):229–39; and Frances Leon Swadesh, *Los Primeros Pobladores: Hispanic Americans of the Ute Frontier* (Notre Dame, IN: University of Notre Dame Press, 1974), 178–79. Studies that focus upon the American period and the twentieth century include Nan Elsasser, Kyle MacKenzie, and Yvonne Tixier y Vigil, *Las Mujeres: Conversations from a Hispanic Community* (Old Westbury, NY: Feminist Press, 1980); Joan M. Jensen, "Women Teachers, Class, and Ethnicity: New Mexico, 1900–1950," *Southwest Economy and Society* 4(Winter 1978–79):7–10; Sarah Deutsch, *No Separate Refuge: Culture, Class, and Gender on an Anglo-Hispanic Frontier in the American Southwest, 1880–1940* (New York: Oxford University Press, 1987), 41–62. On the role of women in the Mexican American family across the Southwest, see Alfredo Mirandé and Evangelina Enríquez, *La Chicana: The Mexican-American Woman* (Chicago: University of Chicago Press, 1979), 58–60, 106–17; and Richard Griswold del Castillo, *La Familia: Chicano Families in the Urban Southwest 1848 to the Present* (Notre Dame, IN: University of Notre Dame Press, 1984), 26–34, 62–63.

6. Fabiola Cabeza de Baca, *We Fed Them Cactus* (Albuquerque: University of New Mexico Press, 1954), 156, 161.

7. Minutes, New Mexico State Board of Education, 5 September 1913, 27 November 1913, 13 May 1915, 1 February 1915, 2 August 1915, and 9 June 1916, NMSRCA.

8. Carolyn Zeleny, "Relations between the Spanish-Americans and Anglo-Americans in New Mexico: A Study of Conflict and Accommodation in a Dual-Ethnic Situation" (Ph.D. diss., Yale University, 1944; reprint ed. New York: Arno Press, 1974), 282.

9. Robert Arthur Moyers, "A History of Education in New Mexico" (Ph.D. diss., George Peabody College for Teachers, 1941), 496; and "Relating to Educational Legislation Enacted at the Last State Legislature," State Board of Education, New Mexico, *Education Bulletin* 1(1)(March 1915):6, in Education Bulletins 1915–1949, # 1, Department of Education Papers, Exp. #6, NMSRCA.

10. "Relating to Educational Legislation Enacted at the Last State Legislature," 7–8; and Moyers, "A History of Education in New Mexico," 647–48.

11. Moyers, "A History of Education in New Mexico," 496.

12. "An Act for the Employment of Spanish-Speaking Teachers in Certain Rural Schools," Chapter 146, 300, Laws of the State of New Mexico Passed by the Fourth Regular Session, 1919; and "Educational Laws and Resolutions Passed by the Fourth State Legislature of New Mexico," State Board of Education, New Mexico,*Educational Bulletin* 4(5)(March 1919):n.p., in Educational Bulletins 1915–1949, # 1, Department of Education Papers, Exp. #6, NMSRCA.

13. "El Coronel Bronson M. Cutting Explica y Sostiene el Programa Educacional del Gobernador Larrazolo," *La Bandera Americana*, 14 March 1919.

14. "El Gobernador Larrazolo y La Educacion," *La Bandera Americana,* 23 May 1919.

15. "Summary of New School Law," , Department of Education, *Educational News Bulletin* 3(4)(Apr. 1919):2, in Correspondence—Letter & Circulars sent by the Dept. of Education [Scrapbook] 1915-1920, Department of Education Papers, Exp. # 8, NMSRCA.

16. Minutes, State Board of Education, 9 June 1919.

17. Alfred Jelfs to State Board of Education, 9 April 1917, in Coronel file, Department of Education Papers, Exp. 56, Folder 1, NMSRCA.

18. Minutes, State Board of Education, 18 December 1917.

19. "Manual of the Common School: Course of Study for the Public Schools of New Mexico," State Board of Education, New Mexico, *Educational Bulletin* 3(5)(March 1917):20-34, in Department of Education Papers, Exp. 50, NMSRCA.

20. D. B. Morrill, "Teaching English to Spanish Children," *New Mexico Journal of Education* 14(Nov. 1917):9.

21. D. B. Morrill, "Teaching the Spanish-American Child," *New Mexico Journal of Education* 13(April 1917):10.

22. Ibid., 9-10.

23. D. B. Morrill, "The Spanish Language Problems," *New Mexico Journal of Education* 14(May 1918):6.

24. "Americanization Day in the Schools of New Mexico," State Board of Education, New Mexico, *Bulletin* 5(3)(Sept. 1919):1, in Educational Bulletins, 1915-1949, Department of Education Papers, Exp. #6, NMSRCA. On the efforts of the federal Bureau of Education to instill patriotism and conformity during the war, see David M. Kennedy, *Over Here: The First World War and American Society* (New York: Oxford University Press, 1980), 53-59.

25. "Proposed Program of Procedure Adopted by the Administrative School Officials and Teachers in Conference with the State Department of Education at Santa Fe, New Mexico, August 15 to 17, 1918," State Board of Education File, Governor Washington E. Lindsey Papers, NMSRCA.

26. "La Prensa Hispano-Americana Atención," *La Bandera Americana,* 4 July 1919.

27. Patricia Cadigan Armstrong, *A Portrait of Bronson Cutting through His Papers, 1910-1927* (Albuquerque: University of New Mexico, Department of Government, Division of Research, 1959), 31-35.

28. Cutting, quoted in Richard Lowitt, *Bronson M. Cutting: Progressive Politician* (Albuquerque: University of New Mexico Press, 1992), 105-6.

29. George J. Sánchez, *Becoming Mexican American: Ethnicity, Culture, and Identity in Chicano Los Angeles, 1900-1945* (Oxford: Oxford University Press, 1993), 99-101.

30. Montana Hastings, "New Mexico Child Welfare Service; Bulletin 1; The Organization of the State Child Welfare Work," State Board of Education, New Mexico, *Bulletin* 6(3)(Sept. 1920):9, in Educational Bulletins, 1915-1949, #1, in Department of Education Papers, Exp. #6, NMSRCA; and Sandra Schackel, *Social Housekeepers: Women Shaping Public Policy in New Mexico, 1920-1940* (Albuquerque: University of New Mexico Press, 1992), 14-15, 24.

31. George J. Sánchez, *Becoming Mexican American,* 101.

32. Hastings, "New Mexico Child Welfare Service," 10-11.

33. William H. Sheldon, "The Intelligence of Mexican Children," *School and Society* 19(Feb. 1924):139, 141-42.

34. The imposition of a uniform curriculum began in the urban schools of major U.S. cities as early as the 1860s and progressed throughout the nation. For a discussion of curriculum development, see David B. Tyack, *The One Best System: A History of American Urban Education* (Cambridge, MA: Harvard University Press, 1974), 45-47.

35. *Annual Report of the Territorial Superintendent of Public Instruction to the Gov-*

ernor of New Mexico, 1907-08 (Santa Fe: New Mexican Printing Co., 1909), 35; and Moyers, "A History of Education in New Mexico," 533-34.

36. Raymond E. Callahan, *Education and the Cult of Efficiency* (Chicago: University of Chicago Press, 1962), 112-18.

37. Minutes, New Mexico Board of Education, 10 June 1916, NMSRCA.

38. Bagley, William C., *Report on the New Mexico State Educational Institutions to the New Mexico Special Revenue Commission* (Santa Fe: New Mexican Publishing Corp., 1921), 12, 29, 37.

39. Moyers, "A History of Education in New Mexico," 715-18.

40. *New Mexico School Code* ([Santa Fe]: Superintendent of Public Instruction, 1923), 1-36.; and Tom Wiley, *Public School Education in New Mexico* (Albuquerque: University of New Mexico, 1965), 36-38, 42-43.

41. *New Mexico Course of Study for Elementary Schools* ([Santa Fe]: State Department of Education, 1930), 14, in Department of Education Papers, Exp. 50, NMSRCA.

42. *New Mexico Common Schools Course of Study* ([Santa Fe]: State Board of Education, 1921), 89-90, in Department of Education Papers, Exp. 50, NMSRCA.

43. Jensen, "Women Teachers, Class, and Ethnicity," 7-9; and Elsasser, MacKenzie, and Tixier y Vigil, *Las Mujeres,* 25, 87.

44. Josephine Córdova, interview by Erlinda Gonzales-Berry, 7 March 1992, "And Gladly Did We Teach: Gender, Culture, and Educational Policy in New Mexico, 1910-1940," Oral History Program, Center for Southwest Research, University of New Mexico.

45. *Course of Study,* 1930, 105-6.

46. Frank Reeves, *History of New Mexico: Vol. III: Family and Personal History* (New York: Lewis Historical Publishing Co., 1961), 243-44.

47. Clark S. Knowlton, "Patrón-Peón Pattern among the Spanish Americans of New Mexico," *Social Forces* 41(1962-63):13-14.

48. The patrón system is recounted as a positive symbiotic relationship by José Ortiz y Pino III, *Don José: The Last Patrón* (Santa Fe: Sunstone, 1981).

49. News Clippings re: Nina Otero Warren, #105, Bergere Family Collection, NMSRCA; and Charlotte Whaley, *Nina Otero-Warren of Santa Fe* (Albuquerque: University of New Mexico Press, 1994), 64-66, 73-75.

50. Scrapbook #6—Nina Otero Warren's congressional campaign, #122, Bergere Family Collection, NMSRCA.

51. Nancie L. González, *The Spanish-Americans of New Mexico: A Heritage of Pride* (Albuquerque: University of New Mexico Press, 1967), x; and Richard L. Nostrand, *The Hispano Homeland* (Norman: University of Oklahoma Press, 1992), 4,45, 68-69.

52. Nina Otero-Warren, *Old Spain in Our Southwest* (New York: Harcourt Brace and Company, 1936), 10.

53. Ibid., 51.

54. David J. Weber, *The Spanish Frontier in North America* (New Haven: Yale University Press, 1992), 346; Arrell Morgan Gibson, *The Santa Fe and Taos Colonies: Age of the Muses, 1900-1942* (Norman: University of Oklahoma Press, 1983), 11-17, 21-22, 70-73, 89-93; and Marta Weigle, "The First Twenty-Five Years of the Spanish Colonial Arts Society," in *Hispanic Arts and Ethnohistory in the Southwest,* ed. Marta Weigle (Santa Fe: Ancient City Press, 1983), 182-83.

55. Mary Austin, Adelina Otero-Warren, and Aurora Lucero, "New Mexico Folk Song," *El Palacio* 7(1919):152-59; and Helen Cramp McCrossen, "Native Crafts in New Mexico," *The School Arts Magazine* 30(March, 1931):456-58.

56. Gibson, *Santa Fe and Taos,* 174.

57. Adelina Otero, "My People," *Survey* 66(May 1931):149.

58. Ibid., 150.
59. Adelina Otero Warren, "Curriculum for the Elementary Schools of Santa Fe County," 1929, p. 1, File #42, Bergere Family Collection, NMSRCA.
60. Ibid., 2.
61. Weigle, "The First Twenty-Five Years," 188, 190-91; and Suzanne Forrest, *The Preservation of the Village: New Mexico's Hispanics and the New Deal* (Albuquerque: University of New Mexico Press, 1989), 53-54.
62. Nina Otero-Warren to Concha Ortiz y Pino, 20 February 1941, File #43, Bergere Family Collection, NMSRCA.
63. "Personal Resume" and Scrapbook, Concha Ortiz y Pino de Kleven, Papers, Special Collections, Zimmerman Library, UNM.
64. Otero Warren, "Curriculum for the Elementary Schools of Santa Fe County," n.p.
65. Ibid.
66. "La Convención Anual de los Maestros," *La Bandera Americana*, 1 November 1929.
67. "New Mexico Too Poor To Permit Favoritism, Waste or Graft, Says McCollum to Council," *New Mexico State Tribune*, 30 October 1929.
68. "Convention Program," *New Mexico School Review* 9(Oct. 1929):8-9, 14-18.
69. "Teachers Pick Duke City For 1930 Session," *New Mexico State Tribune*, 2 November 1929.
70. Ibid.
71. "Language Not Bar to Good School Work," *New Mexico State Tribune*, 2 November 1929.
72. "Reading Poor in This State Tireman Says," *New Mexico State Tribune*, 2 November 1929.
73. "Officers of N.M.E.A.," *New Mexico School Review* 9(Nov. 1929):8.

Chapter 3

1. George I. Sánchez, *Forgotten People: A Study of New Mexicans* (Albuquerque: University of New Mexico Press, 1940), 10-14, 18-33, 37-40.
2. James Nelson Mowry, "A Study of the Educational Thought and Action of George I. Sánchez" (Ph.D. diss., University of Texas, 1977), 23-26; and Gladys R. Leff, "George I. Sánchez: Don Quixote of the Southwest" (Ph.D. diss., North Texas State University, 1976), 36-37.
3. James F. Zimmerman to Leo M. Favrot, 11 February 1930, in 1033.1, School of Education, 1929-1930, Box 598, Folder 6357, Ser. 1.4, General Education Board Papers, Rockefeller Archives Center, Pocantico Hills, New York (hereafter GEB).
4. Raymond B. Fosdick, *Adventure in Giving: The Story of the General Education Board* (New York: Harper & Row, 1962), 8-9, 83-85; James D. Anderson, "Northern Foundations and the Shaping of the Southern Black Rural Education, 1902-1935," *History of Education Quarterly* 18(Winter 1978):374, 378-81; and James D. Anderson, *The Education of Blacks in the South, 1860-1935* (Chapel Hill: University of North Carolina Press, 1988), 81-82, 86, 92.
5. During negotiations over funding for the San Jose Training School, GEB officials Jackson Davis and Leo Favrot compared conditions for Hispanos in New Mexico with those of African-Americans in the South, justifying the GEB's involvement in New Mexico on that basis. James Zimmerman, Loyd Tireman, State Superintendent Atanasio Montoya, John Milne of the Albuquerque city schools, and Dean S. P. Nanninga of the UNM School of

Education were involved in the negotiations. Jackson Davis and Leo M. Favrot, memo, 25-30 January 1930 in 1033.1, School of Education (UNM) 1929-1936, Box 598, Folder 6357, GEB.

6. See for example Algernon Coleman, *English Teaching in the Southwest: Organization and Materials for Instructing Spanish-speaking Children* (Washington, DC: American Council on Education, 1940), 4-5; Annie Reynolds, *The Education of Spanish-Speaking Children in Five Southwestern States*, U.S. Department of the Interior, Office of Education Bulletin 11 (Washington, DC: U.S. Government Printing Office, 1933), 39-45; Herschel T. Manuel, *Education of Mexican and Spanish-Speaking Children in Texas* (Austin: University of Texas Press, 1930), 17, 25; and Sánchez, *Forgotten People*, 31.

7. Reynolds, *The Education of Spanish-speaking Children*, 38-39.

8. William H. Sheldon, "The Intelligence of Mexican Children," *School and Society* 19(Feb. 1924): 139.

9. Ibid, 141-42. Sheldon used the Cole-Vincent group test which, he claimed, enabled him to examine two hundred children in eight hours, while the Binet required an hour per child. Sheldon conducted all the tests himself, with the exception of classes where the students did not know English. In those the teachers gave the test, because they were able "to make themselves understood by use of a sort of Spanish-English dialect colloquially called 'spic,' or mongrel Spanish." (ibid., 140) Any of these factors—the haste in giving the tests, the variety of examiners, or the use of language not understood by the examinees—would have invalidated the tests by modern standards. See Paul R. Ehrlich and S. Shirley Feldman, *The Race Bomb: Skin Color, Prejudice and Intelligence* (New York: Quadrangle Books, 1969), 68-80.

10. Examples include Thomas R. Garth, "Racial Differences in Mental Fatigue," *Journal of Applied Psychology* 4(June-Sept. 1920):235-44; Thomas R. Garth, "White, Indian and Negro Work Curves," *Journal of Applied Psychology* 5(March 1921):14-25; Thomas R. Garth, "A Comparison of the Intelligence of Mexican and Mixed and Full Blood Indian Children," *Psychological Review* 30(Sept. 1923):388-401; Zella K. Jordan Flores, "The Relation of Language Difficulty to Intelligence and School Retardation in a Group of Spanish-Speaking Children" (Ph.D. diss., University of Chicago, 1926; reprint ed., San Francisco: R & E Research Associates, 1975); O. K. Garretson, "A Study of Causes of Retardation among Mexican Children in a Small Public School System in Arizona," *Journal of Educational Psychology* 14(Jan. 1928):31-40; Eunice Elvira Parr, "A Comparative Study of Mexican and American Children in the Schools of San Antonio, Texas" (Ph.D. diss., University of Chicago, 1926); and Helen Lois Koch and Rietta Simmons, "A Study of the Test Performance of American, Mexican, and Negro Children," *Psychological Monographs* 35(1926):1-116.

11. Mowry, "A Study of the Educational Thought and Action of George I. Sánchez," 26-27.

12. George I. Sánchez, "Group Differences and Spanish-Speaking Children—A Critical Review," *Journal of Applied Psychology* 16(1932):549-50.

13. George I. Sánchez, "Scores of Spanish-Speaking Children on Repeated Tests," *The Pedagogical Seminary and Journal of Genetic Psychology* 60(March 1932):229.

14. Ibid., 224-25.

15. Sánchez, "Group Differences," 550-51.

16. George I. Sánchez, "Bilingualism and Mental Measures; A Word of Caution," *Journal of Applied Psychology* 17(1934):765-66, 770.

17. Ibid., 770-71.

18. George I. Sánchez to J. F. Zimmerman, 22 January 1931, in NM 1, Division of Information and Statistics, 1931-33, Box 100, Folder 900, Series 1, GEB.

19. W. W. Brierly to Georgia Lusk, State Superintendent, 24 April 1931, and Georgia Lusk, John Milne, and J. F. Zimmerman to General Education Board, 6 March 1931, in NM 1, Box 100, Folder 900, Ser. 1, GEB.

20. James F. Zimmerman to Leo M. Favrot, GEB, 13 March 1935, in NM 1, Box 100, Folder 901, Ser. 1, GEB.

21. *Report of the State Superintendent of Public Instruction for the Eleventh Biennium Period Beginning July 1, 1930 and Ending June 30, 1932 Prepared by the Division of Information and Statistics* (Santa Fe: State Superintendent of Public Instruction, 1932), 8.

22. George I. Sánchez to W. W. Brierly, GEB, 16 July 1932, in NM 1, Box 100, Folder 900, Ser. 1, GEB.

23. George I. Sánchez to Leo M. Favrot, 17 October 1932, in NM 1, Box 100, Folder 900, Ser. 1, GEB. Leo M. Favrot was southern field agent for the General Education Board and acted as the contact person between the GEB and those persons connected with GEB projects in New Mexico through the 1930's. He became a close friend and confidant of George Sánchez.

24. George I. Sánchez, "The Age-Grade Status of the Rural Child in New Mexico ; Public Elementary Schools, 1931-32," Educational Research Bulletin, New Mexico State Department of Education (1932), n.p., in Department of Education Papers, Report-Age Grade Status of the Rural Child 1931-1932 #5, NMSRCA.

25. George I. Sánchez to Leo M. Favrot, 23 December 1932, NM 1, Box 100, Folder 900, Ser. 1, GEB.

26. Tom Wiley, *Public School Education in New Mexico* (Albuquerque: University of New Mexico Press, 1965), 43-46.

27. Ibid., 39-41, 43.

28. George I. Sánchez, "Future Legislative Program for Financing Public Education in New Mexico," *University of New Mexico Bulletin,* Education Series 8(3)(Sept. 1934): 97-98.

29. Ibid., 98-101.

30. Leff, "George I. Sánchez," 141-48. Prior to this time, the permanent school fund in New Mexico was derived from property taxes.

31. Leff, "George I. Sánchez," 141-52.

32. George I. Sánchez to Leo M. Favrot, 26 April 1933, in NM 1, Box 100, Folder 900, Ser. 1, GEB.

33. Sánchez to Favrot, 26 April 1933.

34. "Proceedings at Hearing Before the Committee Appointed by the Board of Regents of the University of New Mexico for the Purpose of Investigating the Racial Attitude Survey," May 3-5, 1933, 48-49, Special Reports: Hearing on Racial Prejudice, Governor Arthur Seligman Papers, NMSRCA; and Richard M. Page, "Brief Prepared for Investigating Committee, in Defense of the Race Study," May 1933, 2-3, Box #161, Folder 1, Richard M. Page Papers, Special Collections, UNM.

35. *Albuquerque Tribune,* 27 April 1933.

36. Page, "Brief," 14.

37. Phillip B. Gonzales, "Spanish Heritage and Ethnic Protest in New Mexico: The Anti-Fraternity Bill of 1933," *New Mexico Historical Review* 61(Oct. 1986):288-89, 292-93.

38. See Lynne Marie Getz, "Politics, Science, and Education in New Mexico: The Racial-Attitudes Survey of 1933," *History of Higher Education Annual* 10(1990):53-70.

39. "Proceedings," 142-43; and George I. Sánchez to Leo M. Favrot, 11 May 1933, NM 1, Box 100, Folder 900, Ser. 1, GEB.

40. George I. Sánchez to Leo M. Favrot, 11 May 1933.

41. Leo Favrot to George Sánchez, 28 December 1932, NM 1, Box 100, Folder 900, Ser. 1, GEB; and Leff, "George I. Sánchez," 111-12.
42. George I. Sánchez, "The Education of Bilinguals in a State School System" (Ed.D. diss., University of California, Berkeley, 1934), 7, 13.
43. Ibid., 1-22.
44. Ibid., 23.
45. Ibid., 24.
46. Ibid., 30, 103.
47. George I. Sánchez to Jackson Davis, 9 November 1934, in NM 1, Box 100, Folder 901, Ser. 1, GEB.
48. George I. Sánchez, "Teachers!" *New Mexico School Review* 15(Oct. 1935):22-23.
49. "Fiftieth Annual Convention of the N.M.E.A," *New Mexico School Review* 15(Sept. 1935):8.
50. George I. Sánchez, "Management and Mismanagement in a State Business—Education," 15 October 1934, typescript in NM 1, Box 100, Folder 901, Ser. 1, GEB.
51. William A. Keleher, *New Mexicans I Knew: Memoirs, 1892-1969* (Albuquerque: University of New Mexico Press, 1983), 139.
52. "Progress of the N.M.E.A. Legislative Program," *New Mexico School Review* 14(Dec. 1934):8; "N.M.E.A. Legislative Program Compared with Educational Legislative Enactments," *New Mexico School Review* 14(Mar. 1935):8-9; Leff, "George I. Sánchez," 167-69; and Wiley, *Public School Education,* 53-56.
53. *Santa Fe New Mexican,* 8 February 1935, 9 February 1935, 11 February 1935.
54. *Santa Fe New Mexican,* 20 March 1935; and George I. Sánchez to New Mexico State Board of Education, 19 March 1935, copy in NM 1, Box 100, Folder 901, Ser. 1, GEB.
55. George I. Sánchez to Leo M. Favrot, 20 March 1935, in NM 1, Box 100, Folder 901, Ser. 1, GEB.
56. *Santa Fe New Mexican,* 20 February 1935.
57. Filemon T. Martinez, "Train a Native Educator, and Hire a Politician," *Santa Fe New Mexican,* 28 March 1935.
58. New Mexico State Board of Education Minutes, March 18-19, 1935, NMSRCA; and Leff, "George I. Sánchez," 172.
59. George I. Sánchez to James F. Zimmerman, 23 September 1935, George I. Sánchez file, Box 20, University Secretary Record Group 28-48, UNM.
60. *Santa Fe New Mexican,* 1 November 1935.
61. George I. Sánchez, "Educational Intangibles," *New Mexico School Review* 15(Dec. 1935):19, 31.
62. George I. Sánchez to Leo M. Favrot, 5 March 1935; George I. Sánchez to Leo M. Favrot, 9 July 1937; and Leo M. Favrot, memo from interview with George Sánchez, 27 July 1937, in 303 Julius Rosenwald fund, 1937-38, Box 212, Folder 2043, Ser. 1.2, GEB.
63. George I. Sánchez to Leo M. Favrot, 19 December 1938, in 634 George Sánchez, 1937-44, Box 286, Folder 2983, Ser. 1.3, GEB.
64. *Albuquerque Tribune,* 12 December 1938; and *Santa Fe New Mexican,* 22 December 1938.
65. *Santa Fe New Mexican,* 6 January 1939.
66. Ibid.
67. *La Revista de Taos,* 16 February 1939.
68. New Mexico State Board of Education Minutes, 20 January 1939, NMSRCA.
69. Michael Welsh, "A Prophet Without Honor: George I. Sánchez and Bilingualism in New Mexico," *New Mexico Historical Review* 69(Jan. 1994):29-32.
70. Sánchez, *Forgotten People,* 78-79.

71. Ibid., 81.

72. Jackson Davis, memo from interview with J. F. Zimmerman, 2–3 September 1940, in 1033 University of New Mexico, 1938–54, Box 598, Folder 6356, Ser. 1.4, GEB.

Chapter 4

1. See for example Algernon Coleman, *English Teaching in the Southwest: Organization and Materials for Instructing Spanish-Speaking Children* (Washington, DC: American Council on Education, 1940), 4–5; Annie Reynolds, *The Education of Spanish-Speaking Children in Five Southwestern States*, U.S. Department of the Interior, Office of Education Bulletin 11 (Washington, DC: U.S. Government Printing Office, 1933), 39–45; Herschel T. Manuel, *Education of Mexican and Spanish-Speaking Children in Texas* (Austin: University of Texas Press, 1930), 17, 25; and George I. Sánchez, *Forgotten People: A Study of New Mexicans* (Albuquerque: University of New Mexico Press, 1940), 31.

2. Reynolds, *The Education of Spanish-Speaking Children*, 38–39.

3. Ibid., 41.

4. Loyd Spencer Tireman, Application for Fellowship, 14 Feb. 1933, in 1033.2, Study of Bilingual Schools, 1932–34, Box 599, Folder 6362, Series 1.4, GEB.

5. David L. Bachelor, *Educational Reform in New Mexico: Tireman, San José, and Nambé* (Albuquerque: University of New Mexico Press, 1991), 12, 132, 142.

6. Loyd S. Tireman, "Mi Amigo el Hispano," 1–3, pamphlet, in 1033.1, University of New Mexico, School of Education, Reports and Pamphlets, Box 599, Folder 6361, Ser. 1.4, GEB.

7. Loyd S. Tireman, "Reading in the Elementary Schools of New Mexico," *Elementary School Journal* 30(1930):621–23.

8. Ibid., 623, 625.

9. Ibid., 625.

10. Ibid., 9–10.

11. Tireman, *Teaching Spanish-Speaking Children*, (Albuquerque: University of New Mexico Press, 1948), 36–37, 51. Tireman acknowledged his reliance on the work of George Sánchez in cautioning educators on the use of IQ tests, 19, 22–23.

12. Raymond B. Fosdick, *Adventure in Giving: The Story of the General Education Board* (New York: Harper & Row, 1962), vii, 2–3.

13. John Milne and Atanasio Montoya to Dr. F. P. Bachman, 29 April 1929 in 1033.1, School of Education (UNM) 1929–1936, Box 598, Folder 6357, GEB; and letters from various New Mexico educators to General Education Board, 1905–1929, in 1033 University of New Mexico, 1905–1935, Box 598, Folder 6355, Series 1.4, GEB.

14. Jackson Davis and Leo M. Favrot, Memo of 23–25 Jan. 1930 visit to New Mexico, in 1033.1, Box 598, Folder 6357, Ser. 1.4, GEB.

15. J. F. Zimmerman to Jackson Davis, 28 April 1930; L. S. Tireman to Leo M. Favrot, 8 May 1930; Telegram Zimmerman to Favrot, 17 May 1930; Davis to Zimmerman, May 1930; and Zimmerman to W. W. Brierly, 29 July 1930, all in 1033.1, Box 598, Folder 6357, Ser. 1.4, GEB.

16. Leo M. Favrot to Loyd S. Tireman, 5 June 1931, in 1033.1, Box 599, Folder 6361, Ser. 1.4, GEB.

17. Zimmerman to Brierly, 29 July 1930.

18. Loyd S. Tireman, "The San José Training School," *University of New Mexico Bulletin*, Training School Series 1(1)(Oct. 1930):8–9.

19. Loyd Tireman, *We Learn English: A Preliminary Report of the Achievement of*

Spanish-Speaking Pupils in New Mexico (Albuquerque: University of New Mexico, San José Training School, 1936), 6.

20. Loyd S. Tireman, "Report to the Board of Directors," October 1930, in 1033.1, Box 599, Folder 6361, Ser. 1.4, GEB.

21. John E. Earl, B. F. Haught, and L. S. Tireman, "Results of Group Tests Given in the Original Survey of San José School," *University of New Mexico Bulletin,* Training School Series 1(2)(March 15, 1931):11–12; and Tireman, *We Learn English,* 7–8.

22. Earl, Haught, and Tireman, "Results of Group Tests," 18–26.

23. Loyd S. Tireman, "First Annual Report of the San José Training School," 1931, 2, in 1033.1, Box 599, Folder 6361, Ser. 1.4, GEB.

24. Ibid., 2–3.

25. Tireman, "First Annual Report," 1931, 4; Tireman, "Report to the Board of Directors," Oct. 1930; L. S. Tireman and Marie M. Hughes, "A Reading Program for Spanish-Speaking Pupils," *Elementary English Review* 14(April, 1937):138; and L. S. Tireman, Newel Dixon, and Vera Cornelius, "Vocabulary Acquisition of Spanish-Speaking Children," *Elementary English Review* 12(May, 1935):118.

26. Marie M. Hughes, *Teaching a Standard English Vocabulary with Initial Reading Instruction* (Las Cruces, New Mexico: Bronson Printing Company, 1932), 9–10.

27. Loyd S. Tireman to Leo M. Favrot, 3 December 1931, in 1033.1, UNM School of Education, 1931–36, Box 598, Folder 6358, Ser. 1.4, GEB.

28. Leo M. Favrot, "Inspection of San José Training School, Albuquerque, New Mexico," field report, 31 October 1932, in 1033.1, Box 598, Folder 6358, Ser. 1.4, GEB.

29. L. S. Tireman, Mela Sedillo Brewster, and Lolita Pooler, "The San José Project," *New Mexico Quarterly* 3(Nov. 1933):214.

30. Loyd S. Tireman to Leo M. Favrot, 26 October 1933, in 1033.2, Box 599, Folder 6362, Ser. 1.4, GEB.

31. "Digest of the Stenographic Report of the Minutes of the Fourth Annual Meeting of the Board of Directors of the San José Project, June 19, 1934," in 1033.1, Box 598, Folder 6358, Ser. 1.4, GEB.

32. Ibid.

33. L. S. Tireman, "Preliminary Report for the First Four Years of the San José Experimental School," May 1935, 9–10, in 1033.1, Box 599, Folder 6361, Ser. 1.4, GEB.

34. Tireman, *Teaching Spanish-Speaking Children,* 54.

35. Ibid., 127.

36. Tireman, "Preliminary Report for the First Four Years," 11.

37. Tireman, *Teaching Spanish-Speaking Children,* 130–31.

38. Reynolds, *The Education of Spanish-Speaking Children,* 29; and Arnold H. Leibowitz, *Educational Policy and Political Acceptance : The Imposition of English as the Language of Instruction in American Schools* (Washington, DC: Center for Applied Linguistics, 1971), 9–14.

39. Loyd S. Tireman to Leo M. Favrot, 7 Sept. 1934, in 1033.1, Box 598, Folder 6358, Ser. 1.4, GEB.

40. Loyd S. Tireman to Leo M. Favrot, 7 Nov. 1934, in 1033.1, Box 598, Folder 6358, GEB.

41. James F. Zimmerman to Leo M. Favrot, 31 January 1935, in 1033.1, Box 598, Folder 6358, Ser. 1.4, GEB.

42. James F. Zimmerman to W. W. Brierly, 24 June 1935, in 1033.1, Box 598, Folder 6358, Ser. 1.4, GEB. The San José School also lost the support of one of its most influential backers when Senator Bronson Cutting died in a plane crash in May 1935. Although he had promised continued support to the school, his estate never provided it with any funds.

43. Loyd S. Tireman to Leo M. Favrot, 16 April 1936, in 1033.1, Box 598, Folder 6358, Ser. 1.4, GEB.

44. Leo M. Favrot to Loyd S. Tireman, 18 October 18, 1938, in 1033.1, UNM School of Education, 1937-40, Box 599, Folder 6359, Ser. 1.4, GEB.

45. Tireman, *Teaching Spanish-Speaking Children*, 28-32.

46. Bachelor, *Educational Reform in New Mexico*, 30, 40, 44-45.

47. New Mexico's Hispanos had entered the migrant labor stream, but during the Depression these supplemental economic outlets decreased. Tireman hoped education would allow Hispanos to find alternatives to migrant labor. For an account of patterns of employment for Hispanos before 1940, see Sarah Deutsch, *No Separate Refuge: Culture, Class and Gender on an Anglo-Hispanic Frontier in the American Southwest, 1880-1940* (New York: Oxford University Press, 1987). On education for the immigrant workforce, see Robert L. Church and Michael W. Sedlak, *Education in the United States: An Interpretive History* (New York: Free Press, 1976), 194-201, 304-8; and Harvey Kantor, "Vocationalism in American Education: The Economic and Political Context, 1880-1930," in *Work, Youth and Schooling,* ed. Harvey Kantor and David B. Tyack (Stanford, CA: Stanford University Press, 1982), 14-36.

48. L. S. Tireman and Mary Watson, *A Community School in a Spanish-Speaking Village* (Albuquerque: University of New Mexico Press, 1948), 15-16.

49. Loyd S. Tireman, "First Annual Report of the San José Training School," 1931, 10, 13, in 1033.1, Box 599, Folder 6361, Series 1.4, GEB.

50. Ibid., 13-14.

51. Teachers' Diaries, Records of San José Training School, in UNM Department of Special Education Collection, #306, Box #1, Folder 3, Special Collections, Zimmerman Library, UNM.

52. Tireman, "First Annual Report of the San José Training School," 14.

53. Loyd S. Tireman to Leo M. Favrot, 3 December 1931, in 1033.1, Box 598, Folder 6358, Ser 1.4, GEB.

54. Esther Lanigan Stineman, *Mary Austin: Song of a Maverick* (New Haven: Yale University Press, 1989), 152-54, 176; and Thurman Wilkins, "Mary Hunter Austin," in *Notable American Women: A Biographical Dictionary* (Cambridge, MA: Belknap Press, 1971), 1:67-69.

55. Mary Austin, "Mexicans and New Mexico," *Survey* 66(1931):144, 187.

56. Mary Austin, "Rural Education in New Mexico," *University of New Mexico Bulletin,* Training School Series, 2(1)(Dec. 1931):28-29.

57. Deutsch, *No Separate Refuge,* 190-95.

58. Suzanne Forrest, *The Preservation of the Village: New Mexico's Hispanics and the New Deal* (Albuquerque: University of New Mexico Press, 1989), 33-34, 48-50.

59. Margaret Abreu, "The Father of the Kindergarten System in New Mexico," *New Mexico School Review* 11(Dec. 1931):29.

60. Tireman, "First Annual Report of the San José Training School," 1.

61. Tireman, "Preliminary Report of the First Four Years," 12.

62. "University of New Mexico: Project for Improving Instruction of Spanish-Speaking Children in the Public Schools of the State—Appraisal," 1938, 1-3, in 1033.1, UNM School of Education, 1937-1940, Box 599, Folder 6359, Ser. 1.4, GEB.

63. "Valencia County Teachers Visit San José Training School," *New Mexico School Review* 11(Dec. 1931):21; "Socorro County Teachers Visit San José," *New Mexico School Review* 13(Mar. 1934):25; "De Baca Teachers Visit San José," *New Mexico School Review* 13(Apr. 1934):18; "Conference on Education, Santa Fe," *New Mexico School Review*

14(Sept. 1934):12; "Valencia County Rural Schools," *New Mexico School Review* 15(Mar. 1936):16; "With the State Department of Education," *New Mexico School Review* 16(Oct. 1936):22.

64. Reynolds, *The Education of Spanish-Speaking Children*, 29.

65. "Preliminary Report for the First Four Years," n.p.

66. "State Curriculum Revision," *New Mexico School Review* 14(Apr. 1935):14; *Report of the State Superintendent of Public Instruction for the Thirteenth Biennium Period Beginning July 1, 1934 and Ending June 30, 1936* (Santa Fe: State Superintendent of Public Instruction, 1936), 31; H. R. Rodgers to Leo M. Favrot, 23 December 1935, and L. S. Tireman to Leo M. Favrot, 27 January 1936, in NM2, Curriculum Revision, Rural Elementary Schools, 1935-40, Box 100, Folder 902, Ser. 1.1, GEB

67. Loyd S. Tireman to Leo M. Favrot, 27 January 1936, and L. S. Tireman to Leo M. Favrot, 14 March 1936, in NM2, Box 100, Folder 902, Ser. 1.1, GEB; and New Mexico State Board of Education, Minutes, February 14, 1938, NMSRCA.

68. Loyd S. Tireman to Leo M. Favrot, 2 June 1939, in NM2, Box 100, Folder 902, Ser. 1.1, GEB.

69. *Santa Fe New Mexican*, 15 February 1938; *Report of the State Superintendent of Public Instruction . . . 1936*, 31-32; and *Report of the State Superintendent of Public Instruction for the Fourteenth Biennium Period Beginning July 1, 1936 and Ending June 30, 1938* (Santa Fe: State Superintendent of Public Instruction, 1938), 31.

70. *Report of the State Superintendent of Public Instruction . . . 1938*, 17-18.

71. Ibid., 20.

72. Loyd S. Tireman to Leo M. Favrot, 2 June 1939; and memo of interview, Jackson Davis and L. S. Tireman, 3 September 1940, in NM2, Box 100, Folder 902, Ser. 1.1, GEB.

73. Grace Corrigan to Leo M. Favrot, 21 June 1939, and A. R. Mann to Grace Corrigan, 7 July 1939, in NM2, Box 100, Folder 902, Ser. 1.1, GEB.

74. Untitled report attached to letter, Grace J. Corrigan to W. W. Brierly, 10 November 1939, in NM2, Box 100, Folder 902, Ser. 1.1, GEB; and Grace J. Corrigan, "Handbook of Essentials in Language Arts," *Bulletin Issued by the Curriculum Division of the State Department of Education*, 1942, in Exp. 51-1, Department of Education Papers, NMSRCA.

75. Georgia L. Lusk, "Curriculum Development in the Elementary Schools of New Mexico," New Mexico Department of Education, *Bulletin* 2, 1944, 320-30, in Exp. 50, Department of Education Papers, NMSRCA.

Chapter 5

1. On the educational programs of the New Deal, see Paula Fass, *Outside In: Minorities and the Transformation of American Education* (New York: Oxford University Press, 1989), 115-42; and David Tyack, Robert Lowe, and Elisabeth Hansot, *Public Schools in Hard Times: The Great Depression and Recent Years* (Cambridge, MA: Harvard University Press, 1984), 92-138. On the goals of the General Education Board, see Lynne Marie Getz, "Extending the Helping Hand to Hispanics: The Role of the General Education Board in New Mexico in the 1930s," *Teachers College Record* (Spring 1992):500-15.

2. Counts issued his famous exhortation at a meeting of the Progressive Education Association in February 1932. Tyack, Lowe, and Hansot, *Public Schools in Hard Times*, 18-21.

3. W. Fred Totten and Frank J. Manley, *The Community School: Basic Concepts, Function, and Organization* (Galien, MI: Allied Educational Council, 1969), 16-17.

4. Loyd S. Tireman, "First Annual Report of the San José Training School," 1931, 14, in 1033.1, Box 599, Folder 6361, Ser. 1.4, GEB.
5. L. S. Tireman, "Mi Amigo el Hispano," 5, 1033.1, Box 599, Folder 6361, GEB.
6. Ibid., 7-8.
7. Ibid., 7.
8. L. S. Tireman, *Teaching Spanish-Speaking Children* (Albuquerque: University of New Mexico Press, 1948), 194.
9. Tireman, "Mi Amigo el Hispano," 9.
10. Anita Dominguez Chavez, interview with Erlinda Gonzales-Berry, 24 June 1993, "And Gladly Did We Teach: Gender, Culture, and Educational Policy in New Mexico, 1910-1940," Oral History Program, Center for Southwest Research, University of New Mexico (hereafter OHPUNM).
11. Mary Sanchez, interview with Erlinda Gonzales-Berry, 20 March 1992, OHPUNM.
12. Dora Vásquez Chacón, interview with Erlinda Gonzales-Berry, 18 March 1992, OHPUNM.
13. Ibid.
14. L. S. Tireman to James F. Zimmerman, 28 January 1931, Departments—Education File, Box 1, University Secretary Record Group, Special Collections, Zimmerman Library, UNM.
15. Loyd S. Tireman, "Report to the Board of Directors," October 1930, in 1033.1, UNM School of Education—Reports and Pamphlets, Box 599, Folder 6361, Ser. 1.4, GEB.
16. Marie M. Hughes, "The County Extension Program of the San José Project," [1933], in 1033.1, Box 599, Folder 6361, Ser. 1.4, GEB.
17. Tireman, "First Annual Report of the San José Training School," 1931, 22.
18. Leo M. Favrot, "Inspection of San José Training School, Albuquerque, New Mexico," October 1932, in 1033.1, UNM School of Education, 1929-1936, Box 598, 6358, Ser. 1.4, GEB.
19. Jennie Gonzales, "What I Hope to Accomplish: Address Given at the Rural Section of the New Mexico Educational Association," 2 November 1932, 2, 5, in 1033.1, Box 599, Folder 6361, Ser. 1.4, GEB.
20. Ibid., 8-10.
21. Ibid., 2, 4, 6, 9.
22. Ibid., 8-10.
23. "Mrs. Gonzalez Appointed State Rural School Supervisor," *New Mexico School Review* 14(Jan. 1935):15.
24. Loyd S. Tireman, "Introduction" to Hughes, "The County Extension Program," [1933].
25. Hughes, "The County Extension Program," n.p.
26. Loyd S. Tireman to Leo M. Favrot, 16 June 1933, in 1033.1, Box 598, Folder 6358, Ser. 1.4, GEB.
27. Donald Mackay, "Rural Education," 13(Oct. 1933):27.
28. *Report of the State Superintendent of Public Instruction for the Twelfth Biennium Period Beginning July 1, 1932 and Ending June 30, 1934* (Las Vegas, NM: Optic Publishing Co., 1934), 22.
29. "Nuevo Método de Preparación para los Alumnos Hispanos," *La Bandera Americana*, 25 July 1930.
30. Virginia Gonzáles, interview with Erlinda Gonzales-Berry 10 December 1994, OHPUNM.

31. Ruth Miller Martinez, "Taos County Rural Schools, 1938-39: Suggestions to Teachers No. 4—Supplementing Suggestions No. 3," pamphlet in Nina Otero-Warren Papers, Bergere Family Papers #43, NMSRCA. Emphasis in original.
32. Ibid., 1.
33. Ibid., 2-5.
34. *Taos Review*, 29 September 1938.
35. *Taos Review*, 2 March 1939.
36. Loyd S. Tireman to Leo M. Favrot, 29 April 1937, in 1033.1, Box 599, Folder 6359, Ser. 1.4, GEB; Cyrus McCormick to James F. Zimmerman, 29 April 1937, Mr. and Mrs. Cyrus McCormick File, University Secretary Record Group, Box 10, UNM.
37. "University of New Mexico: Project for Improving Instruction of Spanish-Speaking Children in the Public Schools of the State-Appraisal," 1938, 4, in 1033.1, UNM School of Education, 1937-1940, Box 599, Folder 6359, Ser. 1.4, GEB.
38. Loyd S. Tireman, "Proposed Reorganization of the San José Project," 4 May 1937, 3, in 1033.1, Box 599, Folder 6359, Ser. 1.4, GEB.
39. L. S. Tireman and Mary Watson, *A Community School in a Spanish-Speaking Village* (Albuquerque: University of New Mexico Press, 1948), 1-8.
40. Ibid., 11.
41. Rita Carabajal Apodaca, "The Nambé Community School (1937-1942): A Study of a Community-Relevant Curriculum," (Ph.D. diss., University of New Mexico, 1986), 56.
42. Cyrus McCormick to L. S. Tireman, 13 April 1938, in 1033.1, Box 599, Folder 6359, Ser. 1.4, GEB.
43. L. S. Tireman, "Nambé . . . A Community School," 1939, 8, pamphlet in 1033.1, School of Education, Reports and Pamphlets, Box 599, Folder 6361, Ser. 1.4, GEB.
44. Ibid., 8-9.
45. Apodaca, "Nambé Community School," 62, 66-67
46. Florence McCormick to James F. Zimmerman, 4 June 1940, Mr. and Mrs. Cyrus McCormick File, Box 10, University Secretary Record Group, UNM.
47. Tireman and Watson, *A Community School*, 23, 50.
48. Ibid., 53-57.
49. Ibid., 163-64.
50. Apodaca, "Nambé Community School," 206-7.
51. Teachers' Diaries, Nambé Project, 1937-38, UNM Department of Special Education Collection, #306, Box # 5, UNM.
52. Teachers' Diaries, Nambé Project, 1937-38, #306, Box #5, UNM.
53. Teachers' Diaries, Nambé Project, 1937-38, #306, Box #5, UNM.
54. Tireman and Watson, *A Community School*, 123-28.
55. Jackson Davis, "Nambé Demonstration School," Field Report, 3 September 1940, in 1033.1, Box 599, Folder 6359, Ser. 1.4, GEB.
56. David L. Bachelor, *Educational Reform in New Mexico: Tireman, San José, and Nambé* (Albuquerque: University of New Mexico Press, 1991), 97.
57. Apodaca, "Nambé Community School," 176-78.
58. Bachelor, *Educational Reform*, 180.
59. Tireman and Watson, *A Community School*, 20.
60. Apodaca, "Nambé Community School," 166.
61. According to David Bachelor, Tireman "tended to treat women in a manner that in contemporary terms could be labeled sexist." Bachelor, *Educational Reform*, 142.
62. Davis, "Nambé Demonstration School," n.p.
63. "FMR, Interview with Prof. L. S. Tireman," 25 July 1940, 1033.1, Box 599, Folder 6359, GEB.

Chapter 6

1. On the impact of the New Deal in New Mexico, see Sandra Schackel, *Social Housekeepers: Women Shaping Public Policy in New Mexico, 1920-1940* (Albuquerque: University of New Mexico Press, 1992), 141-62; Sarah Deutsch, *No Separate Refuge: Culture, Class and Gender on an Anglo-Hispanic Frontier in the American Southwest, 1880-1940* (New York: Oxford University Press, 1987), 162-99; and Suzanne Forrest, *The Preservation of the Village: New Mexico's Hispanics and the New Deal* (Albuquerque: University of New Mexico Press, 1989).

2. David Tyack, Robert Lowe, and Elisabeth Hansot, *Public Schools in Hard Times: The Great Depression and Recent Years* (Cambridge, MA: Harvard University Press, 1984), 103-4; and Paula S. Fass, *Outside In: Minorities and the Transformation of American Education* (New York: Oxford University Press, 1989), 116-39.

3. See Anthony J. Badger, *The New Deal: The Depression Years, 1933-1940* (New York: Hill and Wang, 1989), 306-9. Badger argues that localism undermined and constrained New Deal programs; he believes that the New Deal did not achieve its major goals, because it failed to implement centralized federal authority in the states.

4. George I. Sánchez, "School Census Distribution in N.M. for 1931," *New Mexico School Review* 11(Jan. 1932):18-19; *Report of the State Superintendent of Public Instruction for the Twelfth Biennium Period Beginning July 1, 1932 and Ending June 30, 1934* (Santa Fe: State Superintendent of Public Instruction, 1934), 13-14, 16-17; *Report of the State Superintendent of Public Instruction For the Fourteenth Biennium Period Beginning July 1, 1936 and Ending June 30, 1938* (Santa Fe: State Superintendent of Public Instruction, 1938), 12-14. Statistics on the number of Hispano pupils for the year 1937-38 were not available.

5. G. L. Fenlon, "The Financial Crisis in the Schools," *New Mexico School Review* 13(Nov. 1933):12-15.

6. Schackel, *Social Housekeepers*, 142-44; and "Préstamos Gran Ayuda a Escuelas," *La Bandera Americana*, 1 Feb. 1934.

7. Forrest, *Preservation of the Village*, 107.

8. The political corruption that plagued many New Deal programs unintentionally harmed the public schools on occasion. In 1935 Democratic Governor Clyde Tingley angered educators—including George Sánchez and the NMEA—when he diverted money earmarked for schools into accounts for matching FERA money. Federal inspectors frequently made the trip to New Mexico to investigate complaints that relief jobs had gone for patronage or some other accusation. See *Santa Fe New Mexican*, 15-25 Jan. 1935, 15 Mar. 1935, 21 June 1935, 29 Oct. 1936; George I. Sánchez to Governor Clyde Tingley, 25 July 1935; Memorandum, undated; and Governor Clyde Tingley to George I. Sánchez, 10 Aug. 1935, in Supt. of Public Instruction File, Governor Clyde Tingley Papers, 1935-38, NMSRCA.

9. Governor Clyde Tingley to Carey Holbrook, 17 July 1935, and Will W. Alexander to Governor Clyde Tingley, 30 July 1935, in WPA Administration—Correspondence, 1935, Governor Clyde Tingley Papers, NMSRCA; Santa Fe New Mexican, 27 June 1935.

10. *La Bandera Americana*, 8 Aug. 1935.

11. "Report and General Survey of the Public School Buildings in Mora County, New Mexico," in Special Reports, 1935, Governor Clyde Tingley Papers, NMSRCA.

12. Floyd Santisteven to Governor Clyde Tingley, 29 July 1935, WPA Correspondence, 1935, Governor Clyde Tingley Papers, NMSRCA.

13. Lea Rowland to Col. F. C. Harrington, 5 Mar. 1937, in New Mexico—Schools,

January 1939–February 1944, WPA—State Series, Record Group 69, National Archives, Washington, D.C. (hereafter NA); and *Santa Fe New Mexican*, 1 Apr. 1940.

14. Works Progress Administration, "Proposed Scope of the Emergency Education Program in the Works Progress Administration," Bulletin #19, 25 July 1935, 1, in WPA Correspondence, 1935, Governor Clyde Tingley Papers, NMSRCA.

15. Ibid., 4–9.

16. "La Importancia de la Educación," *La Bandera Americana*, 4 Oct. 1934; "Un Buen Hecho," *La Bandera Americana*, 21 Mar. 1935; and "Educational Relief Projects Restored," *Santa Fe New Mexican* 21 June 1935.

17. María E. Montoya, "The Roots of Economic and Ethnic Divisions in Northern New Mexico: The Case of the Civilian Conservation Corps," *Western Historical Quarterly* 26(Spring 1995):21–25.

18. Rio Arriba Sub-District Educational Advisers Association, "Minutes of Meeting," 25 August 1936, in WPA—Education—#151, NMSRCA.

19. Nina Otero-Warren, "Program for Literacy Classes," report to Tom L. Popejoy, State Director of Adult Education, 1936, Folder #49, Bergere Family Collection, NMSRCA; Nina Otero-Warren to President James F. Zimmerman, 31 May 1938, in Board of Regents—WPA, 1936–40, Box 6, University Secretary Record Group, Special Collections, Zimmerman Library, UNM; and Nina Otero-Warren to Dr. Mildred Wiese, Specialist, Curriculum and Teacher Education WPA, 14 Mar. 1939, in Adult Education—New Mexico—1939, 651.341, WPA State Series, RG 69, NA.

20. Nina Otero-Warren, "Accomplishments in Elimination of Illiteracy in New Mexico, up to June 1st, 1939," 3, in Education and Retraining Program, 1935–39, 651.34, WPA State Series, RG 69, NA.

21. Forrest, *Preservation of the Village*, 47–55, 70–72, 88–90.

22. "Let's Keep It New Mexico, Is Eloquent Plea of Lea Rowland," *Santa Fe New Mexican* 8 Jan. 1937.

23. James F. Zimmerman to President H. L. Kent, New Mexico State College, 21 Feb. 1933, in Brice Sewell File, Box 15, University Secretary Record Group, UNM.

24. Mary Austin to Governor Arthur Seligman, 28 Jan. 1933, in State Department of Education, Governor Arthur Seligman Papers, NMSRCA.

25. Brice H. Sewell, "Why Vocational Education?" *New Mexico School Review* 14(Feb. 1935):6; and Brice H. Sewell to Governor Clyde Tingley, 2 June 1937, in Department of Vocational Education File, Governor Clyde Tingley Papers, NMSRCA.

26. Brice Sewell, "Vocational Education: Do You Know?" *New Mexico School Review* 12(May 1933):23.

27. *Report of the State Superintendent, . . . 1934*, 38.

28. Manuel Lujan, "Santa Fe County Rural Schools," *New Mexico School Review* 14(Sept. 1935):14.

29. "Espanola School News, 1936–37," *New Mexico School Review* 16(Mar. 1937):27.

30. *Report of the Superintendent of Public Instruction . . . 1938*, 33.

31. Brice Sewell, "Vocational Education Adjusts Its Program to Meet the Needs of Industry," *New Mexico School Review* 17(Feb. 1938):26.

32. Sewell, "Vocational Education," 22; and Sewell, "Why Vocational Education?" 7.

33. "Miss Zelpha Bates Assumes Home Economics Supervisory Work," *New Mexico School Review* 12(Oct. 1932):25.

34. Zelpha Bates, "The Practical Value of Training in Homemaking," *New Mexico School Review* 14(Feb. 1935):15.

35. "First Cultural Center to Open Saturday in Taos," *Santa Fe New Mexican*, 15 May 1935.

36. "State Conference on Adult Education, June 28–29, 1935," *University of New Mexico Bulletin*, Education Series 9(1935):27–28.

37. Brice H. Sewell, "A New Type of School," *New Mexico School Review* 14(Oct. 1935):49–50; and "218 Men Here Live by Weaving," *Santa Fe New Mexican*, 3 Jan. 1936.

38. Cleofas Jaramillo, quoted by Genaro M. Padilla, *My History, Not Yours: The Formation of Mexican American Autobiography* (Madison: University of Wisconsin Press, 1993), 196.

39. "Hispanic Folklore Society to Help Get People in Costume," *Santa Fe New Mexican*, 21 June 1935.

40. Virginia K. Whitney and Josephine Koogler, *Women in Education: New Mexico* (Wichita Falls, TX: Nortex, 1977), 44–45.

41. Aurora Lucero-White, "Folkcultural Program Instituted by the Department of Education," *Report of the State Superintendent of Public Instruction . . . 1934*, 21.

42. Ibid., 21.

43. "Pojoaque School to Present Folk Play of Guadalupe Virgin Sunday, Reviving the Old Lore of Valley," *Santa Fe New Mexican*, 10 Dec. 1938.

44. "Spanish-Colonial Arts to Be Preserved According to Plans of 40 Persons at the Curtins'," *Santa Fe New Mexican*, 11 Feb. 1938.

45. Brice H. Sewell, "New Los Lunas Vocational School Building," *New Mexico School Review* 15(Jan. 1936):6.

46. Forrest, *Preservation of the Village*, 121; and Bruno David Ussher, "Federal Music Project, Region V: Report on New Mexico," 11 Aug. 1936, Cultural Projects, 1942–43, 651.311, WPA State Series, RG 69, NA.

47. Bruno David Ussher, "Report of W.P.A. Federal Music Project for New Mexico," 3 June 1936, Cultural Projects, 1942–43, 651.311, WPA State Series, RG 69, NA.

48. Ussher, "Federal Music Project, Region V: Report," 11 Aug. 1936.

49. Mrs. Alec Brown to David Bruno Ussher, 9 June 1936, Cultural Projects, 1942–43, 651.311, WPA State Series, RG 69, NA.

50. T. P. Gallagher to Bruno David Ussher, 9 June 1936, Cultural Projects, 1942–43, 651.311, WPA State Series, RG 69, NA.

51. Forrest, *Preservation of the Village*, 115–16.

52. "New Mexico Youthogram," May 1937, 8, in Publications—New Mexico, Box 112, National Youth Administration, Record Group 119, NA.

53. Ibid., 10.

54. "New Mexico Youthogram," August 1937, 2, 5, in Publications—New Mexico, Box 112, NYA, Record Group 119, NA.

55. Charlotte Whaley, *Nina Otero-Warren of Santa Fe* (Albuquerque: University of New Mexico Press, 1994), 144.

56. "New Mexico Youthogram," August 1937, 3, and "New Mexico Youthogram," September 1936, 3, in Publications—New Mexico, Box 112, NYA, Record Group 119, NA.

57. L. R. Alderman to James J. Connelly, 13 Nov. 1940; and Nina Otero-Warren to Isabel L. Eckles, 19 Sept. 1940, in Family Life Education—New Mexico, 651.3142, WPA State Series, RG 69, NA.

58. Nina Otero-Warren, "My Work on the Island: An Account of the WPA Adult Education and Public School Projects in Puerto Rico," 1941, Folder #54, Bergere Family Collection, NMSRCA.

59. R. Flores, "Let Us Win Friendship through Language," 1942, in Spanish Teaching, 1941–42, 211.45, WPA, RG 69, NA.

60. Mrs. Florence Kerr to James J. Connelly, 20 Feb. 1942; and Isabel Lancaster Eckles to Mrs. Florence Kerr, 24 Feb. 1942, in Spanish Teaching, 1942–43, 651.3145, WPA State Series, RG 69, NA.

61. "La Educación en los Distritos Rurales," *La Bandera Americana* 16 May 1930; and "Regreso a la Escuela," *La Bandera Americana* 4 Sept. 1931.

Conclusion

1. On educational patterns in California and Texas that influenced New Mexico, see Lynne Marie Getz, "Progressive Ideas for New Mexico: Educating the Spanish-Speaking Child in New Mexico in the 1920s and 30s" (Ph.D. diss., University of Washington, 1989), 173–209.

2. W. E. B. DuBois, *The Souls of Black Folk* (New York: Bantam, 1989), 66.

3. Ibid., 72–74.

4. Ibid., 76.

5. Walter Feinberg, *Reason and Rhetoric: The Intellectual Foundations of 20th Century Liberal Educational Policy* (New York: John Wiley & Sons, 1975), 109–11.

6. Paula Fass, *Outside In: Minorities and the Transformation of American Education* (Oxford University Press, 1989), 66–68.

Bibliography

I. Manuscript Collections

Abbreviations:

NA	National Archives, Washington, DC.
NMSRCA	New Mexico State Records Center and Archives, Santa Fe.
NMSU	Rio Grande Historical Collections, New Mexico State University, Las Cruces.
UNM	Special Collections, Zimmerman Library, University of New Mexico, Albuquerque.

Bergere Family Papers. NMSRCA.
Chaves, Jose Felipe. Papers. UNM.
de Baca, Governor Ezquiel. Papers. NMSRCA.
Dillon, Governor R. C. Papers. NMSRCA.
García, Fabian. Papers. NMSU.
General Education Board Papers. Rockefeller Archives Center, Pocantico Hills, New York.
Hadley, Hiram. Papers. NMSU.
Hannett, Governor Arthur T. Papers. NMSRCA.
Hinkle, Governor James F. Papers. NMSRCA.
Hockenhull, Governor A. W.. Papers. NMSRCA.
Larrazolo, Governor Octaviano A. Papers. NMSRCA.
Las Cruces Public Schools (Ward School). Collection. NMSU.
McDonald, Governor William. Papers. NMSRCA.
Mechem, Governor Merritt C. Papers. NMSRCA.
Miles, Governor John. Papers. NMSRCA.
Miller, Ruth. Papers. UNM.
National Youth Administration. Record Group 119. NA.
New Mexico, State Board of Education. Minutes. NMSRCA.
New Mexico, State Department of Education. Papers. NMSRCA.
New Mexico, Territorial Archives. NMSRCA.
Ortiz y Pino, Concha. Papers. UNM.
Page, Richard M. Papers. UNM.
Ritch, W. G. Collection. Microfilm. UNM.
Seligman, Governor Arthur. Papers. NMSRCA.
Tingley, Governor Clyde. Papers. NMSRCA.

University of New Mexico, Department of Education. Teachers' Diaries from San Jose and Nambé Schools. UNM.
University of New Mexico, University Secretary Records Group. UNM.
Vigil, Donaciano. Papers. NMSRCA.
Women in New Mexico. Vertical Files. UNM.
Woodward, Dorothy. Papers. NMSRCA.
Works Progress Administration. Record Group 69. NA.
Works Project Administration. Writers' Project. NMSRCA.

II. Oral History

"And Gladly Did We Teach: Gender, Culture, and Educational Policy in New Mexico, 1910–1940." Project directors: Erlinda Gonzales-Berry and Tey Diana Rebolleda. Oral History Program, Center for Southwest Research, University of New Mexico.

III. Newspapers

Albuquerque [Morning] Democrat
Albuquerque Journal
Albuquerque Tribune
La Bandera Americana
El Eco del Río Grande
El Eco del Valle
Las Vegas Daily Optic
New Mexico Independent
New Mexico State Record
New Mexico State Tribune
La Revista de Taos
Santa Fe [Daily] New Mexican
Taos Review

IV. Books

Acuña, Rodolfo. *Occupied America: The Chicano's Struggle toward Liberation.* San Francisco: Canfield Press, 1972.
Anderson, James D. *The Education of Blacks in the South, 1860–1935.* Chapel Hill: University of North Carolina Press, 1988.
Armstrong, Patricia Cadigan. *A Portrait of Bronson Cutting through His Papers, 1910–1927.* Albuquerque: University of New Mexico, 1959.
Arsenian, Seth. *Bilingualism and Mental Development: A Study of the Intelligence and the Social Background of Bilingual Children in New York City.* New York: Teachers College, Columbia University, 1937.
Bachelor, David L. *Educational Reform in New Mexico: Tireman, San José, and Nambé.* Albuquerque: University of New Mexico Press, 1991.
Badger, Anthony J. *The New Deal: The Depression Years, 1933–1940.* New York: Hill and Wang, 1989.
Bagley, William C. *Report on the New Mexico State Educational Institutions to the*

New Mexico Special Revenue Commission. Santa Fe: New Mexican Publishing Corp., 1921.

Bagley, William C., and George C. Kyte. *The California Curriculum Study.* Berkeley: University of California Press, 1926.

Bancroft, Hubert Howe. *History of Arizona and New Mexico, 1530–1888.* Albuquerque: Horn & Wallace, 1962.

Bannister, Robert C. *Sociology and Scientism: The American Quest for Objectivity, 1880–1940.* Chapel Hill: University of North Carolina Press, 1987.

Baur, John E. *Growing Up with California: A History of California's Children.* Los Angeles: Will Kramer, 1978.

Beck, Warren A. *New Mexico: A History of Four Centuries.* Norman: University of Oklahoma Press, 1962.

Bobbitt, J. Franklin. *Curriculum-Making in Los Angeles.* Chicago: University of Chicago Press, 1922.

———. *The San Antonio Public School System: A Survey.* San Antonio: San Antonio School Board, 1915.

Bogardus, Emory. *The Mexican in the United States.* Los Angeles: University of Southern California, School of Research Studies, 1934.

Borrego, Eva R. *Teaching English as a Foreign Language to Children: First Three Grades.* Ph.D. diss., Catholic University, 1968; reprint ed., San Francisco: R and E Research Associates, 1974.

Brigham, Carl C. *A Study of American Intelligence.* Princeton, NJ: Princeton University Press, 1923.

Cabeza de Baca, Fabiola. *We Fed Them Cactus.* Albuquerque: University of New Mexico Press, 1954.

Callahan, Raymond E. *Education and the Cult of Efficiency: A Study of the Social Forces That Have Shaped the Administration of the Public Schools.* Chicago: University of Chicago Press, 1962.

Camarillo, Albert. *Chicanos in California: A History of Mexican-Americans in California.* San Francisco: Boyd & Fraser Publishing Co., 1984.

Cardoso, Lawrence A. *Mexican Emigration to the United States, 1897–1931.* Tucson: University of Arizona Press, 1980.

Carlson, Robert A. *The Americanization Syndrome: A Quest for Conformity.* London: Croom Helm, 1987.

Carter, Thomas P. *Mexican Americans in School: A History of Educational Neglect.* Princeton, NJ: College Entrance Examination Board, 1970.

Chávez, John R. *The Lost Land: The Chicano Image of the Southwest.* Albuquerque: University of New Mexico Press, 1984.

Church, Robert L., and Michael W. Sedlak. *Education in the United States: An Interpretive History.* New York: Vintage Books, 1961.

Clark, Kenneth B. *Prejudice and Your Child.* 2d ed. Boston: Beacon Press, 1963.

Cohen, Sol, ed. *Education in the United States: A Documentary History.* New York: Random House, 1974.

Coleman, Algernon. *English Teaching in the Southwest: Organization and Materials for Instructing Spanish-Speaking Children.* Washington, DC: American Council on Education, 1940.

Cravens, Hamilton. *The Triumph of Evolution: American Scientists and the Heredity-*

Environment Controversy, 1900–1941. Philadelphia: University of Pennsylvania Press, 1978.
Cremin, Lawrence A. *American Education: The Metropolitan Experience, 1876–1980*. New York: Harper & Row, 1988.
———. *American Education: The National Experience, 1783–1876*. New York: Harper & Row, 1980.
———. *The Transformation of the Schools: Progressivism in American Education, 1876–1957*. New York: Vintage Books, 1961.
Crunden, Robert M. *From Self to Society, 1919–1941*. Englewood Cliffs, NJ: Prentice Hall, 1972.
———. *Ministers of Reform: The Progressives' Achievement in American Civilization, 1889–1920*. New York: Basic Books, 1982.
Curti, Merle. *The Social Ideas of American Educators* Totowa, NJ: Littlefield, Adams & Co., 1978.
Davis, Philip, ed. *Immigration and Americanization*. Boston: Ginn and Co., 1920.
Davis, W. W. H. *El Gringo: New Mexico and Her People*. Lincoln: University of Nebraska Press, 1982.
Deutsch, Sarah. *No Separate Refuge: Culture, Class and Gender on an Anglo-Hispanic Frontier in the American Southwest, 1880–1940*. New York: Oxford University Press, 1987.
Dewey, John. *Democracy and Education: An Introduction to the Philosophy of Education*. New York: The Macmillan Co., 1916.
———. *The School and Society*. Chicago: University of Chicago Press, 1900.
Divine, Robert A. *American Immigration Policy, 1924–52*. New Haven: Yale University Press, 1957.
DuBois, W. E. B. *The Souls of Black Folk*. New York: Bantam, 1989.
Eby, Frederick. *The Development of Education in Texas*. New York: The Macmillan Company, 1925.
Ehrlich, Paul R., and S. Shirley Feldman. *The Race Bomb: Skin Color, Prejudice and Intelligence*. New York: Quadrangle Books, 1969.
Elsasser, Nan, Kyle MacKenzie, and Yvonne Tixier y Vigil. *Las Mujeres: Conversations from a Hispanic Community*. Old Westbury, N.Y.: The Feminist Press, 1980.
Falk, Charles J. *The Development and Organization of Education in California*. New York: Harcourt, Brace & World, 1968.
Fass, Paula. *Outside In: Minorities and the Transformation of American Education*. New York: Oxford University Press, 1989.
Feinberg, Walter. *Reason and Rhetoric: The Intellectual Foundations of 20th Century Liberal Educational Policy*. New York: John Wiley & Sons, 1975.
Fincher, E. B. *Spanish-Americans as a Political Factor in New Mexico, 1912–1950*. Ph.D diss., New York University, 1950; reprint ed., New York: Arno Press, 1974.
Flores, Zella K. Jordan. *The Relation of Language Difficulty to Intelligence and School Retardation in a Group of Spanish-Speaking Children*. Ph.D. diss., University of Chicago, 1926; reprint ed., San Francisco: R & E Research Associates, 1975.
Foley, Douglas E., Clarice Mota, Donald E. Post, and Ignacio Lozano. *From Peones to Politicos: Class and Ethnicity in a South Texas Town, 1900–1987*. Austin: University of Texas Press, 1988.
Forrest, Suzanne. *The Preservation of the Village: New Mexico's Hispanics and the New Deal*. Albuquerque: University of New Mexico Press, 1989.

Fosdick, Raymond B. *Adventure in Giving: The Story of the General Education Board.* New York: Harper & Row, 1962.
Fuller, Wayne E. *The Old Country School: The Story of Rural Education in the Middle West.* Chicago: University of Chicago Press, 1982.
Gallegos, Bernardo P. *Literacy, Education, and Society in New Mexico, 1693-1821.* Albuquerque: University of New Mexico Press, 1992.
Gamio, Manuel. *Mexican Immigration to the United States: A Study of Human Migration and Adjustment.* New York: Dover, 1971.
———. *The Mexican Immigrant: His Life Story.* Chicago: University of Chicago Press, 1931.
García, Mario T. *Desert Immigrants: The Mexicans of El Paso, 1880-1920.* New Haven: Yale University Press, 1981.
———. *Mexican Americans: Leadership, Ideology, & Identity, 1930-1960.* New Haven: Yale University Press, 1989.
Gibson, Arrell Morgan. *The Santa Fe and Taos Colonies: Age of the Muses, 1900-1942.* Norman: University of Oklahoma Press, 1983.
Gonzalez, Gilbert G. *Chicano Education in the Era of Segregation.* Philadelphia: Balch Institute Press, 1990.
———. *Progressive Education: A Marxist Interpretation.* Minneapolis: Marxist Educational Press, 1982.
González, Nancie L. *The Spanish-Americans of New Mexico: A Heritage of Pride.* Albuquerque: University of New Mexico Press, 1967.
Gordon, Lynn. *Gender and Higher Education in the Progressive Era.* New Haven: Yale University Press, 1990.
Gossett, Thomas F. *Race: The History of an Idea in America.* New York: Schocken Books, 1963.
Greer, Colin. *The Great School Legend: A Revisionist's Interpretation of American Education.* New York: Basic Books, 1972.
Gregg, Josiah. *Commerce of the Prairies.* Ann Arbor, MI: University Microfilms, 1966.
Gribble, Stephen C. *Teacher Qualifications and School Attendance in New Mexico, 1918-1946.* Albuquerque: University of New Mexico Press, 1948.
Griswold del Castillo, Richard. *La Familia: Chicano Families in the Urban Southwest, 1848 to the Present.* Notre Dame, IN: University of Notre Dame Press, 1984.
Gutiérrez, Ramón A. *When Jesus Came, The Corn Mothers Went Away: Marriage, Sexuality, and Power in New Mexico, 1500-1846.* Stanford, CA: Stanford University Press, 1991.
Gutman, Herbert H., ed. *Work, Culture and Society in Industrializing America.* New York: Vintage, 1977.
Hadley, Anna R., Carolin H. Allen, and C. Frank Allen. *Hiram Hadley.* Boston: The Authors, 1924.
Hartmann, Edward G. *The Movement to Americanize the Immigrant.* New York: Columbia University Press, 1948.
Higham, John. *Strangers in the Land: Patterns of American Nativism, 1860-1925.* New York: Atheneum Press, 1965.
Hofstadter, Richard. *The Age of Reform.* New York: Vintage Books, 1955.
———. *Anti-Intellectualism in American Life.* New York: Vintage Books, 1962.
Hood, E. Lyman. *The New West Education Commission, 1880-1893.* Jacksonville, FL: H. & W. B. Drew Co., 1905.

Horgan, Paul. *Lamy of Santa Fe: His Life and Times*. New York: Farrar, Straus and Giroux, 1975.
Horn, Calvin. *New Mexico's Troubled Years: The Story of the Early Territorial Governors*. Albuquerque: Horn & Wallace, 1963.
Horsman, Reginald. *Race and Manifest Destiny: The Origins of American Racial Anglo-Saxonism*. Cambridge, MA: Harvard University Press, 1981.
Hughes, Marie M. *Teaching a Standard English Vocabulary with Initial Reading Instruction*. Las Cruces, NM: Bronson Printing Company, 1932.
Jensen, Joan M., and Darlis A. Miller, eds. *New Mexico Women: Intercultural Perspectives*. Albuquerque: University of New Mexico Press, 1986.
Johnson, Leighton H. *Development of the Central State Agency for Public Education in California, 1849-1949*. Albuquerque: University of New Mexico Press, 1952.
Jones, Maldwyn A. *American Immigration*. Chicago: University of Chicago Press, 1960.
Kaestle, Carl E. *Pillars of the Republic: Common Schools and American Society, 1780-1860*. New York: Hill and Wang, 1983.
Kamin, Leon J. *The Science and Politics of I.Q.* New York: John Wiley & Sons, 1974.
Kantor, Harvey, and David B. Tyack, eds. *Work, Youth and Schooling*. Stanford, CA: Stanford University Press, 1982.
Karier, Clarence. *The Individual, Society and Education: A History of American Educational Ideas*. 2d ed. Urbana: University of Illinois, 1986.
Karier, Clarence, comp. *Shaping the American Educational State, 1900 to the Present*. New York: The Free Press, 1975.
Keefe, Susan E., and Amado M. Padilla. *Chicano Ethnicity*. Albuquerque: University of New Mexico Press, 1987.
Keleher, William A. *New Mexicans I Knew: Memoirs, 1892-1969*. Albuquerque: University of New Mexico Press, 1983.
Kennedy, David M. *Over Here: The First World War and American Society*. New York: Oxford University Press, 1980.
Kettleborough, Charles, comp. and ed. *The State Constitutions*. Indianapolis: B. F. Bowen, 1918.
Kloss, Heinz. *The American Bilingual Tradition*. Rowley, MA: Newbury House, 1977.
Kluckhohn, Florence. *Variations in Value Orientations*. Evanston, IL: Row, Peterson, 1961.
La Farge, Oliver. *Santa Fe: The Autobiography of a Southwestern Town*. Norman: University of Oklahoma Press, 1959.
Lamar, Howard R. *The Far Southwest, 1846-1912*. New Haven: Yale University Press, 1966.
Larson, Robert W. *New Mexico's Quest for Statehood, 1846-1912*. Albuquerque: University of New Mexico Press, 1968.
Lavender, David. *The Southwest*. Albuquerque: University of New Mexico Press, 1980.
Leibowitz, Arnold H. *Educational Policy and Political Acceptance: The Imposition of English as the Language of Instruction in American Schools*. Washington, DC: ERIC Clearinghouse for Linguistics, Center for Applied Linguistics, 1971.
Leonard, Olen, and C. P. Loomis. *Culture of a Contemporary Rural Community: El Cerrito, New Mexico*. Rural Life Studies 1. Washington, DC: U.S. Department of Agriculture, Bureau of Agricultural Economics, 1941.

Lopez, Thomas R. *Prospects for the Spanish American Culture of New Mexico.* San Francisco: R & E Research Associates, 1974.
Lowitt, Richard. *Bronson M. Cutting: Progressive Politician.* Albuquerque: University of New Mexico Press, 1992.
Lux, Guillermo. *Politics and Education in Hispanic New Mexico: From the Spanish American Normal School to the Northern New Mexico Community College.* El Rito and Espanola, NM: Northern New Mexico Community College, 1984.
Manuel, Herschel T. *Spanish-Speaking Children of the Southwest: Their Education and the Public Welfare.* Austin: University of Texas Press, 1965.
———. *The Education of Mexican and Spanish-Speaking Children in Texas.* Austin: University of Texas Press, 1930.
Mayhew, Katherine Camp, and Anna Camp Edwards. *The Dewey School: the Laboratory School of the University of Chicago, 1886–1903.* New York: D. Appleton-Century Co., 1936.
McCombs, Vernon M. *From Over the Border: A Study of the Mexicans in the United States.* New York: Missionary Education Movement, 1925.
McWilliams, Carey. *North From Mexico: The Spanish-Speaking People of the United States.* Philadelphia: J. B. Lippincott, 1949.
Meier, Matt S., and Feliciano Rivera. *The Chicanos: A History of Mexican Americans.* New York: Hill and Wang, 1972.
Meinig, Donald W. *The Southwest: Three Peoples in Geographical Change, 1600–1970.* New York: Oxford University Press, 1971.
Mirandé, Alfredo, and Evangelina Enríquez. *La Chicana: The Mexican American Woman.* Chicago: University of Chicago Press, 1979.
Murguía, Edward. *Assimilation, Colonialism and the Mexican American People.* Austin: University of Texas, Center for Mexican American Studies, 1975.
Nasaw, David. *Schooled to Order: A Social History of Public Schooling in the United States.* New York: Oxford University Press, 1979.
Nostrand, Richard L. *The Hispano Homeland.* Norman: University of Oklahoma Press, 1992.
Oakes, Jeannie. *Keeping Track: How Schools Structure Inequality.* New Haven: Yale University Press, 1985.
Ortiz y Pino III, José. *Don José: The Last Patrón.* Santa Fe: Sunstone, 1981.
Otero-Warren, Nina. *Old Spain in Our Southwest.* New York: Harcourt, Brace and Company, 1936.
Padilla, Genaro M. *My History, Not Yours: Mexican American Autobiography.* Madison: University of Wisconsin Press, 1993.
Parr, Eunice Elvira. *A Comparative Study of Mexican and American Children in the Schools of San Antonio, Texas.* Ph.D. diss., University of Chicago, 1926; reprint ed., San Francisco: R & E Research Associates, 1971.
Raftery, Judith Rosenberg. *Land of Fair Promise: Politics and Reform in Los Angeles Schools, 1885–1941.* Stanford, CA: Stanford University Press, 1992.
Ravitch, Diane. *The Revisionists Revised: A Critique of the Radical Attack on the Schools.* New York: Basic Books, 1978.
Reese, William J. *Power and the Promise of School Reform: Grassroots Movements During the Progressive Movement.* Boston: Routledge & Kegan Paul, 1986.
Reeves, Frank. *History of New Mexico.* 3 vols. New York: Lewis Historical, 1961.

Reisler, Mark. *By the Sweat of Their Brow: Mexican Immigrant Labor in the United States, 1900–1940.* Westport, CT: Greenwood Press, 1976.

Reynolds, Annie. *The Education of Spanish-Speaking Children in Five Southwestern States.* U.S. Department of the Interior, Office of Education, Bulletin 11. Washington, DC: U.S. Government Printing Office, 1933.

Rodriguez, Richard. *Hunger of Memory: The Education of Richard Rodriguez.* Boston: David R. Godine, 1982.

Romo, Ricardo. *East Los Angeles: History of a Barrio.* Austin: University of Texas Press, 1983.

Rosaldo, Renato, Robert A. Calvert, and Gustav L. Seligmann, eds. *Chicano: The Evolution of a People.* Minneapolis: Winston Press, 1973.

Ruiz, Vicki L., and Ellen Carol DuBois. *Unequal Sisters: A Multicultural Reader in U.S. Women's History.* 2d ed. New York: Routledge, 1994.

Samora, Julian, ed. *La Raza: Forgotten Americans.* Notre Dame, IN: University of Notre Dame Press, 1966.

San Miguel, Guadalupe, Jr. *"Let All of Them Take Heed": Mexican Americans and the Campaign for Educational Equality in Texas, 1910–1981.* Austin: University of Texas Press, 1987.

Sánchez, George I. *Forgotten People: A Study of New Mexicans.* Albuquerque: University of New Mexico Press, 1940; reprint ed. 1996.

Sánchez, George J. *Becoming Mexican American: Ethnicity, Culture and Identity in Chicano Los Angeles, 1900–1945.* Oxford, Eng.: Oxford University Press, 1993.

Schackel, Sandra. *Social Housekeepers: Women Shaping Public Policy in New Mexico, 1920–1940.* Albuquerque: University of New Mexico Press, 1991.

Schrieke, Bertram J. O. *Alien Americans: A Study of Race Relations.* New York: The Viking Press, 1936.

Seagoe, May V. *Terman and the Gifted.* Los Altos, CA: William Kaufmann, 1975.

Simmons, Marc. *The Little Lion of the Southwest: A Life of Manuel Antonio Chaves.* Chicago: Swallow Press, 1973.

———. *New Mexico: A Bicentennial History.* New York: W. W. Norton & Co., 1977.

Simmons, Ozzie G. *Anglo-Americans and Mexican Americans in South Texas.* Ph.D. diss., Harvard University, 1952; reprint ed.: New York: Arno Press, 1974.

Sokal, Michael M., ed. *Psychological Testing and American Society, 1890–1930.* New Brunswick: Rutgers University Press, 1987.

Spring, Joel. *Education and the Rise of the Corporate State.* Boston: Beacon Press, 1972.

Stineman, Esther Lanigan. *Mary Austin: Song of a Maverick.* New Haven: Yale University Press, 1989.

Stocking, George W., Jr. *Race, Culture and Evolution: Essays in the History of Anthropology.* New York: Free Press, 1968.

Swadesh, Frances Leon. *Los Primeros Pobladores: Hispanic Americans of the Ute Frontier.* Notre Dame, IN: University of Notre Dame Press, 1974.

Taylor, Paul S. *An American-Mexican Frontier: Nueces County, Texas.* Chapel Hill: University of North Carolina Press, 1934.

———. *Mexican Labor in the United States: Imperial Valley.* Berkeley: University of California Press, 1928.

———. *Mexican Labor in the United States: Valley of the South Platte.* Berkeley: University of California Press, 1929.

Terman, Lewis M. *The Measurement of Intelligence: An Explanation of and a Complete Guide for the Use of the Stanford Revision and Extension of the Binet-Simon Intelligence Scale.* Boston: Houghton Mifflin Co., 1916.
Thurstone, L. L., and E. J. Chave. *The Measurement of Attitude: A Psychophysical Method and Some Experiments with a Scale for Measuring Attitude toward the Church.* Chicago: University of Chicago Press, 1929.
Tireman, L. S. *Teaching Spanish-Speaking Children.* Albuquerque: University of New Mexico Press, 1948.
———. *We Learn English: A Preliminary Report of the Achievement of Spanish-Speaking Pupils in New Mexico.* Albuquerque: University of New Mexico, San José Training School, 1936.
Tireman, L. S., and Mary Watson. *A Community School in a Spanish-Speaking Village.* Albuquerque: University of New Mexico Press, 1948.
Totten, W. Fred, and Frank J. Manley. *The Community School: Basic Concepts, Function, and Organization.* Galien, MI: Allied Educational Council, 1969.
Trejo, Arnulfo D, ed. *The Chicanos As We See Ourselves.* Tucson: University of Arizona Press, 1979.
Twitchell, Ralph E. *The Leading Facts of New Mexican History.* Vol. 2. Cedar Falls, IA: The Torch Press, 1912.
Tyack, David. *The One Best System: A History of American Urban Education.* Cambridge, MA: Harvard University Press, 1974.
Tyack, David, Robert Lowe, and Elisabeth Hansot. *Public Schools in Hard Times: The Great Depression and Recent Years.* Cambridge, MA: Harvard University Press, 1984.
Vaughan, John H. *The History and Government of New Mexico.* [n.p.]: State College, New Mexico, 1925.
Violas, Paul C. *The Training of the Urban Working Class: A History of Twentieth Century Education.* Chicago: Rand McNally, 1978.
Weber, David J. *Myth and the History of the Hispanic Southwest: Essays by David J. Weber.* Albuquerque: University of New Mexico Press, 1988.
———. *The Spanish Frontier in North America.* New Haven: Yale University Press, 1992.
Weber, David J., ed. *New Spain's Far Northern Frontier: Essays on Spain in the American West, 1540–1821.* Albuquerque: University of New Mexico Press, 1979.
Weigle, Marta, ed. *Hispanic Arts and Ethnohistory in the Southwest.* Santa Fe: Ancient City Press, 1983.
Welter, Rush. *Popular Education and Democratic Thought in America.* New York: Columbia University Press, 1962.
West, Elliott. *Growing Up with the Country: Childhood on the Far Western Frontier.* Albuquerque: University of New Mexico Press, 1989.
Whaley, Charlotte. *Nina Otero-Warren of Santa Fe.* Albuquerque: University of New Mexico Press, 1994.
Whitney, Virginia, and Josephine Koogler. *Women in Education: New Mexico.* Wichita Falls, TX: Nortex Press, 1977.
Wiebe, Robert. *The Search for Order, 1877–1920.* New York: Hill and Wang, 1967.
Wiley, Tom. *Politics and Purse Strings in New Mexico's Public Schools.* Albuquerque: University of New Mexico Press, 1968.
———. *Public School Education in New Mexico.* Albuquerque: Division of Government Research, University of New Mexico, 1965.

Works, George A., ed. *Texas Educational Survey Report*. 6 vols. Austin: Texas Educational Survey Commission, 1925.
Zeleny, Carolyn. *Relations between the Spanish-Americans and Anglo-Americans in New Mexico: A Study of Conflict and Accommodation in a Dual-Ethnic Situation.* Ph.D. diss., Yale University, 1944; reprint ed., New York: Arno Press, 1974.

V. Articles and Bulletins

Abreu, Margaret. "The Father of the Kindergarten System in New Mexico." *New Mexico School Review* 11(Dec. 1931):29.
Almaráz, Jr., Felix D. "Bilingual Education in New Mexico: Historical Perspective and Current Debate." *New Mexico Historical Review* 53(Oct., 1978):347-60.
Anderson, James D. "Northern Foundations and the Shaping of Southern Black Rural Education, 1902-1935." *History of Education Quarterly* 18(winter 1978):371-96.
Austin, Mary. "Education in New Mexico." *New Mexico Quarterly* 3(Nov. 1933):217-21.
———. "Mexicans and New Mexico." *Survey* 66(May 1931):141-44, 187-90.
———. "Rural Education in New Mexico." *University of New Mexico Bulletin*, Training School Series 2(Dec. 1931):27-30.
Bates, Zelpha. "The Practical Value of Training in Homemaking." *New Mexico School Review* 14(Feb. 1935):15-16.
Biebel, Charles D. "Cultural Change on the Southwest Frontier: Albuquerque Schooling, 1870-1895." *New Mexico Historical Review* 55(July 1980):209-30.
Blanton, Annie Webb. "A Handbook of Information as to Education in Texas, 1918-1922." Texas State Department of Education, *Bulletin* No. 157 (1923).
Bohme, Frederick G. "The Italians in New Mexico." *New Mexico Historical Review* 34(Apr. 1959):61-67.
Brown, Gilbert L. "Intelligence As Related to Nationality." *Journal of Educational Research* 5(Apr. 1922):325-27.
Clark, James E. "New Mexico's Educational Policy." *New Mexico Journal of Education* 7(Feb. 1911):15-19.
Davis, E. E. "A Report on Illiteracy in Texas." *University of Texas Bulletin* 2328(22 July 1923).
Donnelly, Thomas C. "Educational Progress in New Mexico and Some Present Problems." *New Mexico Quarterly Review* 16(autumn 1946):305-17.
Droba, D. D. "Methods for Measuring Attitudes." *The Psychological Bulletin* 29(May 1932):309-23.
DuBois, Philip H. "A Psychologist in Idaho and New Mexico in the 1930's: Some Recollections." *Journal of the Behavioral Sciences* 24(Jan. 1988):107-10.
Earl, John E., B. F. Haught, and L. S. Tireman. "Results of Group Tests Given in the Original Survey of San Jose School." *University of New Mexico Bulletin,* Training School Series 1(Mar. 1931):11-30.
Ellis, Richard N. "Hispanic Americans and Indians in New Mexico State Politics." *New Mexico Historical Review* 53(Oct. 1978):361-64.
Fenlon, G. L. "The Financial Crisis in the Schools." *New Mexico School Review* 13(Nov. 1933):12-15.
Fuller, Wayne E. "Country Schoolteaching on the Sod-House Frontier." *Arizona and the West* 17(summer 1975):121-40.

Garretson, O. K. "A Study of Causes of Retardation among Mexican Children in a Small Public School System in Arizona." *Journal of Educational Psychology* 14(Jan. 1928):31–40.

Garth, Thomas R. "A Comparison of the Intelligence of Mexican and Mixed and Full Blood Indian Children." *Psychological Review* 30(Sept. 1923):388–401.

———. "Racial Differences in Mental Fatigue." *Journal of Applied Psychology* 4(June–Sept. 1920):235–44.

———. "White, Indian and Negro Work Curves." *Journal of Applied Psychology* 5(Mar. 1921):14–25.

Getz, Lynne Marie. "Extending the Helping Hand to Hispanics: The Role of the General Education Board in New Mexico in the 1930s." *Teachers College Record* (spring 1992):500–15.

———. "Politics, Science, and Education in New Mexico: The Racial Attitudes Survey of 1933." *History of Higher Education Annual* 10(1990):51–68.

Gonzales, Phillip B. "Spanish Heritage and Ethnic Protest in New Mexico: The Anti-Fraternity Bill of 1933." *New Mexico Historical Review* 61(Oct. 1986):281–300.

Goodenow, Ronald K. "The Progressive Educator, Race and Ethnicity in the Depression Years: An Overview." *History of Education Quarterly* 15(winter 1975):365–94.

Gray, E. D. McQueen. "How the Curriculum of the Secondary School Might Be Reconstructed." *University of New Mexico Bulletin,* Educational series 1(5)(Oct. 1911):141–65.

———. "The Spanish Language in New Mexico: A National Resource." *University of New Mexico Bulletin,* Sociological Series, 1(2)(Feb. 1912):1–7.

Heffernan, Helen. "A Guide for Teachers of Beginning Non-English Speaking Children." California State Department of Education, *Bulletin* 8(1932).

———. "A Statement of the Philosophy and the Purposes of the Elementary School." *California Journal of Elementary Education* 1(Feb. 1933):109–13.

Hodgin, C. E. "Early School Laws of New Mexico." *University of New Mexico Bulletin,* Educational series 1(Dec. 1906):1–36.

Hofer, Joseph S. "The Child as the Supreme Study in Education." *New Mexico Journal of Education* 8(Jan. 1912):12–17.

Jenkins, Myra Ellen. "Early Education in New Mexico." *NEA-NM School Review* (midwinter 1977):5–11.

Jensen, Joan M. " 'Disfranchisement is a Disgrace': Women and Politics in New Mexico, 1920–1940." *New Mexico Historical Review* 56(Jan. 1981):5–35.

———. "Pioneers in Politics." *El Palacio* 92(1986):12–19.

———. "Women Teachers, Class and Ethnicity: New Mexico, 1900–1950." *Southwest Economy and Society* 4(winter 1978–79):1–13.

Kevles, Daniel J. "Testing the Army's Intelligence: Psychologists and the Military in World War I." *Journal of American History* 55(Dec. 1968):565–81.

Knowlton, Clark S. "Patrón-Peón Pattern among the Spanish Americans of New Mexico." *Social Forces* 41(1962–63):12–17.

Koch, Helen Lois, and Rietta Simmons. "A Study of the Test Performance of American, Mexican, and Negro Children." *Comparative Monographs* 35(1926):1–116.

Lagemann, Ellen Condliffe. "The Plural Worlds of Educational Research." *History of Education Quarterly* 29(summer 1989):183–214.

Lamar, Howard. "Edmund G. Ross as Governor of New Mexico Territory: A Reappraisal." *New Mexico Historical Review* 36(July 1961):178–207.
Lecompte, Janet. "The Independent Women of Hispanic New Mexico, 1821–1846." *Western Historical Quarterly* 22(Jan. 1981):17–35.
Lowitt, Richard. "Bronson Cutting and the Early Years of the American Legion in New Mexico." *New Mexico Historical Review* 64(Apr. 1989):126–42.
Lujan, Manuel. "Santa Fe County Rural Schools." *New Mexico School Review* 14(Sept. 1935):14–15.
Madison, James H. "John D. Rockefeller's General Education Board and the Rural School Problem in the Midwest, 1900–1930." *History of Education Quarterly* 24(1984):181–99.
Marrs, S. M. N. "A Course in English for Non-English-Speaking Pupils, Grades I–III." Texas State Department of Education, *Bulletin*, 268(Feb. 1930):1–126.
Martinez, Filemon T. "Train a Native Educator, and Hire a Politician." *Santa Fe New Mexican*, 28 Mar. 1935.
McCrossen, Helen Cramp. "Native Crafts in New Mexico." *School Arts Magazine* 30(Mar. 1931):456–58.
Montoya, María E. "The Roots of Economic and Ethnic Divisions in Northern New Mexico: The Case of the Civilian Conservation Corps." *Western Historical Quarterly* 26(spring 1995):14–34.
Morrill, D. B. "Teaching English to Spanish Children." *New Mexico Journal of Education* 14(Nov. 1917):9–10.
———. "The Spanish Language Problems." *New Mexico Journal of Education* 14(May 1918):6–7.
———. "Teaching the Spanish American Child." *New Mexico Journal of Education* 13(Apr. 1917):8–11.
Neal, Elma. "Adapting the Curriculum to Non-English Speaking Children." *Elementary English Review* 6(Sept. 1929):183–85.
New Mexico Journal of Education. 1916–20.
New Mexico School Review. 1926–40.
Otero-Warren, Nina. "My People." *Survey* 66(May 1931):149–51.
Otero-Warren, Nina, Mary Austin, and Aurora Lucero. "New Mexico Folk Song." *El Palacio* 7(1919):152–59.
Padilla, Amado M. "Early Psychological Assessment of Mexican-American Children." *Journal of the History of the Behavioral Sciences* 25(Jan. 1988):111–16.
Paschal, Franklin C., and Louis R. Sullivan. "Racial Influence in the Mental and Physical Development of Mexican Children." *Comparative Psychology Monographs* 3(Oct. 1925).
Reisler, Mark. "Always the Laborer, Never the Citizen: Anglo Perceptions of the Mexican Immigrant during the 1920's." *Pacific Historical Review* 45(May 1976):231–54.
Richardson, Ethel. "The Immigrant Child in the Public Schools." California, Superintendent of Public Instruction, *Bulletin* 5B(Feb. 1922).
Rock, Rosalind S. " 'Pido y Suplico': Women and the Law in Spanish New Mexico, 1697–1763." *New Mexico Historical Review* 65(Apr. 1990):145–59.
Ross, J. C. "Industrial Education for the Spanish-Speaking People." *New Mexico Journal of Education* 7(Feb. 1911):19–21.

Sánchez, George I. "Bilingualism and Mental Measures: A Word of Caution." *Journal of Applied Psychology* 17(1934):765–72.
———. "Educational Intangibles." *New Mexico School Review* 15(Dec. 1935):19, 31–32, 37.
———. "Future Legislative Program for Financing Public Education in New Mexico." *University of New Mexico Bulletin,* Education Series 8(3)(Sept. 1934):96–105.
———. "Group Differences and Spanish-Speaking Children—A Critical Review." *Journal of Applied Psychology* 16(Oct., 1932):549–58.
———. "School Census Distribution in N.M. for 1931." *New Mexico School Review* 11(Jan. 1932):18–19.
———. "Scores of Spanish-Speaking Children on Repeated Tests." *The Pedagogical Seminary and Journal of Genetic Psychology* 60(Mar. 1932):223–231.
———. "Teachers!" *New Mexico School Review* 15(Oct. 1935):22–24.
San Miguel, Guadalupe, Jr. "Culture and Education in the American Southwest: Towards an Explanation of Chicano School Attendance, 1850–1940." *Journal of American Ethnic History* 7(spring 1988):5–21.
Schlossman, Steven. "Self-Evident Remedy? George I. Sanchez, Segregation, and Enduring Dilemmas in Bilingual Education." *Teachers College Record* 84(summer 1983):871–907.
Sewell, Brice H. "New Los Lunas Vocational School Building." *New Mexico School Review* 15(Jan. 1936):6.
———. "A New Type of School." *New Mexico School Review* 14(Oct. 1935):49–50.
———. "Vocational Education Adjusts Its Program to Meet the Needs of Industry." *New Mexico School Review* 17(Feb. 1938):26.
———. "Vocational Education: Do You Know?" *New Mexico School Review* 12(May 1933):23.
———. "Why Vocational Education?" *New Mexico School Review* 14(Feb. 1935):6–7.
Seyfried, J. E. "Analysis and Evaluation of New Mexico State School Laws." *University of New Mexico Bulletin,* Education Series 6(2)(Sept. 1932):1–60.
———. "Illiteracy Trends in New Mexico, Including Comparison of Trends in New Mexico with Those in Certain Other States and the United States." *University of New Mexico Bulletin,* Education Series 8(1)(Mar. 1934):1–38.
Sheldon, William H. "The Intelligence of Mexican Children." *School and Society* 19(Feb. 1924):139–42.
Smith, Clara H., and La Rae Olvey. "Milpitas—A Rural School Project in Teacher Training." Department of the Interior, Bureau of Education, *Rural School Leaflet* 27(Apr. 1924):1–19.
Szasz, Margaret Connell. "Albuquerque Congregationalists and Southwestern Social Reform: 1900–1917." *New Mexico Historical Review* 60(July 1980):231–52.
Taylor, Paul S. "Mexicans North of the Rio Grande." *Survey* 66(May 1931):135–40, 197, 200–5.
Terman, Lewis M. "The Use of Intelligence Tests in the Grading of School Children." *Journal of Educational Research* 1(Jan. 1920):20–32.
Thurstone, L. L. "Attitudes Can Be Measured." *American Journal of Sociology* 33(Jan. 1928):529–54.
Tireman, L. S. "The Bilingual Child and His Reading Vocabulary." *Elementary English Review* 32(Jan. 1955):33–35.

———. "Bilingual Children." *Review of Educational Research* 11(June 1941):340–52.
———. "New Mexico Tackles the Problem of the Spanish-Speaking Child." *Journal of Education* 114(Nov. 1931):300–301.
———. "Reading in the Elementary Schools of New Mexico." *Elementary School Journal* 30(1930):621–26.
———. "The San Jose Training School." *University of New Mexico Bulletin*, Training School Series 1(Oct. 1930):7–16.
———. "School Problems Created by the Homes of the Foreign-Speaking Children." *California Journal of Elementary Education* 8(May 1940):234–38.
Tireman, L. S., and Marie M. Hughes. "A Reading Program for Spanish-Speaking Pupils." *Elementary English Review* 14(Apr. 1937):138–40.
Tireman, L. S., Mela Sedillo Brewster, and Lolita Pooler. "The San José Project." *New Mexico Quarterly* 3(1933):207–16.
Tireman, L. S., Newel Dixon, and Vera Cornelius. "Vocabulary Acquisition of Spanish-Speaking Children." *Elementary English Review* 12(May 1935):118–19, 144.
Trulio, Beverly. "Anglo-American Attitudes toward New Mexican Women." *Journal of the West* 12(1973):229–39.
Van Ness, Christine M., and John R. Van Ness. "W. W. H. Davis: Neglected Figure of New Mexico's Early Territorial Period." *Journal of the West* 16(July 1977):68–73.
Vaughan, John H. "New Mexico's Educational Crisis." *New Mexico Journal of Education* 7(Feb. 1911):61–71.
Vollmar, E. R. "First Jesuit School in New Mexico." *New Mexico Historical Review* 27(Oct. 1952):296–99.
Walter, Paul A. F. "First Meeting of the New Mexico Educational Association." *New Mexico Historical Review* 2(Jan. 1927):67–82.
Welsh, Cynthia Secor. "A 'Star Will Be Added': Miguel Antonio Otero and the Struggle for Statehood." *New Mexico Historical Review* 67(Jan. 1992):33–51.
Welsh, Michael. "A Prophet Without Honor: George I. Sánchez and Bilingualism in New Mexico." *New Mexico Historical Review* 69(Jan. 1994):19–34.
Wilkins, Thurman. "Mary Hunter Austin." In *Notable American Women: A Biographical Dictionary* (Cambridge, MA: Belknap Press, 1971) 1:67–69.
Young, Kimball. "Intelligence Tests of Certain Immigrant Groups." *Scientific Monthly* 14(Nov. 1922):417–34.
———. "Mental Differences in Certain Immigrant Groups: Psychological Tests of South Europeans in Typical California Schools with Bearing on the Educational Policy and on the Problems of Racial Contacts in This Country." *University of Oregon Publication*, 1(11)(July, 1922).
Zinn, Maxine Baca. "Gender and Ethnic Identity among Chicanos." *Frontiers* 5(summer 1980):18–24.

VI. Government Documents

California. Industrial Relations Department. *Mexicans in California; Report of Governor C. C. Young's Mexican Fact-Finding Committee*. San Francisco: Department of Industrial Relations, 1930.
New Mexico. State Superintendent of Public Instruction. *Biennial Reports of the Superintendent of Public Instruction to the Governor of New Mexico*. Santa Fe: State

Department of Public Instruction, 1912, 1914, 1916, 1918, 1920, 1922, 1924, 1926, 1932, 1934, 1936, 1938.

———. *New Mexico School Code.* [Santa Fe]: Superintendent of Public Instruction, 1923.

New Mexico. Territorial Superintendent of Public Instruction. *Annual Reports of the Territorial Superintendent of Public Instruction to the Governor of New Mexico.* Santa Fe: New Mexican Printing Co., 1909, 1911.

New Mexico. Territory. *Compilation of the School Laws of the Territory of New Mexico.* Santa Fe: El Boletín Popular Printing Co., 1903.

U.S. Congress. House. Committee on Immigration and Naturalization. *Hearings on the Restriction of Immigration from Countries of the Western Hemisphere.* 70th Cong., 1st sess., 1928.

U.S. Department of Interior. Office of Education. *Annual Report of the Commissioner of Education Made to the Secretary of the Interior.* Washington, DC: U.S. Government Printing Office, 1870, 1882.

U.S. Department of Labor. *Annual Report of the Commissioner General of Immigration.* Washington, DC: U.S. Government Printing Office, 1924.

VII. Unpublished Dissertations and Theses

Apodaca, Rita C. "The Nambé Community School (1937–1942): A Study of a Community Relevant Curriculum." Ph.D. diss., University of New Mexico, 1986.

Atkins, Jane. "Who Will Educate: The Schooling Question in Territorial New Mexico, 1846–1911." Ph.D. diss., University of New Mexico, 1982.

Avant, Louis. "History of Catholic Education in New Mexico Since the American Occupation." M.A. thesis, University of New Mexico, 1940.

Bacon, Frederick Mason. "Contributions of Catholic Religious Orders to Public Education in New Mexico Since the American Occupation." M.A. thesis, University of New Mexico, 1947.

Berman, Martin L. "Arthurdale, Nambé, and the Developing Community School Model: A Comparative Study." Ph.D. diss., University of New Mexico, 1979.

Bustamante, Adrian Herminio. "Los Hispanos: Ethnicity and Social Change in New Mexico." Ph.D. diss., University of New Mexico, 1982.

Drake, Rollen H. "A Comparative Study of the Mentality and Achievement of Mexican and White Children." M.A. thesis, University of Southern California, 1927.

García, Enos E. "History of Education in Taos County." M.A. thesis, University of New Mexico, 1950.

Getz, Lynne Marie. "Progressive Ideas for New Mexico: Educating the Spanish-Speaking Child in the 1920s and 1930s." Ph.D. diss., University of Washington, 1989.

Gonzales, Phillip B. "A Perfect Furor of Indignation: The Racial Attitude Confrontation of 1933." Ph.D. diss., University of California, Berkeley, 1985.

Gonzalez, Gilbert George. "The System of Public Education and its Function within the Chicano Communities, 1920–1930." Ph.D. diss., University of California, Los Angeles, 1974.

Gould, Betty. "Methods of Teaching Mexicans." M.A. thesis, University of Southern California, 1932.

Leff, Gladys R. "George I. Sanchez: Don Quixote of the Southwest." Ph.D. diss., North Texas State University, 1976.

Lopez, Daniel. "The State Department of Education and Public School Educational Policymaking in New Mexico: A Political Perspective." Ph.D. diss., University of New Mexico, 1985.

Lucas, Verlene Diana. "The Development of Public Elementary Curriculum in California, 1930–1970." Ed.D. diss., University of Southern California, 1973.

Mayfield, Thomas J., Jr. "Development of the Public Schools in New Mexico Between 1848 and 1900." Masters thesis, University of New Mexico, 1938.

McCracken, Glen F. "A Comparative Study of Certain Objective Factors of the Protestant and the Public High Schools of New Mexico." Masters thesis, University of New Mexico, 1939.

Mowry, James Nelson. "A Study of the Educational Thought and Action of George I. Sánchez." Ph.D. diss., University of Texas, 1977.

Moyers, Robert Arthur. "A History of Education in New Mexico." Ph.D. diss., George Peabody College for Teachers, 1941.

Parr, Eunice Elvira. "A Comparative Study of Mexican and American Children in the Schools of San Antonio, Texas." Ph.D. diss., University of Chicago, 1926.

Raftery, Judith Rosenberg. "The Invention of Modern Urban Schooling: Los Angeles, 1885–1941." Ph.D. diss., University of California, Los Angeles, 1984.

Sánchez, George I. "The Education of Bilinguals in a State School System." Ed.D. diss., University of California, Berkeley, 1934.

Shamberger, Elizabeth Strong. "A Thirty Year Educational History of Albuquerque." M.A. thesis, University of New Mexico, 1928.

Index

Abreu, Margaret, 111
adult education, 106-7, 109-10, 115-16
Air Corps Spanish Project, 116
Alexander, Will, 104
American Legion, 35, 56
Americanization, 6, 34-36; health education as means of, 23, 35, 79-81, 85
Andrews, Flora, 72
Angel, Frank, 101
Applegate, Frank, 112
Aragón, Julian, 15
Arizona schools, 66
Asplund, Rupert, 61
Atlanta University, 118, 120-21
Austin, Mary, 42, 70-71, 80-82, 108, 111-12

Bachelor, David L., 67, 78
Bagley, William C., 37
Bancroft, Hubert Howe, 6
Barnard, Henry, 3
Bates, Zelpha, 109
Becero, Gerónimo, 5
Beeson, Ulrich, 84
Bergere family, 114
Bergere, A. M., 40
Bernalillo County, 15, 22, 49, 77
Biddle, Nicholas, 2
Bilingualism, 17, 120-22; in New Mexico schools, 17, 19-21, 30-34, 38, 44-45, 85, 94-95; in New Mexico society, 19-20, 35; in state constitution, 26-27; in San José Training school, 73-76; in WPA projects, 106-17, 115-16
Binet mental test. *See* Stanford-Binet mental test
Brewster, Mela Sedillo, 74
Brown, Mrs. Alec, 113

Cabeza de Baca, Fabiola, 21, 30
California: Home Teacher Act of 1915, 35-37
Campa, Arturo, 46-47, 113
Casias, Maria, 98, 100
Catholic Church: involvement in schools, 15, 18, 26, 129n. 30
CCC. *See* Civilian Conservation Corps
Cedro community school, 92-93
Chacón, Dora, Vásquez. *See* Vásquez Chacón, Dora
Chapman, Kenneth, 112
Chaves, Amado, 17, 18, 20
Chaves, José Francisco, 18
Chávez, Anita Dominguez. *See* Dominguez Chávez, Anita
Chicano movement, 123
Child Welfare Service, 35-36
Chimayo weavers, 81
Civilian Conservation Corps (CCC), 105-6, 116
Clark, James E., 19, 21-22, 24
Clark, L. W., 84
Common school movement, 2, 3, 18
Conway, John V., 29
Córdova, Josephine, 39
Coronado Cuarto Centennial, 123
Coronel, Alexia, 32-33
Corrigan, Grace, 84, 94, 102
Counts, George S., 88
Cubberley, Ellwood P., 37
Curriculum Laboratory, 83-84
Curriculum: as means of Americanization, 23, 43, 78-79; as means of cultural preservation, 43-44; uniform, 36-37; 1923 School Code, 37-38; Curriculum Revision Project of 1936-1939, 83-85, 95; Elementary School Curriculum of 1944, 85; of

165

Curriculum (*continued*)
  San José Training School. *See* San José Training School
Curtin, Leonora, 112
Cutting, Bronson, 32, 35, 56–57, 70–71, 139n. 42

Davis, Jackson, 65, 69, 102, 134n. 5
Davis, William Watts Hart, 4
Deutsch, Sarah, 103
Dewey, John, 8–9, 24, 43, 78, 88, 97, 119
Dillon, R. C., 46
"Direct Method" of English instruction, 33–34, 39, 118
Dixon, Newell, 73
Dominguez Chávez, Anita, 90
DuBois, W. E. B., 118–21
Dwire, Isaac W., 22

Eckles, Isabel Lancaster, 116
Emergency Education Program. *See* Federal Emergency Relief Administration
English-only policy, 17, 21, 26–27, 31–32, 76
Espinosa, Carmen, 112
Espinosa, Gilbert, 71

Favrot, Leo M., 53, 56–57, 61, 63, 70, 76, 84, 121, 134n. 5, 136n. 23
Federal Emergency Relief Administration (FERA), 104, 110; Emergency Education Program, 105–6, 115, 144n. 8
Federal Music Project, 113–114
FERA. *See Federal Emergency Relief Administration*
Fergusson Act of 1898, 13
folklore, 110–13
Forrest, Suzanne, 103, 107
Franciscans, 4

Gallagher, T. P., 113–14
Gallegos, Bernardo P., 5
General Education Board (GEB), 49, 53, 56, 65, 83–84, 87, 102, 121, 136n. 23; support of San José Training School, 69–70, 77, 134n. 5; support of Nambé Community School, 96, 101
genízaros, 4
Gonzales, Jennie, 72, 83, 92–93
Gonzáles, Virginia, 94–95
Gonzales-Berry, Erlinda, 90
Good Neighbor policy, 115
Grant, Joseph, 62

Gray, E. D. McQueen, 24
Gregg, Josiah, 3
Grissom, R. H., 61
Guadalupe County, 22
Gutiérrez, Ramón, 5

Hadley, Hiram, 18–21
Harwood School (Albuquerque), 90
Hastings, Montana, 35–36
Haught, B. F., 46–47
health education, 23; at San José Training School, 79–80; at Nambé Community School, 98
Heffernan, Helen, 59
Hispanas, 131n. 5; as teachers, 30, 90–92, 101
Hispanic Institute of New Mexico, 113
Hispanos: definition of term, 125n. 2; acceptance of church involvement in schools, 15, 17, 129n. 30; alleged resistance to schooling, 2, 6, 7, 15–16, 18–19, 25; stereotyping of, 1, 3–7, 13, 122; traditions and culture of, 4, 6; use of Spanish by, 19
Hodgin, Charles E., 23
Hofer, Joseph S., 23
home economics education, 23, 109–10
Huff, Raymond, 46–47, 60–62, 110
Hughes, Marie M., 73, 83–84, 93–94

Ilfeld, Louis C., 115
intelligence tests, 11, 36, 38, 46, 50, 58, 69, 135n. 9; at San José Training School, 72, 77

Jaramillo, Cleofas Martínez, 111
Jaramillo, Veneslao, 22
Jefferson, Thomas, 2
Jesuits, 15
Johnson, Virginia, 79
Jones, Ann, 79
Julius Rosenwald Fund, 62–63

Keleher, W. A., 110
Kenney, May Bergere, 114
Kemp, Maude, 110
Kercheville, F. M., 95, 106

La Sociedad Folklórica, 111
Lamy, Bishop Jean, 16
Larrazolo, Octaviano, 31–32
League of United Latin-American Citizens (LULAC), 61
local control of schools, 2, 14, 16–17, 19, 103

"Los Pastores," 82, 93, 112
Lucero, Leandro, 20
Lucero-White, Aurora, 111-12
Lujan, Manuel, 111
Luna, Solomon, 22
Lusk, Georgia, 85, 94
Lyon, Thelma London, 106

MacKay, Donald W., 83
Mainz, Virginia, 115
Mann, Horace, 3, 5
Manual, Herschel T., 49
Martínez, A., 109
Martínez, Antonio José, 5
Martínez, Eduardo, 15
Martínez, Filemon, 62
Martínez, L. P., 110
Martinez, Ruth Miller. See Miller-Martinez, Ruth
McCollum, J. R., 46
McCormick, Cyrus, 96-97, 100-101
McCormick, Florence, 96, 98, 100
Meadors, Mamie, 116
Menaul School, Albuquerque, 24
Miles, John, 61
Miller-Martinez, Ruth, 94-95
Milne, John, 60, 69-70, 134n. 5
Montoya, Atanasio, 38, 45-47, 69, 71, 94, 134n. 5
Montoya, Nestor, 35
Mora County, 91, 104-5
Morrill, D. B., 33-34

Nambé Community School, 82; founding of, 96-97; curriculum of, 97-99; bilingual instruction in, 99-100
Nambé Pueblo, 96
Nanninga, S. P., 46-47, 60, 70-71, 134n. 5
National Vocational Education Act, 46
National Youth Administration, 100, 105-6, 109, 114-16
Native Market, 112, 114
New Deal, 2, 11, 87, 103; in New Mexico, 11, 43, 103-7, 115-17, 122
New Mexico Educational Association (NMEA), 18, 23, 33, 59, 83, 144n. 8; founding of, 16; annual meeting of 1929, 45-47, 68; and equalization bill of 1932, 33, 56; and equalization bill of 1935, 61; annual meeting of 1935, 62
New Mexico Municipal and County School Superintendents Association, 63

New Mexico Normal University at Las Vegas, 53
New Mexico State Board of Education, 30, 32-33, 37-38, 52, 54, 56, 60, 63, 83-84, 111
New Mexico State Constitution, 26-27
New Mexico State Department of Education, 34, 38, 45, 52, 54, 60-61, 77, 82-84, 94, 102, 107, 111; Department of Vocational Education, 112
New Mexico State University at Las Cruces, 18, 94
New Mexico Taxpayers' Association, 55, 61
New Mexico, University of. See University of New Mexico
NYA. See National Youth Administration

Oñate, Juan de, 4, 15
Ortiz y Pino, Concha, 44
Ortiz, Cordelia, 97, 99-101
Otero family, 40
Otero-Warren, Adelina "Nina," 46, 47, 80, 85, 95, 114, 120; early life, 40; as Santa Fe County School Superintendent, 41-45; *Old Spain in Our Southwest*, 41; and Spanish colonial arts revival, 42-43, 112; method of bilingual instruction, 44-45; work for WPA, 106-7, 115-16
Owens, J. E., 61-62

Pacheco, Lionides, 95
Padilla, Camilo, 71, 81
Padilla, Genaro, 111
Page, Richard, 56-57
Parker, J. P., 22
Pierce, John, 3
Pike, Zebulon, 3
Pile, William, 6
Pooler, Lolita, 74
Popejoy, Thomas L., 114
Prince, L. Bradford, 16-17, 22
Progressive education, 2, 8-11, 44, 78-79
Public Works Administration, 104
Puerto Rico, 115-16
PWA. See Public Works Administration

Redick, Charles B., 45
Reid, J. T. 63, 65, 106
Reynolds, Annie, 50, 66-67, 76
Ritch, William G., 7, 15
Rockey, Dautin W., 106
Rodgers, H. R., 60, 62, 83, 93, 110

Roosevelt, Franklin Delano, 11, 105
Roosevelt, Theodore, 34
Ross, Edmund G., 16
Ross, J. C., 24
Rousseau, Edna, 46–47
Rowland, Lea, 107
Rush, Benjamin, 2
Ryan, Helen Chandler, 113

San José Training School, 53, 56, 87–88, 96, 99, 108, 115, 139n. 42; founding of, 69–70, 134n. 5; Board of Directors of, 71, 74, 92; testing program of, 71–72, 77–78; curriculum of, 72–76; bilingual instruction in, 73–76, 85, 121–22; health education in, 79–80; vocational education program of, 80, 82–83, 107; teacher training program, 91–93; impact on New Mexico education, 82–85
San Miguel County, 15, 20, 111
Sánchez, George Isidore, 47, 67, 70, 87, 120–21, 136n. 23, 144n. 8; early life, 49; on intelligence testing, 48, 51, 58–59, 69; as Director of Division of Information and Statistics, 52, 55, 58, 61; on rural schools, 53–54; and equalization bill of 1932–1933, 55–56; involvement with Page racial survey, 56–58; *Forgotten People*, 48, 64; on bilingualism and bilingual instruction, 58–59; as president of NMEA, 59, 62, 110; and equalization bill of 1935, 60–61; legacy in New Mexico, 64–65
Sánchez, George J., 36
Sánchez, Mary, 90–91
Sánchez, Mrs. Philip, 104
Sangre de Cristo Mountains, 96
Santa Fe County, 29, 41–45, 80, 96, 101, 109, 111, 114
Santa Fe Fiesta, 42–43, 111
Santa Fe Railroad, 61, 104
Santa Fe Ring, 16
Santisteven, Floyd, 105, 110
Schackel, Sandra, 103
School Code of 1923, 54–55. *See also* Curriculum
Seligman, Arthur, 55–57, 108
Sena, A. A., 31
Sewell, Brice H., 82–83, 107, 120; early life, 108; on vocational education, 108–9; and adult education, 110–11; and Spanish colonial arts revival, 111–13
Sheldon, Lionel A., 36

Sheldon, William H., 36, 50, 135n. 9
Sienna, M., Sister, 109
Sierra County, 22
Sininger, Harlan, 83
Sisters of Loretto, 15
Smith-Hughes Act, 108
Socorro County, 91
Spanish colonial arts revival, 42, 82, 107, 111
Spanish Colonial Arts Society, 42–43, 81, 112
Spanish-American Normal School at El Rito, 22, 37–38, 61–62
Stanford-Binet mental test, 58, 72
Strayer, George D., 37
Stroup, A. B., 22
Sweeney, R. P., 112

Taos County Teachers' Association, 95
Taos County, 22, 64, 90, 94–95, 105, 110; Carnegie Project on, 63–65
Taos Cultural Center, 110
Thurstone, L. L., 57
Tingley, Clyde, 45, 47, 60–62, 71, 104, 144n. 8
Tireman, Loyd Spencer, 46–47, 56–57, 87, 91, 110, 113, 120–22, 134n. 5, 140n. 47; early life, 67; view of Hispanos, 67–68, 78–79, 88–90; as Director of San José Training School, 71–83; reading pedagogy of, 68–69, 72–73; on intelligence testing, 69, 77–78; on bilingual instruction, 73–76, 85; curriculum revision project and 83–85; Nambé Community School, 96–102; impact on New Mexico education, 85–86. *See also* San José Training School; Nambé Community School)
Tolle, Vernon O., 60
Treaty of Guadelupe Hidalgo, 123
Tugwell, Rexford G., 104
Tuskegee Institute, 121

U.S. Bureau of Education, 34, 50, 66, 76, 83; Department of Vocational Education, 109
University of California at Berkeley, 58
University of New Mexico, 18, 23, 45–46, 49, 56–58, 63–65, 67, 77, 82–84, 90, 92, 95–96, 108; Tireman Learning Materials Library, College of Education, 67
University of Texas, 64
Ussher, Bruno David, 113

Valencia County, 91
Vásquez Chacón, Dora, 91

Vaughan, John H., 19
Vette, Bette, 114
Vigil, Agnes, 114
Vigil, Celina, 109
vocational education, 23–24, 82, 108–9, 115, 119–21

Wagner, Jonathan, 38
Warren, Rawson, 40
Washington University, St. Louis, 108
Washington, Booker T., 118
Watson, Mary, 97, 100–1
Wheelwright, Mary, 112

White, Aurora Lucero. *See* Lucero-White, Aurora
Wood, Vera, 73
Works Progress Administration (WPA), 100, 104–5, 109, 115–16; Educational Program, 106–7, 113
WPA. *See* Works Progress Administration

YWCA, 114

Zimmerman, James F., 45, 47, 49, 57, 62–65, 69, 71, 77, 82–83, 91, 108, 134n. 5

www.ingramcontent.com/pod-product-compliance
Lightning Source LLC
Chambersburg PA
CBHW070332230426
43663CB00011B/2290